Sincerely, Luther

NARRATIVE LETTERS OF THE GREAT REFORMER

NEAL E. SNIDER

CONCORDIA PUBLISHING HOUSE · SAINT LOUIS

Founded in 1869 as the publishing arm of The Lutheran Church—Missouri Synod, Concordia Publishing House gives all glory to God for the blessing of 150 years of opportunities to provide resources that are faithful to the Holy Scriptures and the Lutheran Confessions.

Published by Concordia Publishing House
3558 S. Jefferson Ave., St. Louis, MO 63118-3968
1-800-325-3040 • www.cph.org

Manufactured in the United States of America

1 2 3 4 5 6 7 8 9 10 28 27 26 25 24 23 22 21 20 19

In loving memory
of my father and mother

Frank and Mabel Snider
Pembina, ND

Foreword

One of my old teachers, a historian, liked to divide the word "history" into two: his story. For Christians, the events and circumstances that make the news don't just happen accidentally. Somebody is looking, making a story that has an end.

My teacher knew firsthand how things can get scrambled, losing rhyme or reason. He grew up on a mountain in China where, with other members of his family, he became a missionary. When the Communists took over in the late 1940s, all of them had to flee. Their stone houses were taken over by the Chinese military.

There is an old hymn that includes this line: "That though the wrong seems oft so strong, God is the ruler yet." Though things don't always make sense to us, it is God's story. He makes even the wicked to serve His purposes. So Joseph, when he was reunited with his brothers after they had sold him into slavery, said, "You meant evil against me, but God meant it for good" (Genesis 50:20).

That is how God shapes His story. There is always a cross, some event or circumstance that makes it all look confusing and dreadful. But even more certainly, with the cross there is a resurrection. Good Friday and Easter go side by side.

Neal Snider, who has put together the stories in this book, is a long-term pastor who has served several congregations, finishing his vocation in the Northwest. His life has been spent listening to the texts of Scripture, studying them carefully to preach them week by week. He has stood with his parishioners under the cross and preached both Christ's cross and His resurrection.

But Neal always had an ear for another story that goes with the biblical one. When he was in seminary, preparing to become a preacher, Neal had a great old teacher, like mine, who taught him to read Martin Luther and the history of the Reformation as His story, God's story. It was Luther, among others long before him, who recognized that the shape of the biblical story and our own stories alike are cruciform, that is, shaped like the cross and ending in the resurrection.

When jazz musicians talk about players who are really good, who not only sound good but also know their way around the music, they says that person has chops. The player knows the techniques that go into playing well. Neal Snider has chops.

So when you read this book, you are going to learn the most important things in Luther's story. You will meet his father, a hard-nosed miner named Hans from East Central Germany five hundred years ago, and his mother, Margarethe, who came from an educated family. You will learn how Luther, whom Hans wanted to be a lawyer, got stuck in a thunderstorm and vowed to become a monk. Then the confusion came down on him. The more he studied Scripture and the harder he worked at trying to become what he wanted to be, the worse it got. That was his cross, and it nearly killed him. But then studying Scripture day and night, he heard another word that came to him as the resurrection. The word he heard was the Gospel of God's compounding goodness in Jesus, crucified and risen.

Neal will take you along, following Luther, to a famous meeting wonderfully named, the Diet of Worms. Then he will introduce you to Katharina von Bora, a former nun so strong that no one even today calls her Mrs. Martin Luther, though she was.

But it is Neal's turn now. Even if you have heard it before, even if you already know the end of the story, it is a lot of fun to hear Neal tell it. While Neal is telling it, let Luther take you into the old, old story—the oldest and best. Though you may die, in Christ you will surely live.

James Arne Nestingen

Preface

The first of the letters from Luther was printed in a congregational newsletter in July 1997. Subsequent letters came with almost monthly regularity until March 1999. In late February of that year, the publisher of the congregational newsletter sent me a note saying, "At some point in the next two or three issues, Martinus Lutheri will probably need to retire or go on at least a one-page diet." Was Luther miffed by that unintentional slight? I cannot say, but I did not receive another letter until 2004. I received two in that year, and I thought that Luther may have chosen to continue sending me letters, but alas, I received only two. More than a decade passed, and I had given up all hope of ever hearing from the great reformer again. To my great surprise and delight, I received a torrent of letters in January 2015 that continued with few interruptions until August 2017.

I cannot say that I have received the last letter from Luther, but the way he concluded Letter 110 implies that he has written his last—at least his last letter to me.

Luther made it quite clear in the first letter that what he wrote was not intended to be personal letters to me alone. His very first words were "My beloved brothers and sisters in the New World." I concluded that it is my responsibility to make what he wrote available to all who care to read his words.

In these letters, Luther (he and other major personalities of that day were referenced by their last names) shares a bit about his early life, his inner struggles with his relationship to God, his contest with the powerful Roman Church of his day, and his life vis-à-vis the political rulers that both threatened and protected him. He also shares comments on some of what he wrote. His writing of treatises, sermons, and letters was prolific. One scholar said that Luther wrote more than 450 treatises, more than 3,000 sermons, and more than 2,600 letters.[1] Clearly, he could not include all that he wrote in a few short letters. I was never privy to the answers to any "why" questions, and I was never provided with any way that I could respond to his letters with questions of clarification.

1 Gritsch, vii.

I cannot say whether Luther would approve of what I am about to say, but I will preface my remark with a comment made by Bishop Hans Lilje, from Germany, at the Lutheran World Federation Assembly in Minneapolis in 1957. "We are faithful to Martin Luther not when we focus on him, but when our focus is on Jesus Christ." Perhaps that is another way of saying that nothing is true because Martin Luther said it; it is true only because most of what he said is a faithful witness to the Gospel of Jesus Christ. Luther himself said that he would recant in a heartbeat if he could be shown by Scripture or clear reason that what he wrote was unfaithful to the historic faith, transmitted in the Bible from the time of the apostles. Martin knew that he was a sinner like the rest of us. But because God has no one with whom to work in this world other than sinners, he chose Martin to be His servant in bringing necessary reform to the one holy catholic and apostolic Church.

Luther has so much more to say than what is included in these letters. When he makes comments about some of his treatises, sermons, or letters, he gives only a brief summary. Serious students of the faith would do well to read what he said in the full context of his writings. We are thankful that a great deal of what Luther wrote is available in the American Edition of *Luther's Works*. Every Lutheran congregation should seriously consider having those volumes available in its church library. Seventy-nine volumes are available from Concordia Publishing House in St. Louis and Fortress Press in Minneapolis.

Neal E. Snider
31 October 2017

Acknowledgments

I am eternally grateful

to God, whose Spirit has called me through the Gospel, enlightened me with His gifts, and sanctified and preserved me in the one true faith;

to faithful Roman Catholic monks who planted the Christian faith and maintained fidelity to the apostolic faith during a thousand years when power, politics, and greed ensnared the hierarchy of the church;

to Martin Luther, whose sensitive spirit recognized the terrible consequences of human sin and found relief, comfort, and the certainty that God forgives sins by divine grace through faith in Jesus Christ;

to my parents, Frank and Mabel Snider, who first taught me to pray and attend Sunday School and divine worship and who nurtured my faith by their example;

to my pastors as a youth, in particular Waldemar Anderson, who guided me through the difficult years of adolescence, and G. H. "Giggs" Bretheim, my mentor, who showed me the image of a good pastor;

to my college professor, Paul Sonnack, who gave me a thirst for the history of the church, and my seminary professor, John Stensvaag, who taught me how to interpret the Bible.

I am temporally grateful

to my wife of sixty years, Judy, who endured my absence while I was working on the manuscript and who read the manuscript and made very helpful suggestions for its improvement;

to Concordia Publishing House for accepting the manuscript for publication and to my editor, Scot Kinnaman, who allows an author to be the author;

to Victory Lutheran Church and Senior Pastor Larry Kassebaum, who provided me with office space and the resources of the congregation while I was working on the manuscript, and to Elly Nawrocki, a most competent office manager, and Eileen Hernandez, communication specialist, both of whom offered me outstanding support;

to you, dear readers, who care enough about the Reformation of the Church and the solid foundation for the faith recovered by the great reformer to read what Martin has to say in the twenty-first century.

+ Soli Deo Gloria +

Letter 1

My beloved brothers and sisters in the New World: I greet you from my resting place. Some think that resting place to be in Wittenberg, Germany. I assure you that my resting place is far superior to Wittenberg.

I must say that I am embarrassed that you have used my name to refer to the Church of Jesus Christ. Unfortunately, the use of my name in reference to the church began even in my own day. I objected as much then as I do today. I recall writing to my beloved people in Wittenberg when I was absent from them for several months. A rebellion had broken out among my supporters in late December 1521. That grieved me greatly. I wrote them a long letter, *A Sincere Admonition by Martin Luther to All Christians to Guard against Insurrection and Rebellion*.[1] In that letter, I wrote, "In the first place, I ask that men make no reference to my name; let them call themselves Christians, not Lutherans." I followed by adding, "How then should I—poor stinking maggot-fodder that I am—come to have men call the children of Christ by my wretched name?"[2] That rebellion (I'll tell you more about that sometime later) caused me to write an entire treatise, *Receiving Both Kinds in the Sacrament*.[3] In that treatise I said, "True, by any consideration of body or soul you should never say: I am Lutheran, or Papist. For neither of them died for you, or is your master. Christ alone died for you, he alone is your master, and you should confess yourself a Christian."[4] Alas, it makes little difference what I think; people will do what they are wont to do, and my embarrassment continues.

I do sense a danger in the use of the name Lutheran, however. You may be so attracted to my name that you forget the priority of Jesus Christ, the Lord of the Church. You may even use my name to cut yourself off from others in the communion of saints. I grieve in my grave for there are those who identify themselves with my name who are no more Christian than Satan himself. They neither worship God nor receive the Holy Sacrament of Christ's body and blood. They neither hear the Word,

1 LW 45:53.

2 LW 45:53.

3 LW 36:237.

4 LW 36:265.

read the Word, believe the Word, nor live nor die by the Word of God. Even though they use my name, let them be accursed, because they already are.

I have identified myself above by the Latin spelling of my name, which I occasionally used during my professional career. (I use the term "professional career" only because you will understand what I mean by that phrase. I never used it, and I never would! Mine was a calling by God to be a faithful witness to the Word of God and to Jesus Christ, my Lord; I never considered my calling to be a profession.) My first name was given to me by my parents when they took me to the Church of Sts. Peter and Paul in Eisleben, Germany (the town in which I was born on 10 November) to be baptized by Pastor Bartholomy Rennebecher on St. Martin's Day, 11 November 1483.

The family name was spelled several different ways. My grandfather Heine Luder spelled the name with a *d*. Other spellings in my day, including my own variant spellings, were Ludher, Lueder, Lutter, and Lauther. After 15 October 1517, I occasionally spelled my name Eleutherius (the free one). One of the first times I used that spelling was in a letter written in January 1518 to my friend Spalatin, chaplain in the court of my sovereign, Prince Frederick.

I should tell you a bit about my parents. I need say little about my mother, Margarethe, because little is known about her in your day. Perhaps that is my fault because I seldom spoke of her and made almost no reference to my ancestors on my mother's side of the family.

My father, Hans (called Gross-Hans to distinguish him from his brother by the same name, who was called Klein-Hans), was a miner. When I was very young, my father worked in the mines around Eisleben. I was less than a year old when my family moved to Mansfeld. If you have difficulty with the geography of Germany, perhaps one of your German friends can be of assistance to you. In brief, those two towns are mostly south and a bit west of Berlin.

In Mansfeld, my father was a working part-owner of a mine. We were not wealthy, nor were any of the working class of my day. However, my family had modest wealth compared to my neighbors.

I spent my early years in Mansfeld. I'll have to tell you about that on another occasion. I must now return to my rest, and you must return to your work of bearing witness to God's saving truth against all the lies that the forces of darkness present to you and your neighbors in your day, just as those same forces were present in my day.

Letter 2

In my first letter, I mentioned that our family moved from Eisleben to Mansfeld, Germany, when I was less than a year old. In Mansfeld, I began school at an early age. I do not recall my exact age, but in my day most children began school at about age 7. Some think that I began school as early as age 4. That seems rather young, but I do recall being carried to school in the arms of Nicholas Oemler. (Incidentally, Nick later became my brother-in-law.) The school was only three or four blocks from our family home. If I had been six or seven years old, I hardly would have had need to be carried. I may have been four and a half, but I cannot recall that for certain.

The school that I attended was called the *Trivialschule*, not because the material we learned was trivial, but because our course of instruction was called the Trivium. The Trivium included grammar, logic, and rhetoric. Grammar taught us how to write correctly, logic taught us how to think clearly, and rhetoric taught us how to speak coherently and persuasively. Of course, we also studied Latin. No one could be considered educated if he could not read and write Latin, the universal language of my day. Music was also part of our daily curriculum.

Frankly, I did not like school in those early years. Children were beaten and thrashed if they had not learned their lessons well. I received my share. In 1524, I wrote a treatise, *To the Councilmen of All Cities in Germany That They Establish and Maintain Christian Schools*.[1] In that treatise I said, "Today, schools are not what they once were, a hell and purgatory in which we were tormented with *casualibus* [noun cases] and *temporalibus* [verb tenses] and yet learned less than nothing despite all the flogging, trembling, anguish, and misery."[2] Someone recorded me speaking at my dinner table in my adult years and quoted me as saying, "Some teachers are as cruel as hangmen. I was once beaten fifteen times before noon, without any fault of mine, because I was expected to decline and conjugate although I had not yet been taught this."[3]

---

1 LW 45:341.

2 LW 45:369.

3 LW 54:457.

You might be interested to note that Huldrych (Ulrich) Zwingli, the great reformer of the church in Switzerland, was born on 1 January 1484, less than two months after my birth. I met Huldrych in 1529 in an attempt to join our two reform movements. We agreed on much of the faith but could not reach an agreement on the Lord's Supper. I'll tell you more about that later.

Several events of monumental significance occurred when I was about eight or nine years old. Actually, I was not aware of them in my lifetime. Two of those events you know very well; two, I expect, will be news to you. I'll tell you about them next time. Until then, keep the faith.

Letter 3

I promised to tell you about four events that happened when I was eight or nine years old. I knew about none of them when they happened and about only one of them subsequently. Remember, no one in my day had television, radio, or daily newspapers as you have. News traveled by foot.

On 11 August 1492, Rodrigo Borgia became pope and took the name Alexander VI. You may know that I had some real battles with popes later in my life. But because I was only a youth, I knew nothing of Alexander's election to his exalted position, nor did I care. I mention Alexander VI only because he represented the papacy at the point of its greatest depravity. Don't confuse the popes in your day with the popes in my day. Those in your day represent a vast improvement.

Alexander VI was an opportunist without scruples. He had no pastoral heart, and he used the papacy for his own personal ends. He was the father of several children both before and after his election to the papacy. He had a daughter named Lucrezia and a son named Cesare among them. Although Cesare (almost certainly) killed his own brother, his father protected him and even gave him the position of cardinal (a bishop with extraordinary honors) in the Roman Church.

While there is so much more that I could tell you about Alexander VI, I do want to mention a bit of trivia that will be of interest to you. The reason that Brazil is the only country in South America where the population speaks Portuguese while the rest of South America speaks Spanish relates to a decision made by Alexander VI. He declared that all newly discovered lands west of a meridian 370 leagues west of the Cape Verde Islands (off the west coast of Africa) would belong to Spain, while east of that meridian the lands would belong to Portugal. Look at a map of South America, and note how far east Brazil extends. I forget so easily that we used terms in my day that are not familiar to you. The distance of one league was the distance that a person could walk in one hour. I know, that is not very precise, but that was one of our ways of measuring distance. The treaty that formalized that line of demarcation is called the Treaty of Tordesillas.

That line of demarcation resulted from a second event that happened when I was nine years old. You know of that event better than I. Christopher Columbus, sailing for the king and queen of Spain, discovered what you know as America. Columbus thought that he had discovered a western route to India. That explains why the people Columbus met when he arrived were called Indians.

The third major event in 1492 was the end of the Moorish Kingdom of Spain. After Muhammad founded the religion of Islam in the seventh century AD, his followers moved across North Africa and crossed the Strait of Gibraltar. They moved quite far north on the Iberian Peninsula, thereby threatening Western Christianity. (Later in my life the Muslim Turks threatened Western Europe from the East. I'll tell you more about that much later.) But in 1492, the Muslim threat in Spain was eliminated as the Muslim Moors were repulsed into Africa.

Since the Muslim Kingdom had its center in Granada, in southern Spain, I sometimes wonder whether the popular song lyrics that some of you may recall from your youth, "Granada will live again, the glory of yesterday," has reference to that kingdom. My wonder is piqued even more because Islam seems to be making strong advances in Western Europe. Well, if Christians do not pray and bear witness to our Lord Jesus Christ, Islam may be the agent of God's judgment on a lifeless and faithless people. Be alert, my friends, God has previously used pagans to punish His faithless people!

The fourth event of 1492 was the expulsion of all Jews from Spain. I shall not comment more about that expulsion except to say that in Europe, in my day, Jews were not liked. I was a child of my time, as you are of yours. I was no different. In the early years of the Reformation, I did write a tract *That Jesus Christ Was Born a Jew*. I wrote rather kindly about the Jews in that tract. But in my later years, I spoke very harshly against the Jews. Many Lutherans in your day are embarrassed by what I said. I guess that I'll have to tell you more about that later also.

Next time, I'll resume telling you about my schooling. Until then, keep the faith. Remember to be faithful to Jesus Christ, not to Martinus.

Letter 4

I digressed a bit last time to tell you about several important events that happened when I was eight or nine years old.

I was thirteen in 1497 when my parents sent me to school in Magdeburg. I do not recall my father giving any reason for sending me away to school. Perhaps, since my father had become moderately prosperous, he felt that he could afford one of the best schools for his son; the Magdeburg school had a good reputation.

I spent only one year at Magdeburg. Most people think that this was a rather uneventful year for me. In most ways, perhaps, it was. But the course of one's life can be changed by the most unlikely events. The year in Magdeburg was important in my development because during that year I came under the influence of a group known as the *Nullbrüder*. You will know them as "Brethren of the Common Life." They were simple Christian people who emphasized Bible reading and the return to a simple, pious life. Some of those men taught in the school I attended. I cannot say that the *Nullbrüder* had a profound influence on my life, but I never forgot their simple way of life that so contrasted with the pomp and splendor of the religious establishment of my day.

Again, since I was only a teenager, but an impressionable teenager, the *Nullbrüder* emphasis on Bible reading may have influenced me more than I ever realized.

I am much like you; I cannot be too certain of all the formative factors in my youth. But I do know that I did share with the *Nullbrüder* that deep appreciation and commitment to the Bible as the Word of God. I suppose that nothing more characterizes my entire life than that unswerving faithfulness to the Bible as the Word of God. Nearly a quarter of a century after my year in Magdeburg, I stood before the emperor of the Holy Roman Empire and said, "My conscience is captive to the Word of God." But, that's a story for later.

In Magdeburg, I saw what I considered a most unusual sight. A member of the nobility had become a monk. Prince William of Anhalt had left the relative leisure of the nobility to become a Franciscan friar. He carried a sack like all mendicants (beggars) do, asking for food. I was only fourteen, but I recall saying in later life, "With my own eyes I saw him . . .

carrying a sack like a donkey. He had so worn himself down by fasting and vigil that he looked like a death's head, mere bone and skin. No one could look upon him without feeling ashamed of his own life."[1]

I cannot remember for certain, but I think that I saw a copy of the Bible for the first time during that year 1497 in Magdeburg.[2]

It may be a bit of trivia to you, but in the same year, 1497, my closest companion in my later life was born. His name was Philip Schwartzerd. If you know my native tongue, you will recognize his name means "black earth." Philip became a great student of the Greek language. He was much more competent with Greek than I. Consequently, when I translated the New Testament into German, Philip was an invaluable assistant. Philip was so taken with Greek that he even changed his last name to Melanchthon (which has the same meaning in Greek as Schwartzerd does in German). You'll hear more about Philip in later years.

This seems like a good time to stop writing. After that one year in Magdeburg, I was sent to school in Eisenach. I loved Eisenach. I'll tell you about my school experience in Eisenach next time.

Keep the faith! Tell the story!

---

1 Bainton, 33.

2 Schwiebert, 119.

LETTER 5

Following my one year in Magdeburg (1497), my parents sent me to school in Eisenach. I do not recall whether I was ever told the reason my father made this change. (I don't think my mother had any influence in the change in my schooling.) In my day, teenagers didn't question the decisions made by their parents.

I may speculate that I was sent to Eisenach in 1498 because my father had an uncle living there. My mother had some relatives in Eisenach as well. Perhaps my father thought that I could live with that old great-uncle or some of the other relatives. However, uncle Konrad Hutter was too poor to keep me, and I expect that my mother's relatives were equally poor.

Eisenach always had a special place in my heart. I must say that I loved Eisenach. Maybe that was because I was a teenager in what you would call "high school" years.

I did well in school, but I would certainly not say that I was brilliant. Many years later, one of my colleagues, Philip Melanchthon, told about my years in Eisenach. He said, "Here he rounded out his Latin studies; and since he had a penetrating mind and rich gifts of expression, he soon outstripped his companions in eloquence, language, and poetic verse."[1]

That was a nice compliment by my friend Philip, but I have no idea how he could be so certain. He didn't even know me at the time. Indeed, I was a serious student and did well, but those comments about a "penetrating mind" and "rich gifts of expression" I fear were read back into my teenage years from what Philip knew of me in later life.

I did enjoy music throughout my life, and I must say, I was above average in musical ability.

That musical ability had a utilitarian value for me while at Eisenach as a student. It was a common practice for students to go from house to house singing with the expectation that we would be given food and drink for our singing. (Did you ever wonder where your practice of Christmas caroling originated? Our singing, of course, was not only during the Christmas season but yearlong.)

---

1 Schwiebert, 125.

I was recognized for my exceptional singing ability and was invited to room and take meals with two different families in Eisenach. You may not be surprised that there was a condition attached. I was expected to tutor one of the children in one of those families.

I did well enough in school to be recommended for study at the university level.

I must make one additional comment about Eisenach. The small town (the population in my day was about four thousand[2]) stood at the base of a hill on which the Wartburg Castle had been built several hundred years before my birth. This was the fortress in which I was to be held—somewhat against my will—about a quarter of a century later. That quasi-imprisonment followed my conviction as a heretic. Actually I was *not* imprisoned; it was my prince's way of keeping me safe. I will tell you more about that later.

There were two fine universities in the part of Germany in which I lived. One was in Leipzig, and the other in Erfurt. In the spring of 1501, I entered the University of Erfurt in the Department of Liberal Arts. I was matriculated as "Martinus Ludher ex Mansfeld." I'll tell you more about Erfurt and my university studies next time.

Now I must return to my rest. As for you, keep the faith!

---

2 Brecht 1:17.

Letter 6

I mentioned in my previous letter that I entered the University of Erfurt in the spring of 1501.

Erfurt was among the three or four largest cities in Germany, with a population of about twenty thousand.[1] The University of Erfurt was one of five in Germany at that time. In my area, there were only two for my consideration: Leipzig and Erfurt.[2] My father preferred Erfurt, probably because it was closer to our hometown.

University students in your day could not possibly understand the regimented lifestyle of students in my day. I lived in a boardinghouse with other students. We were required to arise at 4:00 a.m. and be in bed by 8:00 p.m. We all dressed the same, wearing a uniform, and our food was prescribed.

When I entered the university, indeed throughout my four years as a university student, I had not the least thought of becoming a monk, priest, or theologian. My father wanted me to become a lawyer. I did enter law school after completing my master's degree in 1505.

I completed my baccalaureate studies in the fall of 1502, ranking thirtieth in a class of fifty-seven. That is about as average as one can get. I continued on to the next level of university studies and received my master of arts degree in January 1505. I showed myself to be a somewhat better student on that level. I finished second in a class of seventeen.[3]

My father was proud of my success, and henceforth when speaking to me in my native tongue, he never addressed me with the familiar *Du* (you) but with the more respectful *Sie* (you).[4]

I should tell you just briefly about the educational or philosophical bias of the University of Erfurt in my day. (All educational institutions and teachers represent some bias. Beware of those who claim to be ob-

---

1 Brecht 1:23.

2 Loewenich, 46.

3 Gritsch, 5.

4 Bainton, 24.

jective and unbiased. They represent the greatest danger.) I mention this bias at the risk of oversimplification only because I think that it influenced me in my understanding of God and God's revelation of himself in my later theological studies.

There were two schools of thought in my day. One was called *via antiqua* (the old way). It was based on the thought of Thomas Aquinas, who lived about three hundred years before my time. Thomas taught that human reason could be used to bring a person to faith in God. The other approach to learning was called *via moderna* (the new way). It was based on the thought of the English Franciscan William of Ockham (Occam). William taught that human reason is of no value in the realm of faith. The professors at Erfurt represented the *via moderna*. It will not be surprising to you that I also took that position. Are we not all products of our teachers? I was no different than you in that regard. In my later theological reflection, you will probably detect my bias against reason in the realm of faith.

Next time, I'll tell you about my entrance into the monastery. Until then, keep the faith!

Letter 7

When I received my master of arts degree from Erfurt University in January 1505, I was expected to lecture in the Arts faculty for two years. At the same time, I had a choice to continue my education in one of the three professions available in my day: medicine, law, and theology. I was never attracted to medicine as a career, although I did have a son, Paul, who became a physician. Theology did not fit my father's plans for my future. He had determined that I should become a lawyer and had already purchased for me a *Corpus Juris*, a set of law books.[1] Up until that time, I had never indicated any objection to my father's plan for my life, and I do not recall that I had ever expressed any interest in pursuing a career in theology.

On 20 May 1505, I began my study of law. One month later, on 20 June, I returned to my parental home in Mansfeld. I do not even recall the purpose of that journey, but I remained at home for about ten days. On my return to Erfurt on 2 July, only a few miles from Erfurt, near Stotternheim, I found myself in a terrifying rainstorm. A bolt of lightning struck so close to me that I was knocked to the ground. In fear I cried out, "St. Anne, help me, and I will become a monk." St. Anne, the mother of the Virgin Mary, was the patron saint of miners. You recall that my father was a miner. Consequently, it was she on whom I called in my moment of fear.

I returned to Erfurt and told my friends of my decision. They were distraught because they knew that to enter a monastery meant my withdrawal from the world. It was almost like a death; they would see me no more. I recall saying to them as we parted, "Today you see me, but never again!"[2] Of course that parting was painful for me, as it was for my friends. But my course had been set; I was resolute in my decision.

The distress of my friends paled in comparison to the reaction of my father. He was livid. In fact, my decision to enter the monastery created a monumental rift between my father and me. We did not speak to each other for a rather long time. Only with the greatest reluctance did my father eventually accept my decision. However, I don't think that he ever fully approved of it.

---

1 Bainton, 24.

2 Brecht 1:50.

After making the decision to enter the monastery, I then had to decide which monastic order I would enter. Finally, on 17 July 1505, I applied for admission to the "Black Cloister" in Erfurt, the chapter house of the Hermits of St. Augustine.

Next time, I'll tell you a bit about my early months in the monastery and what I expected to gain by entering. Until then, keep the faith.

Letter 8

I mentioned that I had entered the Augustinian monastery in Erfurt, Germany, in July 1505. About six weeks later, I was admitted to a one-year probationary period called the *novitiate*. Did you ever wonder from where your word *novice* came? Yes, indeed, I was a novice monk for that first year. Only after that first year was I allowed to make the threefold, lifelong vows of poverty, chastity, and obedience. Thereupon, I became a full-fledged friar. (The word *friar* comes from the Latin word *frater*, which means brother.)

The monastic life was austere and severe. I was duly informed of the nature of monastic life when I began my novitiate. My choice of a monastic life was a voluntary act on my part, and I understood the severity of that life before I made my vows.

Upon entering the monastery, my head was shaved, save for a band of hair no more than two fingers width. That band of hair was called a tonsure (*tonsure* in Latin means shearing). I was also given a white woolen shirt that reached to the ankles. That "habit" was worn night and day. When in public, we monks covered the habit with a black cowl and hood.

I was given a private cell about six feet by ten feet. It was unheated, including in the winter. There was no bed, only a straw sack on which to lie, and woolen blankets. A table, chairs, candlestick, and storage cabinet completed my cell.

The externals were the easy part. Life was almost entirely religious and regimented. (At that stage in my life, I believed, as everybody believed, that life could be divided into two neat categories: the religious and the secular.) The other brothers and I attended public prayers at seven times each day from before dawn to after dark. On Sundays, the regimen was increased. Besides the prayer time, there was Bible study and confession, along with the menial tasks required of all brothers—to keep "home" clean and provide for the daily needs of the community, to provide and prepare food, clean the common areas, and so on.

Certainly, you must wonder why anyone would submit to such an austere life with its intense demands. (I haven't begun to tell you all the detailed requirements.) There was one reason: to win approval of almighty God, by acquiring enough merits so that I could one day live in the presence of that demanding Sovereign of the Universe. I was terrified of that Sovereign. I knew my unworthiness. If only he would see my religious devotion and, on the basis of that devotion, count me worthy! My conscience agonized over the prospect of spending eternity in hell. Nothing was too high a price to pay to escape that torment. I was delighted that I could take the religious way of finding peace with God. (Later I'll tell how that attempt failed miserably.) I did discover, however, that an extraordinarily high price had been paid for my escape from that torment. Someone other than me made that payment.

There is so much more that I could tell you about the monastic life, but now I am weary. I must return to my rest. Next time, I'll tell you about my assignment to become a priest. Until then, keep the faith.

Letter 9

You recall that I made the monk's lifelong vow of poverty, chastity, and obedience in the fall of 1506, following my year as a novitiate. When I made that vow, the Rule of the Augustinian Order was placed in my hands. The prior of the monastery (prior means first, the principal, superintendent, spiritual father, final authority in a local monastic community) said to me, "If you keep this rule, I promise you eternal life." Those were the only words I wanted to hear. I can still visualize myself making my vow, prostrated on the floor in front of the altar of the church, my arms stretched wide in the form of a cross. The prior stood on the steps above me. He asked, "What do you seek?" I responded, "God's grace and your mercy." The prior then raised me to my feet and asked me a few questions about whether I was married or had any legal obligations or any secret diseases. When I affirmed that I was free from all those impediments, the prior described the rigors to which I must submit. (I described some of those rigors in my previous letter.) The prior then asked me if I was ready to accept the burdens that he had described. I answered, "Yes, by the help of God."

I will tell you later how I was released from those vows. After that release, I had only Christ and His death for me to which I could cling. I exchanged the promise to the prior, which was contingent on keeping the monastic rule, for the promise of Christ, who took all the burden of "keeping the rule" on my behalf. I then had only to trust what Christ had done for me. That was the greatest liberation I ever experienced.

But now I am getting ahead of myself. I promised to tell you about becoming a priest. When I entered the monastery as a novice in 1505, I wanted only to be a simple, humble monk performing the religious exercises required to assure the eternal salvation of my soul. But, remember, I had taken the vow of obedience.

Shortly after my permanent acceptance of the monastic life in the fall of 1506, I was told that I was to become a priest. (The monastery had both brothers and fathers. The fathers were those who had been ordained into the priesthood.)

Preparation for the priesthood was different in my day than in yours. Your clergy spend about four years after college studying the Bible, theological issues, the history of the church, and practical aspects of the public ministry of the Word of God and the Sacraments. After that, they are ordained by the church for service within the church. I was ordained a priest on 3 April 1507, only about six months after I was selected for the priesthood; theological studies followed.

There are some distinct advantages to your system. I must say that there were some very uneducated priests serving in my day, indeed to the point of embarrassment. God is not honored by ignorance. (Of course, I do not know from firsthand experience, but I have heard that your system of theological education does not guarantee absence of ignorance. I do expect, however, that your system of training helps a great deal.)

There is at least one advantage to the system of ordination practiced in my day. It separates the ministry from academic proficiency. There were no academic honors associated with ordination. It was simply the call of the church, under the guidance of the Spirit of God, to select those who would be ordained by the church and given the power to celebrate the Mass. The only obligation of a priest in my day, other than hearing confession, was to celebrate the Mass.

Mind you, saying the Mass was no small responsibility, nor was it a weekly, Sunday obligation. The Mass fairly encompassed the entire life of every believer. So fundamental and foundational was the Mass to the religious life of every believer that I think I will write my next letter telling you about the understanding of the Mass in my day.

I celebrated my first Mass on 2 May 1507. I'll tell you what a traumatic experience that was for me when I tell you more about the understanding of the Mass. As for you, keep the faith.

Letter 10

I was terror stricken when I celebrated my first Mass as a priest in 1507. What right did I have—I, a miserable sinner—to hold in my hands the holy body and sacred blood of Jesus Christ, the sinless Son of God? Not only could I hold Christ in my hands, but now, as a priest of the Holy Roman Catholic Church, I also had power not given even to angels. I had the power to transform the substance of the bread and wine into the body and blood of Christ.

The certainty of my sinfulness in the presence of a holy God, and my new power to transubstantiate the elements of bread and wine into the body and blood of Christ, so terrorized me that I wanted to bolt from the altar. I would have done just that had my superior not prevented me.

Thirty years later, I recalled that first Mass and said, in casual conversation with friends, "Later when I stood there during the mass and began the canon [the Canon of the Mass was the central moment when the priest spoke the words that were believed to transubstantiate the bread and wine into the body and blood of Jesus], I was so frightened that I would have fled [from the altar] if I hadn't been admonished by the prior. For when I read the words, 'Thee, therefore, most merciful Father,' etc., and thought I had to speak to God without a Mediator, I felt like fleeing from the world like Judas. Who can bear the majesty of God without Christ as Mediator? In short, as a monk I experienced such horrors; I had to experience them before I could fight them."[1]

You might wonder what caused me such anguish. Let me try to explain. Remember, in the spring of 1507, I was twenty-three years old, a loyal son of the Church of Rome. My understanding of God and of the Mass changed dramatically in subsequent years, but at the time I became a priest I understood God and the Mass in the same way as the vast majority of my contemporaries. God was depicted as a stern and terrifying judge who demanded holiness of mortals. Without that holiness, God would consign souls to the fires of hell.

I never wavered from the certainty that a holy God demands righteousness from men and women, but I did later understand that such righteousness is not attainable by any human effort but can be received

1 LW 54:234.

only as a gift. I'll tell you more about that when I share with you how that realization broke upon me a few years later.

I must say, however, that if folks in my day quaked before a holy God, forgetting the fatherly loving kindness of that God, I fear that in your day that holiness and distance created by your sin has been forgotten. God is understood too much as merely a buddy, a pal, or an equal. I was appalled to hear that some even refer to the Almighty as "the man upstairs." What a scandal! If my age was over-terrorized by the holiness of God, your age has lost all sense of holiness, and the appropriate reverence, if not terror, that is appropriate to that holiness.

At any rate, the terror at my first Mass as a priest derived partially from that sense of holiness before which I then stood. The second factor that contributed to my fear was the understanding of the Mass itself. Again, my understanding of the Mass changed in later years, but in 1507 I remained a child of my time.

For many centuries, the Church of Rome had taught that there are seven sacraments. They all convey God's grace. But five of the seven were offered only once during a lifetime: Baptism at birth, confirmation at the beginning of adolescence, marriage as one enters adulthood, holy orders for those who were set apart for the priesthood, and extreme unction (anointing with oil at the point of "extremis") at the end of life. Only penance and the Eucharist remained as sacraments to be repeated frequently throughout life, and penance was intently linked to the Eucharist. The Eucharist became *the* sacrament. It virtually encompassed all of one's religious life and, indeed, the life of the church. The forgiveness of sins depended on the right reception of that sacrament. So holy was the sacrament that the laity could receive only the body of Christ; the blood of Christ was reserved for the priests. (That had been the practice for about four hundred years prior to my day.) The priest who celebrated the Eucharist must be morally pure, must say the right words without stammering or missing a word, and must not let his mind wander. He must go to confession himself before Mass and receive absolution for his sins. Should he then miss a word or find his mind wandering, he would be guilty of the gravest sin.

I knew my sinfulness. I knew my unworthiness. I quaked as I stood in the presence of a holy God. I wanted to run, but I was prevented. So I completed my first Mass, but I was emotionally drained.

I'm exhausted even recalling that event. I must now return to my rest. Next time, I'll tell you a bit about my life as an Augustinian monk after I was ordained a priest. Until then, keep the faith.

Letter 11

Following my ordination in 1507, when I was twenty-three years old, my superiors in the Augustinian monastic order selected me for advanced biblical and theological training. For five and a half years, I was a student until I received the degree of doctor of theology on 12 October 1512. Most of that time was spent in the Augustinian monastery in Erfurt.

After one and a half years of study, I was sent to the University of Wittenberg for about one year to be a lecturer. There I lectured on the ethics of the ancient Greek philosopher Aristotle. I must tell you that my heart was not in that teaching, because my first love was the Bible. But, as an obedient monk, I did as I was directed.

Those years in Erfurt were uneventful, but I was miserable. I did complete the four steps that led to the doctor of theology degree, but my spirit was always heavy. In those years, indeed until after I received my final academic degree, I knew God only as a stern, demanding deity, and I knew Jesus as a severe judge. Day after day, I labored under that terror, which tore my life. I had no peace because I was never sure that I had done enough to satisfy that demanding and severe God. I do not know how to tell you in English the anguish of soul that I experienced. In my native language, it was called *Anfechtung*. Ask one of your German friends to translate that word for you into English. In the Latin language, the word is *tentatio*. However, because shamefully few schools offer Latin in your day, I do not expect you to be familiar with that word. Regardless of how you translate the word, the experience was like a perpetual spiritual death march, a deep religious foreboding and depression that engulfed me. I felt as though God had abandoned me. I could not rid myself of the terror that had seized my life.

When I lectured on the Book of Psalms, my first teaching assignment at the University of Wittenberg, I came upon Psalm 22. I shuddered when I read the words, "My God, My God, why have You forsaken Me? Why are You so far from saving Me, from the words of My groaning? O My God, I cry by day, but You do not answer, and by night, but I find no rest" [Psalm 22:1–2]. I remembered that those were the words Jesus spoke as He hung upon the cross. Jesus, too, suffered *Anfechtung* just like me. But if my *Anfechtungen* nearly drove me to despair, how much more powerful was that suffering for Jesus? I had only the weight of my own sin to bear. Jesus bore the sins of the world. There was God abandoned by God; who can understand it? One of my biographers in your day has said that Christ's descent into hell was "nothing other than his sense of alienation from God."[1] I don't recall ever having said that, but it sounds about right.

That recognition that Jesus experienced *Anfechtungen*, as I had, helped, I think, to form what many in your day call the theology of the cross. If I remember, I will tell you more about the theology of the cross when I tell you about a disputation I had in Heidelberg in 1518.

Later in life, I described my terror with these words: "There in the convent I was the most wretched man on earth, passing whole nights in weeping and feeling that everything was hopeless, which condition no one could alleviate. . . . For I no longer knew Christ except as a stern judge from whom I wanted to flee, yet was unable to escape."[2]

I am fatigued even recalling those bitter years in the monastery, striving to please a remote God who had me sentenced to hell in spite of all my prayers and religious observances.

Next time, I'll tell you about the trip I made to Rome during those years in Erfurt.

---

1 Bainton, 62.

2 Schwiebert, 153.

Letter 12

Only once did I travel beyond my beloved Germany. Of course, Germany in my day was quite different from the Germany you know. There was no central government. So, technically, there was no Germany. There were only the Germanic people living in a variety of small political units ruled by a prince or duke. In addition, there were a number of free cities that existed independently from any superior political authority. Oh, excuse me; I almost got carried away trying to describe the political situation that characterized the Germanic people in the sixteenth century. I promised to tell you about my only travel outside of Germany.

In the fall of 1510, in November, if I remember correctly, a fellow Augustinian monk and I were sent to Rome as representatives of the Augustinian congregation in Germany. There were fifty-four separate Augustinian communities in Germany. Would you believe that there was a little spat that separated those communities into two groups? (I surely hope that there are no spats between those who use my name in your day.) Twenty-nine congregations were called Reformed Augustinians, and twenty five were called Conventional Augustinians. The Reformed congregations, sometimes called Observants, wanted strict observance of the Augustinian Rule that governed our life together, and they insisted on a high level of education. The Conventional congregations wanted more laxity in following the Augustinian Rule. The decision was made to favor the less stringent rule preferred by the Conventionals and to unite all the Augustinian monasteries in Germany under that interpretation of the Rule.

As I said, a companion and I were selected to go to Rome and appeal the decision to the general of the entire Augustinian Order. I need not tell you how difficult that journey was. The journey was about eight hundred miles from Erfurt to Rome. Nor do I need tell you that the journey was made entirely on foot. On a good day, we could walk about twenty-five miles. But, remember, that walk was in November and December; and we had to cross the snow-covered Alps. The trip took about forty days. I do not recall whether we arrived in Rome prior to Christmas or following the celebration of that most glorious event of the incarnation (taking on flesh; that is, birth) of the Son of God, your Savior and mine.

We presented our appeal to the general of the Augustinian Order, who graciously received us. He put off a response for about a month. During that month, I had time to visit the holy places of that most holy of all cities. (At that time, 1510–11, I really believed that Rome was a holy city.) Rome was the seat of the vicar of Christ on earth, the successor to St. Peter, the pope. Julius II was the pope at that time, but he and most of his cardinals were not in Rome; they were in Bologna on a military expedition. In addition, Rome contained scores, even hundreds, of relics to venerate.

I must tell you about relics. I'm a bit embarrassed to tell you because only a few years later I excoriated relics and their alleged benefits. But in 1510–11, I was a faithful son of Mother Church, and, as best I can remember, I questioned neither the authenticity nor the benefits of venerating those relics. The Roman Church taught that relics were items that had been preserved (mostly) from the time of Christ. The teaching of the church was that the veneration (not quite worship, but adoration and contemplation) of those relics could reduce one's time in purgatory. (At that time, I still accepted the teaching of the Roman Church that most Christians, excepting saints, and they were few, would have to spend an indeterminate time in purgatory after death before entering heaven.)

Let me mention some of the alleged relics that could be venerated in Rome. There were eleven thorns from Christ's crown of thorns, a nail from the cross, pieces of wood from the cross, a sapphire with water and blood from Christ's side, some milk and some hair from the Virgin Mary. These are only a few. There was also a piece from the burning bush of Moses, the table on which Christ instituted the Lord's Supper, and even one of the pieces of silver that Judas received for betraying Jesus. The veneration of that relic alone could save a person 1,400 years from purgatory.

Well, I should not get carried away with relics. Of more lasting impression to me at that time was the perfunctory way in which most of the Roman priests rushed through the Mass, reciting the words and performing the ritual in a mechanical manner. Many of them did not even know Latin; they just recited the words. Some even made a joke of the Mass. That was the negative image of Rome and its clergy that remained with me throughout my life.

About a month after our arrival in Rome, the general of the Augustinian Order curtly denied our appeal, and as loyal sons of the church, we returned home. I think that it was about April 1511 that we arrived back in Erfurt. Shortly thereafter, I was transferred to the University of Wittenberg. I'll tell you about that next time. As for you, keep the faith.

Letter 13

Shortly after I returned to Erfurt from my trip to Rome in the spring of 1511, I was transferred to Wittenberg, which would be my home for the rest of my days. I think that I arrived in Wittenberg in about September. My assignment there was to be a teacher of Bible in the new university established about a decade earlier by my sovereign, Prince Frederick the Wise.

You must understand that politics, jealousies, and rivalries were as rife in my day as they are in yours. I suspect that my transfer had something to do with my participation on the losing side of the controversy between the Reformed and Conventional Augustinian congregations in Germany. No one ever said that to be the reason for my transfer; it is just an assumption on my part. Regardless of the reason for the transfer, it proved to be a blessing from God.

Wittenberg was in the territory of Saxony. But Saxony had been divided between two brothers, Ernest and Albert, in 1485 when I was only two years old. The two Saxon territories were referred to as Ernestine Saxony and Albertine Saxony. To further complicate matters, Ernestine Saxony was referred to as Electoral Saxony because since 1356 the prince who exercised sovereignty in that territory was one of seven electors who filled the throne of the Holy Roman Empire when there was a vacancy. Albertine Saxony was called Ducal Saxony because a duke held the sovereignty in that dukedom.

Leipzig was in Ducal Saxony and boasted one of the most prestigious universities in all of Europe. Electoral Saxony had no university until Prince Frederick established the University of Wittenberg in 1502. I must admit that I believe that university was established in the little city of Wittenberg, population of about two thousand, because of some envy on the part of my beloved protector, Prince Frederick.

From 1507 to 1512, I studied for a doctor of theology degree that would allow me to be a professor of theology. There were four steps in completing that course of study.[1] The first degree granted the title *Biblicus* (lector). That allowed me to teach elementary courses on the Bible.

1 Schwiebert, 148–49.

The second degree toward a doctorate was *Formatus*. That degree showed that I had mastered the terminology of the medieval dictionaries. The third degree was *Sententarius*. Upon completing that degree, I was permitted to lecture on the *Sentences* of Peter Lombard, the standard theological text for all preparing for the priesthood. The fourth and final degree was *Licentiatus*. After completing a rigorous debate with the professors of the graduate school, the doctoral degree was granted. Remember that a debate in my time was more like an oral examination that doctoral candidates must take in your day. More than five years of my life were given to that study; I was then given full right to be a regular lecturer on theology.

I had completed all the requirements for the doctor of theology degree, but I did not have the fifty gulden to pay for the granting of the degree. I know that a gulden means nothing to you, and I know nothing about your monetary system. Perhaps it will help you understand the value of a gulden if I tell you that the price of an ox in my day was one or two gulden.[2]

Upon my promise (actually it was not my promise because I was a monk, pledged to obedience to my superiors, but a promise by my superiors on my behalf) to Frederick the Wise that I would teach at his university the rest of my life, Frederick provided the fifty gulden to pay for the degree. I was finally awarded the degree on 19 October 1512.

To receive the degree, I had to swear to obey the Roman Church and to promote peace among scholars. You may think that subsequent events in my life showed me to be unfaithful to my vows. You might be wise to reserve judgment on that issue.

Next time, I'll tell you about my teaching assignment in Wittenberg. Until then, keep the faith.

---

2 Schwiebert, 107.

Letter 14

You recall that when I entered the monastery in 1507 I had no desire to become a priest or a doctor of theology. All I wanted was to find peace with God. I was assured that I would find that peace through the religious practices of the monastery.

By 1512, I found myself both a priest and a doctor of theology. But my anguish of spirit continued. I was never certain that I had done enough to satisfy a righteous God. There was no doubt in my mind, nor is there to this day, that a holy and righteous God demands the same of those who would live in His presence. As I read the Bible, I came across the phrase "the righteousness of God." I hated that phrase. It reminded me of my unrighteousness and led to deep depression, indeed, almost to despair.

Sometime between 1513 and 1519, I had an experience that changed everything. And when I say *everything*, I am not using hyperbole. It changed not only my life but has also had a profound effect on the whole Christian Church and, so I am told by those who have joined me in subsequent years, has had an effect on all of Western civilization.

You may ask, "If this experience had such a dramatic effect, why can you not be more precise as to when it happened?" First, remembering over five hundred years requires great recall. Second, so many people have written biographies of my life that they have confused even me. Those biographers who have studied my life seem to know more about me than I know about myself. You see, I didn't study my life; I just lived it. The experience about which I spoke is sometimes called the "tower experience." It was so called because my study was in a tower room in the Augustinian monastery in Wittenberg.

In preparing for my lecture on the Psalms, I again came across that awful, threatening, and damning phrase—"the righteousness of God." I think I was preparing a lecture on Psalm 32 or 72. (Again, my biographers have confused me.) In your Bible, you will find the phrase "in Your righteousness deliver me" in Psalm 31:1, and "may he judge Your people with righteousness" in Psalm 72:2. (The numbering of some psalms is different in your Bible than in the Latin version of the Bible that I used.)

In studying that psalm in preparation for my lecture, I referred to Paul's Letter to the Romans where that same phrase, "the righteousness of God," is used. Paul talks about the Gospel (good news) of Jesus Christ and says, "In it [the Gospel] the righteousness of God is revealed from faith for faith, as it is written, 'The righteous shall live by faith'" (Rom. 1:17). Then I was struck like a whack on the side of the head. My righteousness before God is not something that I obtain no matter how much effort I expend, and it is apart from my most noble religious practices. Righteousness is a gift given to me by God; it is the righteousness of Jesus. His righteousness becomes my righteousness, and it is all mine by faith alone in my blessed Savior.

Long after that blessed revelation, or insight as some might call it, I was constrained to prepare a preface to the publication of some of my writings. Less than a year before my death, in March 1545, I prepared that preface. In that preface I wrote, "At last, by the mercy of God, meditating day and night, I gave heed to the context of the words, namely, 'In it the righteousness of God is revealed, as it is written, "He who through faith is righteous shall live."' There I began to understand that the righteousness of God is that by which the righteous lives by a gift of God, namely, by faith. And this is the meaning: the righteousness of God is revealed by the Gospel, namely, the passive righteousness with which [a] merciful God justifies us by faith, as it is written, 'He who through faith is righteous shall live.' Here I felt that I was altogether born again and had entered paradise itself through open gates."[1]

From that point on I was a new person. No longer did "the righteousness of God" strike terror within me; on the contrary, it now sounded like angelic music.

The rhapsody of that recall overwhelms me! I must now return to my rest in that blessed assurance. Next time, I'll tell you a little about my life as I entered the university setting. As for you, keep the faith.

1 LW 34:337.

Letter 15

In the fall of 1512, I was formally received into the faculty of the University of Wittenberg. I was still an Augustinian monk and obligated to obey my superiors.

Johann von Staupitz was my superior, a man whom I loved dearly and respected deeply to the end of my days. I think that he never did quite understand me, my disquietude of spirit, and my struggle with the Church of Rome. But he was a good pastor to me. He must have thought that I had some ability, because it was he who bade me move in directions counter to my own intentions.

All I wanted to do from the day I entered that monastery was to be a simple monk and find peace with God. I was not allowed to do the first, and I never achieved the second, in spite of the religious practices prescribed for us monks.

Father Staupitz insisted that I become a priest, then a doctor of theology, and then he selected me to succeed him as lecturer in Bible at the University of Wittenberg.

It was Staupitz who selected me to be the preacher at the monastery in 1511, even before I began as a professor at that university.

After being received into the faculty, it was my responsibility to select the biblical topic on which I would lecture. I selected the Book of Psalms.

Before beginning my lectures, I had to make preparation. It was not until late summer 1513 that I began teaching. I lectured only two hours a week, sometimes three hours. I completed the first course on Psalms probably in the spring of 1515.

I could tell you how I lectured and how I interpreted the Scriptures at that early stage in my teaching career, but that would only bore you. Let it be sufficient to say that I was a traditional medieval lecturer, and I interpreted the Scriptures in a traditional medieval way.

It did not take me too long to recognize that the traditional way of interpreting the Scriptures allowed one to read more into the Bible than what one got out of the Bible. I became convinced that the only proper way to read and interpret the Bible is to get at its literal meaning. I guess that won't make any sense to you unless I tell you that the medieval way of interpreting Scripture was to get as many as four meanings out of the section being studied. The fourfold interpretation includes the following: the literal historical meaning, an allegorical meaning, a moral meaning, and an anagogical meaning. The literal meaning is obvious. With the allegorical meaning, the words refer to something other than what they mean in a literal sense. You will understand how slippery that can get; the interpreter is free to make the words mean almost anything he or she chooses. With the moral meaning, the interpretation would teach one how to live an ethical life. With the anagogical meaning (anagogical means to lead upward), Scripture is made to refer to the future, perhaps heaven.

Let me try to give you an example of how this fourfold interpretation of the Bible might be used. You remember that the Gospels record several stories of Jesus healing people of blindness. The literal interpretation would mean that someone's physical eyesight had been restored. The allegorical interpretation might suggest that blindness refers to a person's inability or unwillingness to "see" the truths of the Christian faith. A moral interpretation would suggest that one is healed from immorality to a life of purity. The anagogical interpretation might suggest that restoration of sight is the hope of "seeing" the Divine Majesty in heaven.

I must admit that often in my preaching I did not follow my own principle of interpretation. Often I did assert allegorical meanings. Others may judge whether I was right or wrong in doing that. I will defend myself, however, by sharing with you my primary principle of interpretation. I believed that everything in the Bible must be interpreted in the light of Jesus Christ. (Theologians call that the Christological principle of interpretation.)

Why people ever bothered to keep my lecture notes on Psalms I'll never know. They aren't very good. Don't bother reading them; I might be embarrassed. I think that I did improve some in my next lectures on the books of Romans and Hebrews. I'll tell you a bit more about those lectures next time. Until then, keep the faith.

Letter 16

Following my lectures on the Psalms, I began a series on Paul's Letter to the Romans in the spring of 1515 and continued that series until the fall of 1516. I lectured on Mondays and Fridays. The class began at 6:30 a.m. (We went to bed early because we had no central heat to keep our homes warm and, of course, no insulation between the walls and no double-pane windows as you have. Additionally, we had only candles for light.)

Following the series on Romans, I completed a course on what I think was my favorite book of the Bible, my beloved Galatians. That course ran from October 1516 to March 1517. That was immediately followed by lectures on the Book of Hebrews from April 1517 to March 1518. Please don't hold me to those precise dates, but I think they are fairly accurate. Trying to recall dates after five hundred years strains my recollection. Precision of these dates is only trivial anyway.

I must tell you again that I was a child of my era as you are of yours, even though you may not recognize how much you are influenced by the prejudices, biases, practices, and presuppositions of your day. When I began my career as a lecturer on the Bible, I used the same method that my teachers had used when I was a student, a method that had not changed much in three hundred years. By your standards, the method I used would be tiresome, tedious, and boring. (However, I must say that I have spoken to enough people over the past five hundred years to realize that few teachers create excitement in learning even in your day.) Thank God three times a day if you have just one teacher who challenges you to open your mind and expand your intellectual horizon, one who forces you to question the assumptions of your day, and especially opens your mind to challenge the popular prejudices of your day. It did not come overnight, but you might know that I questioned and challenged some of the religious prejudices and presuppositions of my day.

I got distracted; you must excuse me. I was going to tell you about the teaching method that was operative in my day. Usually I had printed for my students the section of the biblical passage on which I intended to lecture. Of course, it was printed in Latin. I had the printer leave good space between the lines and generous margins on both sides of the text. I would then read my notes to the students and expect them to copy them exactly as I recited them. Notes on the meaning of individual words and phrases would be transcribed between the lines. Those notes were called *glosses*. Then I would provide the students with a commentary on the text as I had received them from earlier medieval scholars. Those notes were for inclusion on the wide margins. Those notes were called *scholia*.

During those series of lectures, I began to change my style of teaching. Rather than just reciting the tired, worn-out words of the previous generations, I began to quote the Church Fathers from the early centuries of the Church. I also quoted more freely from the Bible.

It was during those years that a fire began to burn in my belly. Don't get me wrong. I was still gripped by the prejudices of my day. Yet I recognized that something was wrong. Many of those prejudices needed serious reexamination. I was still a loyal son of the Roman Church. But my burning quest to be righteous in the presence of a righteous God drove me to question what was being taught.

The fire in my belly exploded in October 1517. I can't wait to tell you about the excitement, mixed with fear and foreboding, that was mine for the rest of my life after that explosion occurred. But before I do that, I must tell you about a discovery or two during the years of 1516 to 1518 that moved me along the "Road to Reformation," as some have called it. I'll tell you about those discoveries next time. Until then, keep the faith.

LETTER 17

By 1517, my blood was beginning to boil over the way the Holy Scriptures had been interpreted and taught. In that year, I began to write and publish a few pieces. In September, I wrote *A Disputation against Scholastic Theology*. I had intended to tell you about that disputation in this letter, but I think it will make no sense to you unless you understand something about Scholastic theology, or simply Scholasticism.

I think that there are two things that characterized my life in relation to what you call the Reformation of the Church. One was my passionate opposition to the abuses that the Roman Church inflicted on the laity in my day; the other was my fervent opposition to some of the theological teachings of the church. Most people are more interested in abuses, because abuses are juicier, but the theological issues were paramount to me. Scholasticism belongs to the latter.

When I came on the scene in the sixteenth century, Scholasticism had been the foundation of theology for about four hundred years. The simplest way to describe Scholasticism is to say that it was an attempt to reduce all Christian teaching (theology) to rigid truths and falsehoods and to do so by the use of rational argument. Perhaps "synthesis" is the word that best captures the Scholastic attempt. All truth was to be synthesized into one united whole. The object of that attempt, called "the Scholastic synthesis," was to reconcile all Christian teaching with reason and then to arrange it all into a cohesive system that would leave no question unanswered.

The Scholastics argued for the reasonableness of the Christian faith, and they used the philosophy of Aristotle as the form in which the questions were phrased and answered. They used the rules of logic to arrive at the truth.

The method of the Scholastics (sometimes they were called Schoolmen) was to state a proposition and then state its opposite. Then, on the basis of the Bible and the teachings of the Church Fathers, they would argue for a logical conclusion. You can understand where that put the Bible—it was a supporting document for a conclusion rather than the primary document.

Perhaps you can see how plastic or wooden the Christian faith (theology) became. There was no life, vibrancy, or joy in the faith; it was an entirely intellectual enterprise, an intellectual game.

There was a split within Scholasticism between those called Rationalists, who taught that what is real existed in universal ideas, and the Nominalists, who taught that ideas existed in name only; ideas were the result of human experiences.

The Franciscan monk Thomas Aquinas and Duns Scotus, a Dominican monk, represented the Realists. Even they did not agree. Another Franciscan, William of Ockham, represented the Nominalist school. He said that even the greatest Schoolmen could not prove religious doctrines and that Christian doctrine was reserved for faith in what God had revealed. Gabriel Biel was a proponent of Ockham and taught at the University of Erfurt. I studied at Erfurt about fifteen or twenty years after Biel died. I suppose that his emphasis had some influence on me through my teachers who had studied under him.

This may all be a bunch of gobbledygook to you. Sometimes, I get carried away and say far more than needs to be said. I do hope, however, that you understand the stifling nature of Scholasticism and how it reduces our precious faith to a logical game. If I have confused you on the nature of Scholasticism, don't give up. Research a few other places where you will find those who are more able than I to explain Scholasticism at this late date.

Next time, I will tell you about the *Disputation against Scholastic Theology*. As for you, keep the faith.

Letter 18

Now I can tell you about the *Disputation against Scholastic Theology*[1] that I prepared for a disputation on 7 September 1517.

I must tell you a bit about the word *disputation*. That word meant something different in my day than in yours. What we called a disputation you might call a debate, or in the case of a student, an examination. A series of theses, or statements, were presented to a student to be defended in the presence of professors. At other times a disputation might be between theologians. The Ninety-five Theses that I prepared was intended to be a disputation, but nobody showed up for the debate. The *Disputation against Scholastic Theology* consisted of ninety-seven theses that I prepared to be defended by a student to fulfill the requirement for a degree of bachelor of Holy Scripture.

I hope that in my previous letter I provided you with enough information about Scholasticism that I need not comment further on the meaning of "Scholastic theology." It was against that rationalistic distortion of the Christian faith that I wrote the theses to be defended by the student.

The ninety-seven theses were single sentences to be defended in the oral examination. In a few instances, there were two very short sentences.

In that disputation, I challenged three teachings of the Scholastic theologians: that the human will is free (I know that many who use my name in your day still claim that the human will is free. I wrote a more extensive treatise, *The Bondage of the Will*, several years later. I'll tell you about that in a subsequent letter); that righteousness can be obtained by human action; and that the Law (of God) can be fulfilled by human endeavor.

Here are a few of the things that I said about the alleged free will espoused by the Scholastics. I'll number them as you might find them printed in your day.

---

1 LW 31:5–16.

5. "It is false to state that man's inclination is free to choose between either of two opposites. Indeed the inclination is not free but captive."
9. "It (the human will) is nevertheless innately and inevitably evil and corrupt."
18. "To love God above all things by nature is a fictitious term, a chimera, as it were."
21. "No act is done according to (human) nature that is not an act of concupiscence (the residual of human sin that remains even in Christians) against God."
29. "The best and infallible preparation for grace and the sole disposition toward grace is the eternal election and predestination of God."
30. "On the part of man, however, nothing precedes grace except indisposition and even rebellion against grace."
39. "We are not masters of our actions . . . but servants."

Against the Scholastic teaching that humans have the innate capacity to become at least a little bit righteous by our own efforts, I wrote:

40. "We do not become righteous by doing righteous deeds but, having been made righteous, we do righteous deeds."
41. "Virtually the entire *Ethics* of Aristotle is the worst enemy of grace."
44. "Indeed, no one can become a theologian unless he becomes one without Aristotle."

Against the ability of humans to keep the Law (of God) I wrote:

70. "A good law will of necessity be bad for the natural will."
72. "What the law (of God) wants, the will never wants, unless it pretends to want it out of fear or love."
85. "Anyone's will would prefer, if it were possible, that there would be no law and to be entirely free."
87. "Since the law is good, the will, which is hostile to it, cannot be good."

Well, that's a summary of what I said. You may not like it, but I'm just as sure today of what I said in 1517 as when I first wrote it. Think about some of those comments. Talk about them with your Christian friends. If they dislodge some of your pet beliefs, think about them with greater effort. Or, are you too a Scholastic? The name "Scholastic" died out shortly after my time, but the reality of Scholasticism is still alive in your day.

This has been too long, but my blood boils again even thinking about those distortions of our blessed faith. Next time, I'll tell you about one event that happened less than two months after this disputation, an event that set Europe on fire. As for you, keep the faith.

Letter 19

About noon on All Hallows' Eve (I have heard that you folks call it Halloween), the evening before All Saints' Day, 1 November in the year of our Lord 1517, I nailed ninety-five theses, or statements, to the church door of the Castle Church in Wittenberg. Most people date the beginning of the Reformation of the Church to that date.

It matters little to me when people date the beginning of the Reformation, but I certainly wouldn't choose that date. I had some very important things to say in those theses, but I did not consider the issues therein as important as my attack on Scholastic theology, of which I spoke in my last letter to you. I recall saying at one time much earlier that I believed that God had sent me to tear down the Scholastic synthesis.

I certainly didn't expect those theses to circulate among the laity who did not have the theological background to appreciate the issues involved. I wrote the theses in Latin to attract only the educated, and I extended an invitation for those qualified to debate with me the issues that I raised. There was no debate because no one responded to the invitation. Nevertheless, the theses were translated by someone, not me, and spread by word of mouth and by the printers. (I must tell you that if it had not been for Johannes Guttenberg's invention of the movable-type printing press about sixty years earlier there would have been no Reformation of the Church.) Against my intention, the theses spread like wildfire on the prairie, and from that point there was no stopping the conflagration. So, I guess that it is not entirely inaccurate to date the beginning of the Reformation of the Church to the date of that posting, 31 October 1517.

I should tell you, however, that "The Ninety-five Theses" is only a popular description of my posting. More accurately, those theses were entitled *Disputation on the Power and Efficacy of Indulgences*.

I think that before I tell you about the content of those theses, I must explain to you what an indulgence is.

Indulgence refers to the forgiveness of sins. The exceedingly good news (Gospel) to sinners is that God wants to forgive sins. But on what condition? Over the centuries, the collective voice of the Church, based on the witness of the Bible, said that forgiveness was conditioned on repentance. Eventually, repentance grew into a sacrament that included sorrow for sin (contrition), confession of sin, and satisfaction that the sinner must make for the sin. The church would impose the satisfaction required. If sufficient satisfaction had not been made prior to one's death, the remainder of the satisfaction would be required in purgatory.

An indulgence was something that could be done to make satisfaction for sin. Usually, it was stated as so many days or years remitted from purgatory.

In 1517, I had no doubt that the church, speaking through its head, the pope, could impose indulgences as part of the sacrament of penance; nor did I doubt that purgatory awaited all who had not made complete satisfaction for their sin. Later, I thought differently, but not in 1517.

During the time of the Crusades, about four or five hundred years before my time, the indulgence business really exploded. I mentioned that indulgences were to remit so many days or years from purgatory. At the time of the Crusades, the pope declared a plenary indulgence for those who participated in the Crusades. A plenary indulgence is a full and complete indulgence. That is, all time in purgatory is remitted. Only the pope had the authority to grant a plenary indulgence. The practice of granting plenary indulgences continued after the Crusades.

I must tell you about one other issue that relates to this indulgence trafficking. Several hundred years before my time, a "treasury of merits" was invented. That treasury included all the excess merits of the saints. According to Roman Catholic theology, saints had earned more merits than required to cover their sins. Consequently, they spent no time in purgatory, but upon their death they went directly to heaven. The pope could draw from that treasury of merits and apply the merits to sinners who craved for the required indulgences. You will naturally ask, "With so many sinners and so few saints, would that treasury not soon run dry?" To that question the church had said that the merits of Jesus were included in the alleged "treasury." The merits of Jesus are infinite. Consequently, the treasury would never run dry. But that raises a further question. Why the need for the merits of the saints if the merits of Jesus are infinite? I did not ask that question in 1517, and I doubt that anyone has been able to give a satisfactory answer to that question even in your day.

Now I must get back to the issue of indulgences in my day. A dreadful tragedy had developed. Indulgences were being sold for money. People were led to believe that they could buy the forgiveness of sins. I know that the sale of the forgiveness of sins was never an official teaching of the Church of Rome. I care little for "official teachings." I care very deeply how the common people understand the message of the Christian faith. When I saw how indulgences were being sold, and how people actually believed that they had purchased the forgiveness of sins, my German dander was set on edge. I called on my fellow theologians to debate with me Ninety-five Theses that dealt with this whole matter of indulgences.

Even thinking about that tragedy makes me angry and fatigued. I must return now to my rest. Next time, I'll tell you about the content of those so-called Ninety-five Theses. As for you, keep the faith.

Letter 20

Last time, I promised to tell you about the *Disputation on the Power and Efficacy of Indulgences*, which I posted on 31 October 1517. You know that document as the Ninety-five Theses.

Before I tell you about those theses, I must mention several other issues that may help you better understand my concern about the indulgence traffic.

You may know that I lived in Saxony, part of the German lands. In my day, Germany was not one single country as I understand it is in your day. Many different territories and independent cities made up the German lands.

I was less than two years old when in 1485 Saxony was divided into two parts—Ernestine and Albertine Saxony. I lived and taught in Wittenberg from 1512 until my death in 1546. Wittenberg lay in Ernestine Saxony, also called Electoral Saxony because the prince of Ernestine Saxony was one of the seven electors of the Holy Roman Emperor. Fredrick the Wise was my prince. Albertine Saxony was ruled by Duke George.

A Dominican monk by the name of Johann (you say John) Tetzel was selling indulgences in Albertine Saxony. Fredrick the Wise would not permit such sales in his territory, although he had no problem with the many indulgences the pope granted to those who came to venerate the religious objects in the Cathedral Church, which Frederick had richly endowed with relics. In fact, the sale of indulgences would interfere with the indulgences offered in his own Cathedral Church. People from Ernestine Saxony would travel to Albertine Saxony to buy those fraudulent notes. Those common peasants believed that they were actually buying the forgiveness of sins.

It has been said of Johann Tetzel that he had a sales slogan that went something like this: "As soon as the coin in the coffer rings, the soul from purgatory springs." I must confess that I never heard that with my own ears, but if it is not quite exact, it rather accurately represents the marketing strategy of those who engaged in that perfidious dealing.

There was a reason behind this mad sale of indulgences. In Rome, Pope Leo X was building that large and grand cathedral named after St.

Peter. A large amount of money was needed for that construction and the sculptures that surrounded and adorned it. What easier source of revenue than the sale of indulgences?

The second occasion for the need of money was the forbidden purchase of ecclesiastical offices. Three bishoprics became open in 1513, and one person wanted all three. It was forbidden for one person to hold more than one bishopric. It was also forbidden by church law for anyone as young as age 23 to hold any bishopric. Nevertheless, Albert (usually know as Albert of Mainz), who was then only twenty-three years old, wanted all three bishoprics. For the price of about $50,000, the pope saw fit to suspend church law, and he granted Albert the Archbishopric of Magdeburg and the Bishopric of Halberstadt. Who would fill the Archbishopric of Mainz, the leading ecclesiastical office in all Germany? That choice fruit remained "up for grabs." That is still an idiom of your day that I am trying to understand. After some negotiation, the pope appointed Albert to receive the grand prize. The price for this appointment was a mere 23,200 ducats. (I have been told that amounts to about half a million dollars in your money at the beginning of the twenty-first century.) About half of that amount was to be paid in cash and the remainder borrowed from the Fugger bankers. Of course, the Fuggers wanted assurance that their money would be repaid—and at good interest! To secure that loan, the pope ordered a plenary indulgence (plenary means full and complete) in the German lands under Archbishop Albert of Mainz. The sale of indulgences in those lands would transfer one-half of the proceeds directly to Rome to help pay for the construction of St. Peter's, and to finance the extravagant lifestyle of Pope Leo X. The other half was to go to the Archbishop of Mainz to repay the loan from the Fuggers.

I have now given you the setting, the background, and the occasion for the sale of those fraudulent indulgences.

Oh, I'm getting angry again. Next time, I'll get right to the meat and potatoes (that's another idiom that I don't understand) of those theses about the alleged power and efficacy of indulgences. I promise, no more background or setting. As for you, keep the faith.

LETTER 21

The posting of the Ninety-five Theses that disputed the power and efficacy of indulgences was more than an academic exercise. Granted, it was written in Latin and intended for a discussion among those qualified to enter into the debate, namely, those trained in theology. But the issues that I addressed were for the people of my congregation who had been sold a bill of goods (another idiom that I learned several centuries after I left Wittenberg) by those who peddled the sale of indulgences. My dear German people were being fleeced (another idiom that I never knew but now makes sense to me—like sheep being sheared of their wool) of their hard-earned money with the promise that they, and their ancestors now in purgatory, could be spared the suffering of that intermediate state by purchasing a worthless piece of paper, called a letter of indulgence.

It was on 31 October in the year of our Lord 1517 that I posted the theses on the door of the Castle Church in Wittenberg. The selection of 31 October was not a random choice; it was the day before All Saints' Day, when many would flock to the church to venerate (not quite worship, but leaning in that direction) the many relics that my prince, Frederick the Wise, had proudly accumulated for his church. I did not count all the relics, but someone has noted that in 1509 there were 5,005 relics for veneration. If one were to venerate all of them, there could be a reduction in purgatory time of 1,443 years. That was quite a temptation to my parishioners in Wittenberg. (Only three years later, in 1520, I have been told, there were 19,013 holy bones for veneration. If all were venerated, there would be a reduction of 1,902,202 years and 270 days in purgatory.)[1]

I have no intention of reciting all of the Ninety-five Theses that I presented for debate, but I will give you a taste of them by including a few. You can read all of them at your leisure. But don't just read them; stop and think about what you have read. My introduction to the theses was short enough that I can share it with you.

> Out of zeal for the truth and the desire to bring it to light, the following theses will be publicly discussed at Witten-

1 Bainton, 69, 71.

berg under the chairmanship of the reverend father Martin Luther,[2] Master of Arts and Sacred Theology and regularly appointed Lecturer on these subjects at that place. He requests that those who cannot be present to debate orally with us will do so by letter. In the Name of Our Lord Jesus Christ. Amen.[3]

1. **When our Lord and Master Jesus Christ said, "Repent" [Matt. 4:17], he willed the entire life of believers to be one of repentance.** You might ask, "What's new about that?" I might have to get a little bit technical here, but if you will stick with me for just a moment, I think you will understand the issue at stake. Someone in your day has noted that the Latin translation of Matthew 4:17 uses the phrase *poenitentiam agite* and the German translation uses the phrase *tut Busse*, both of which can be translated either "repent" or "do penance." The Roman Church used this word of Jesus to support the sacrament of penance, part of which included satisfaction for sin. In a previous letter, I told you that indulgences were used as a substitute for satisfaction. In the Roman Church's call to "do penance," repentance had been transformed into a religious ritual rather than a total reorientation of one's life. I understood, and still understand, that repentance is a daily requirement for all believers.
2. **This word cannot be understood as referring to the sacrament of penance, that is, confession and satisfaction, as administered by the clergy.**
3. **Yet it does not mean solely inner repentance; such inner repentance is useless unless it produces various outward mortifications of the flesh.** I hope that you understand that I mean to say that repentance is not simply an inner sorrow for one's sin, but an active change in one's way of living. Christian living must be God-centered rather than self-centered. When you try that way of life, you will understand quite rapidly why repentance is not only a daily requirement but an hourly requirement.

---

2 LW 31:25, n. 1 indicates that in this preamble, Luther spelled his name Lutther.

3 LW 31:25.

5. In the fifth thesis I got at the heart of the entire matter: the pope's limited authority in the use of indulgences. At that point in my life, I did not question the use of indulgences, only the misuse. **The pope neither desires nor is able to remit any penalties except those imposed by his own authority or that of the canons.** (The canons are the decrees of the church, some of which go back many centuries. The canons had the force of law.) That is to say that the pope's authority to remit penalties is restricted to only the penalties that he or the canons of the church have imposed. He does not have the authority to remit penalties that God imposes on sin.

16. **Hell, purgatory, and heaven seem to differ the same as despair, fear, and assurance of salvation.** Again, I want to remind you that at this time in my life, I still accepted the church's teaching about the reality of purgatory.

20. **Therefore the pope, when he uses the words "plenary [full] remission of all penalties," does not actually mean "all penalties," but only those imposed by him.** Well, of course, the pope meant all penalties, but my argument was that he had no authority to remit penalties other than those that he had imposed.

21. **Thus those indulgence preachers are in error who say that a man is absolved from every penalty and saved by papal indulgences.**

24. **For this reason most people are necessarily deceived by that indiscriminate and high-sounding promise of release from penalty.**

27. **They preach only human doctrines who say that as soon as the money clinks into the money chest, the soul flies out of purgatory.**

36. **Any truly repentant Christian has a right to full remission of penalty and guilt, even without indulgence letters.**

62. **The true treasure of the church is the most holy gospel of the glory and grace of God.**

82. **Such as: "Why does not the pope empty purgatory for the sake of holy love and the dire need of the souls that are there if he redeems an infinite number of souls for the sake of miserable money with which to build a church? The former reasons would be most just; the latter is most trivial."** You will have to read some of the preceding theses for that last one to make sense, but I made the point that if the pope has the authority to release from purgatory, why does he not release everyone out of Christian love? The church to which I referred is the Papal Basilica of St. Peter in Rome. Much of the indulgence money was used for building or, more accurately, for a major remodeling of that cathedral.

There are some additional very important theses toward the end, but you must do some research on your own.[4]

Next time, I will tell you the responses to these theses.

---

4 LW 31:25–33.

Letter 22

I anticipated a lively debate on the theses that I had presented, but nobody showed up. I don't recall how I felt about that snub, but you might have an idea if you consider how you feel when others pass off as unimportant or irrelevant something that you think to be of great importance.

I suppose that the whole matter would have died had I not sent a copy of the theses to Archbishop Albert of Mainz.

Before I continue, I should tell you a bit about Albert. Albert, the son of a nobleman (the Margrave of Brandenburg), chose the affluent life of a bishop. There was a minimum age for the appointment of a bishop, but in my day money could buy a lot of influence. (I certainly hope that is not true in your day.) There was also the restriction of a person holding only one bishopric. But Albert had access to enough money to "buy" (technically he was appointed by the pope) the Bishopric of Halberstadt and the Archbishopric of Magdeburg. That wasn't enough; Albert wanted the Archbishopric of Mainz as well. He would then be the primate [senior bishop] of all German lands. But even Albert did not have immediate access to that kind of money. He arranged a loan from the large banking firm owned and operated by the Fugger family from Augsburg. How was he to repay the Fuggers? That's where the sale of indulgences came into play. The pope authorized the sale of indulgences in Albert's lands, and Albert engaged Johann Tetzel to be the salesperson. The proceeds from the sale would then be divided equally between the pope, for the rebuilding of St. Peter's Cathedral in Rome, and Albert, for the repayment of his debt to the Fuggers. What a deal for both!

So, I sent a copy of the theses to Albert with the following introduction:

> Father in Christ, and most Illustrious Prince, forgive me that I, the scum of the earth, should dare to approach your Sublimity. The Lord Jesus is my witness that I am well aware of my insignificance and my unworthiness. I make so bold because of the office of fidelity which I owe to Your Paternity.

> May Your Highness look upon this speck of dust and hear my plea for clemency from you and from the pope.[1]

I then urged the archbishop, in the strongest terms, to get rid of the pernicious sale of indulgences. I still recall, as though it were this morning, I began my cry with these words, "God on high, is this the way that souls entrusted to your care are prepared for death? It is high time that you looked into this matter." I concluded by saying, "What shall I do Illustrious Prince, if not to beseech Your Paternity through Jesus Christ our Lord to suppress utterly these instruction lest someone arise to confute this book and to bring Your Illustrious Sublimity into obloquy, which I dread but fear if something is not done speedily?"[2] (I wonder if Albert had any idea who that "someone" might be who would "arise and confute this book.")

Guess what happened to that letter. Albert forwarded it to Rome. God has a way of keeping crucial issues alive. If Albert had not forwarded that letter, I would have been a lone voice barking in the hinterland of Germany; nobody would have paid attention.

Again, if the pope had tossed the letter into the waste, the issue might have died. But the pope did not; he ordered the general of the Augustinian Order to look into the situation in Germany.

Another factor kept the issue alive: the invention of the movable-type printing press by Johannes Guttenberg about thirty years before my birth. I had hoped that the theses would not be reprinted because I did not want to embarrass my Prince, Frederick the Wise. My hope was quashed. Someone translated them into German, and several printers made them public, including printers in Nürnberg, Leipzig, and Basel.[3] Those theses circulated throughout the German lands as though carried by the wind. At that time, I had neither intention nor idea to make the theses public, but the conflagration had begun.

What was my superior to do after being instructed by Rome to suppress this "drunken German monk," as the pope is reported to have called me? Perhaps I can tell you something about that next time.

---

1 Bainton, 84.

2 Bainton, 84–85.

3 LW 31:23.

Letter 23

The Augustinian monasteries, scattered throughout the German lands, convened triennially on the Third Sunday after Easter for mutual support and to conduct the business necessary for all organizations. A meeting of the Augustinians was scheduled for Heidelberg in April 1518. I was the district vicar, and because of that position I was expected to attend. My friends advised me against going to Heidelberg because what appeared to be an aborted attempt to challenge the indulgence traffic was alive and well. My life had been threatened because of my challenge. (Truth always arouses anger in this world, which is alienated from God. That alienation from God appears all too frequently even within the church, laity and clergy included.) Nevertheless, I was intent on attending to my duties as district vicar. Fortunately, I had a prince who provided me with letters of introduction and asked for my safe passage. Nevertheless, it seemed wise for me to travel in disguise. It took me ten days to walk from Wittenberg to Heidelberg.

The pope had directed the general of the Augustinian Order in Rome, Gabriel della Volta, to put a stop to my "heretical" posting. The general contacted my superior, Johann von Staupitz, to have me silenced. I have previously told you that Staupitz was a pastoral superior. Rather than rebuke me, he asked me to prepare a disputation (you may call it a dialogue, debate, or discussion) on the theological issues of sin, free will, and grace to be presented at Heidelberg, but he also asked me to refrain from controversial issues. By "controversial issues," I understood him to mean indulgences. I completed my assignment by preparing forty theses for debate, twenty-eight on theological issues and twelve on issues of philosophy. I'll share with you some of the theological issues and try to explain why I think them to be so very important.[1]

Someone in your day has divided the first twenty-eight in a way that I think represents my intention.[2]

Theses 1–12 relate to the human (apparently good) works and the works of God.

---

1 LW 31: 39–41.

2 Brecht 1:231–34.

1. **The law of God, the most salutary doctrine of life, cannot advance man on his way to righteousness, but rather hinders him.** God's Law has a purpose or function; I will tell you about that at some other point, but it has nothing to do with making people righteous before God.
2. **Much less can human works, which are done over and over again with the aid of natural precepts, so to speak, lead to that end.**
3. **Although the works of man always seem attractive and good, they are nevertheless likely to be mortal sins.** If you don't believe me you might, or might not, believe the prophet Isaiah. He said, "All our righteous deeds are like a polluted garment" (Isaiah 64:6).
4. **Although the works of God always seem unattractive and appear evil, they are nevertheless really eternal merits.** Did not the death of Jesus appear unattractive and evil? Nevertheless, that most unattractive act of God brought the "eternal merit" of our salvation.

Theses 13–18 relate to the human will.

13. **Free will, after the fall, exists in name only, and as long as it does what it is able to do, it commits a mortal sin.** The church in my day taught that if people would do good works to the best of their ability, God would honor that attempt and provide the additional merit to bring them to salvation. I fear that many who use my name in your day believe that delusion. That attempt to please God by doing "the best he or she can" is the greatest sin; it finds salvation in the self rather than in what God has done for sinners through Jesus.
16. **The person who believes that he can obtain grace by doing what is in him adds sin to sin so that he becomes doubly guilty.** Note that little phrase again, "doing what is in him." There is nothing "in you" that is worthy of offering to God. If you think that leads to despair, consider the following thesis.
17. **Nor does speaking in this manner give cause for despair, but for arousing the desire to humble oneself and seek the grace of Christ.** I am quite aware that human pride rebels against receiving something for nothing, but God will have it no other way. I cannot say it any better than I said it in Thesis 18.

18. **It is certain that man must utterly despair of his own ability before he is prepared to receive the grace of Christ.**

Theses 19–28 present the paradox of the opposites. Perhaps you will understand these theses better if you first read what the apostle Paul said to the Christians in Corinth: "God chose what is foolish in the world to shame the wise; God chose what is weak in the world to shame the strong; God chose what is low and despised in the world, even things that are not, to bring to nothing things that are, so that no human being might boast in the presence of God" (1 Corinthians 1:27–29).

19. **That person does not deserve to be called a theologian who looks upon the invisible things of God as though they were clearly perceptible in those things which have actually happened [Rom. 1:20].** I want all to know that God is hidden, and those who have God "figured out" are the most deceived. In *Proofs of the Thesis Debated in the Chapter at Heidelberg*,[3] I said, "The recognition of all these things [God's virtue, godliness, wisdom, justice, goodness, and so forth] does not make one worthy or wise."[4]
20. **He deserves to be called a theologian, however, who comprehends the visible and manifest things of God seen through suffering and the cross.** Again, in the *Proofs* I said, "Now it is not sufficient for anyone, and it does him no good to recognize God in his glory and majesty, unless he recognizes him in the humility and shame of the cross." And again, "For this reason true theology and recognition of God are in the crucified Christ." I can't say it any more clearly than that.
21. **A theologian of glory calls evil good and good evil. A theologian of the cross calls the thing what it actually is.** Again, from the *Proofs*, "He who does not know Christ does not know God hidden in suffering. Therefore he prefers works to suffering, glory to the cross, strength to weakness, wisdom to folly, and, in general, good to evil." It may take you a lifetime of thought and prayer to "get it," but don't give up.

There's more, but you can read the other theses when you have digested the above.

I've had enough for today. Pursue the truth! Keep the faith!

---

3 LW 31:42–58.

4 LW 31:52.

Letter 24

I did not know until the summer of 1518 the great furor I had created in Rome. At issue was my *Disputation on the Power and Efficacy of Indulgences (Ninety-five Theses)*. Perhaps I should not have been surprised. My *Disputation against Scholastic Theology* (September 1517) and the theses that I presented at the Heidelberg Disputation (April 1518) were far more important than the issues relating to indulgences. But indulgences brought money both to Archbishop Albert and the pope. I was reminded again of what the apostle Paul wrote to Timothy, "The love of money is a root of all kinds of evils. It is through this craving that some have wandered away from the faith and pierced themselves with many pangs" (1 Timothy 6:10).

Late in December 1517, the Roman curia had received my Ninety-five Theses from Archbishop Albert. That did not create much of a stir. If the pope even saw the theses, he was not much concerned. He considered it a mere trifle between the Augustinians and the Dominicans. (I was an Augustinian, and Johann Tetzel was a Dominican.)

The Dominicans were much more enraged than Albert. In January 1518, the Saxon chapter of the Dominicans met in Frankfurt, where Tetzel defended one hundred theses against my Ninety-five Theses. There, upon the defense of those theses by Tetzel, the Dominicans denounced me as a heretic in Rome.

The pope was now awakened to the threat I caused to Roman finances. He asked Prierias, the Master of the Sacred Palace, to prepare an "expert" evaluation of what I had written. (Let me clarify two things. First, the Master of the Sacred Palace was the official theological adviser to the pope. Second, Prierias was not his real name. His name was Sylvester Mazzolini. His cognomen was Prierias because his birth city was Priero.)

Prierias prepared *A Dialogue against the Presumptuous Conclusions of Martin Luther about the Power of the Pope*. Prierias declared me a heretic. I received his *Dialogue* in August, and with the *Dialogue* I was summoned to appear in Rome for a hearing within sixty days. Was I frightened? Of course, I was frightened. I, a poor lowly monk, was to appear for a hearing before the greatest power in the Western world! I responded to Prierias, but he was in no mood for a theological discussion or debate.

He simply told me to submit to the ecclesiastical authorities.

I had a friend, Spalatin (his real name was George Burkhardt, but he was known as Spalatin because his hometown was Spalt), who was court chaplain and adviser to my Prince, Frederick the Wise. We had known each other since we were together in Erfurt. Spalatin had been ordained a priest in 1508. I wrote to my friend and asked for his assistance: "I now need your help more than ever, or rather, it is the honor of almost our whole University that needs it along with me. This means that you should use your influence with . . . our Sovereign [Prince Frederick] and his Imperial Majesty [Maximilian I] [to] obtain for me from the Pope the return of my case, so that it is tried before German judges."[1]

God has used politics and world events many times to further His purpose in this world. In my case, I had a prince who was one of the most powerful in Germany. The emperor of the Holy Roman Empire, Maximilian I, was getting old, and my prince was one of seven electors who would select Maximilian's successor. The pope would need the goodwill of Prince Frederick when that election might happen. Maximilian I did die on 12 January 1519. Francis I of France, along with Charles of Spain, were the two prime candidates for the open position. The pope did not want either; he wanted my prince to succeed Maximilian, but Frederick did not want the position. The seven electors finally settled on Charles I of Spain, who became Charles V of the Holy Roman Empire. But Charles was preoccupied in Spain and did not have much effect on the life of the empire for more than a year. Prince Frederick was then the most powerful prince in the empire with whom the pope had to contend.

With the assistance of Prince Frederick, the pope agreed to have my hearing transferred to Augsburg, in southern Germany. I was to appear on 12 October 1518 before Cardinal Cajetan (born James [but then later changed to Thomas] de Vio, from Gaitte, Italy, from which his cognomen was derived).

There was another political event that worked in my favor—or better put, in favor of the Holy Gospel. The Muslim Turks had moved across Eastern Europe and threatened the Holy Roman Empire. Emperor Maximilian I needed a united front against that emerging threat. He had called for a Diet in Augsburg for the summer of 1518 to assure that united support. (A diet has nothing to do with food; it was a deliberative assembly of princes, somewhat of a legislative body.) The threat of the

---

1 Gritsch, 24.

Turks was of far greater consequence to the empire and the pope than my tirade against indulgences.

I'll tell you about the hearing before Cardinal Cajetan in Augsburg later, but before I do that I will share with you several important sermons that I preached in 1518 on the subject of excommunication.

Until I write again, keep the faith.

Letter 25

The furor raised by the publication of my *Disputation on the Power and Efficacy of Indulgences* gave me gastric pain. I had wanted only to debate some issues about the pope's authority to release people from purgatory by the purchase of indulgence letters. Well, frankly, the issues were a bit more extensive, but that was the main thrust of the *Disputation*. I had been charged with heresy, and Johann Tetzel, that infamous seller of indulgence letters, said that he would have me burned at the stake within several weeks. I knew that I must make a further response.

Early in 1518, even prior to going to Heidelberg, I had been working on a further explanation of the Ninety-five Theses. I was ready to publish that explanation in February, but my bishop forbade it. When I returned from Heidelberg, I continued to work on the explanation; despite the prohibition of my bishop, I submitted the manuscript to a printer in April.

My superior, Father Staupitz, was under pressure from Rome to have me silenced. He asked me to write a conciliatory letter to the pope. In respect for my beloved vicar, I complied with his request and sent a letter[1] along with the *Explanations*. I addressed the pope respectfully as "Most Blessed Father, Leo X." In deference to the pope I wrote, "But you will deign, blessed Father, to hear the true case from me, though I am but an uncouth child."[2] I told the pope that it had not been my intention to have the theses published and spread among the common folks. I wrote, "Therefore I published a set of theses, inviting only the more learned to dispute with me if they wished."[3] I further explained that I was not proposing any new doctrine, but only deep personal concerns that needed theological discussion. "For it is a set of theses," I wrote, "not doctrines or dogmas, and they are put, according to custom, in an obscure and enigmatic way."[4]

There are other more pressing issues to share with you. If you have interest in reading the *Explanations*, you have access to them in your own language.[5]

---

1 PE 1:44–48.

2 PE 1:43.

3 PE 1:44.

4 PE 1:47.

5 LW 31:79–252.

I promised to tell you something about the ban, or excommunication, that was practiced in my day. Excommunication had a history in the Christian Church long before my day. Even Jesus spoke of that regrettable necessity. I'll share more about that in a minute. But first, I must tell you what excommunication is and how it had degenerated in my day from an appropriate discipline in the church to a threat against those who did not pay the required tithes and church taxes.

Excommunication bans a person from receiving Holy Communion, the Lord's Supper, until appropriate repentance is made. When an entire community, or even a nation, is placed under that ban, it is called an interdict. An interdict is an invention of church bureaucrats; there is no biblical warrant for such misuse of excommunication.

A historian in your day has rightly said, "Toward the close of the Middle Ages the Roman Curia had developed into one of the leading fiscal institutions in Western Europe, with its channels of revenue carefully guarded through threats of bans, excommunications, and interdicts."[6] When people did not pay their required tithes, they were placed under the ban. If people died while under the ban, they were threatened with certain eternal damnation. I recall saying something like this: "The bans and interdicts flew about like so many bats every fall when the time for the collection of the tithe tax had arrived."[7]

As early as March 1518, long before I was threatened with excommunication, I wrote a sermon on the subject to protect my dear Wittenbergers from the impious threat of the misuse of excommunication; I wrote several others after that first sermon. One that I wrote in December 1519 was published a bit later. It was simply entitled *A Sermon on the Ban*.[8] I'll share a bit of the substance of that sermon with you.

I affirmed the use of excommunication as it was originally intended. I noted Jesus' words in Matthew 18 [:15–17] and Paul's in 1 Corinthians 5 [:11], in addition to several other New Testament statements.[9] Excommunication is a last-resort punishment to bring a sinner back to repentance and full inclusion in the Body of Christ.

I have heard that excommunication, or banning a person from full participation in the life of a Christian congregation, has fallen into disuse

---

6 Schwiebert, 331.

7 Schwiebert, 331.

8 LW 39:5–22.

9 LW 39:8–9.

in your day. I am as grieved at that nonuse as I was with the misuse in my day. A Christian congregation that does not take sin seriously will never call people to repentance or place them under discipline if they do not. People are left to damn themselves if no Christian brother or sister, no community of believers, cares enough to employ tough love (that's another good term that I had never heard until recently) on a Christian who has fallen for the temptations of this world.

Good gracious, I still get carried away with preaching when I should stick to my story. I know that you will forgive me. So, now back to my *Sermon on the Ban*.

The ban should never be used for vengeance or to destroy a person. The reception of the life-giving Sacrament is important beyond words, but the withholding of the Sacrament cannot deprive an individual of God's grace. I wrote,

> Often it may happen that a person under the ban is deprived of the holy sacrament and of burial as well. And yet he may be inwardly certain and blessed in the fellowship of Christ. . . . On the other hand, there are many who freely partake of the sacrament without being outwardly under the ban and yet are inwardly completely estranged from the fellowship of Christ, and thus under the ban—even though they might be buried with golden linen under a high altar with all pomp, bells, and singing.[10]

That is to say that the church can and should impose the tough and strict discipline of excommunication when necessary to restore a sinning member of the Body, but the church cannot deprive anyone of God's grace.

Those who impose the ban are under the watchful eye of the Lord of the Church; they must impose penalty with the greatest caution. I wrote, "To no one is the ban more harmful and dangerous than to those who impose it . . . because they never give this a thought, are completely without fear, and do not consider how they themselves are perhaps worthy of a hundred bans before God."[11] The imposition of the ban is a necessary but fearful undertaking.

That should be enough for you to get the general thrust of what I wrote. You can easily read the whole sermon if you choose; it is not very

---

10 LW 39:9.

11 LW 39:11.

long. I will conclude with a final comment that I wrote, "In short, the higher estate [the excommunicator], in all that it does, is always in greater danger than the lower estate [the excommunicated]; and where the lower estate has to fear once, the higher estate has to fear ten times over. Therefore, those who impose the ban have no reason to be obstinate and arrogant toward those who are under the ban; they should weep about themselves instead. For God's judgment will not fall on the lowly but rather on the mighty."[12]

Do you think those words were lost on my ecclesiastical superiors, even up to the throne of the pope? Not a chance. I knew that I was sealing my own fate; my life would be short. Those who threatened the power of the papacy had been burned at the stake. You need recall only Wycliffe, Hus, and Savonarola.

I still had to face Cardinal Cajetan at Augsburg. I dreaded that meeting. That's for next time.

Keep the faith. It might cost you too.

---

12 LW 39:16.

LETTER 26

I was negligent in my last letter. I left you with three names without telling you anything about them.

John Wycliffe (ca. 1330–31 December 1384) was an English priest who offered some dissent against the teachings of the Roman Church. He died a natural death, but later, in 1415, he was condemned as a heretic at the Council of Constance. His body was exhumed, burned at the stake, and his ashes were thrown into a river. Wycliffe is sometimes called "the morning star of the Reformation."

Jan Hus (ca. 1369–6 July 1415) was a Czech, a follower of Wycliffe who was summoned to the Council of Constance with the promise of safe passage. Upon his arrival, Hus was thrown into prison, condemned as a heretic, and (with the excuse that no promise to a heretic need be kept) burned at the stake.

Girolama Savonarola (1452–98), a Dominican monk, was a great preacher in Florence, in present-day Italy. He denounced corruption among the clergy and the oppression of the poor. He and two other Dominican friars were hanged with fire lit under the gallows.

Those three great men are worthy of your further reading.

Now back to my hearing under Cardinal Cajetan at Augsburg in Bavaria. That was in October 1518.

Political events again worked in my favor. In the summer of 1518, Emperor Maximilian called for a Diet at Augsburg. Pope Leo X had sent Cajetan as his legate [representative] to the Diet. The Turks [Muslims] were advancing on the border of Western Europe, and both the emperor and the pope needed a united front to defend the empire against further Turkish advances. That would take money; new taxes were proposed.

The German representatives to the diet were suspicious because too much money had already been sent from Germany to the pope. Perhaps the request for more money was just another ruse by Rome; the money, they surmised, would not be used for its intended purpose. The German reps therefore attached the *Gravamina* [grievances] that they had previously submitted to Rome in order to secure their support for Turkish tax. My sovereign was perhaps the most prominent of those German statesmen. The pope needed his support, and he was my protector. The pope was caught between a rock and a hard place (another idiom of your day).

In early August, the pope sent a letter to Cajetan authorizing him to conduct my hearing in Augsburg. Cajetan was a very able theologian, one of the best educated in Rome. Nevertheless, he was not allowed to enter into a discussion or debate with me over what I had written or said. He was only to absolve me of my intransigence and sin if I recanted, or have me arrested and held until further word from Rome if I did not recant.

I was never told, but I am quite certain that Prince Frederick received a promise from Cajetan that under no circumstances would he arrest me.[1] I think it was on that understanding that my prince summoned me to come to Augsburg, although he also obtained an imperial letter of safe conduct for me. Frederick left Augsburg in late September prior to my arrival in October.

I don't have the desire to tell you all the lies about me that had been gathered and sent to Rome during the winter and spring of 1518. I will tell you only one perfidious incident that occurred because of my naivete. In July 1518, I visited the Augustinian monastery in Dresden. Dresden was in the "other" Saxony, Ducal Saxony, ruled by Duke George. While there I was invited by Jerome Emser, a chaplain at the court of Duke George, to a friendly dinner. I never turned down a good meal, so I accepted. During the meal, I was lured into a discussion that became an argument over the teachings of St. Thomas and Aristotle. What I did not know was that a member of the Dominican order was eavesdropping behind a door. My comments were recorded, and, as usual, reshaped to put me in the poorest possible light.[2]

Now I will tell you what happened after I arrived and met with Cardinal Cajetan.

The cardinal received me in a gracious and fatherly manner. But when he tried to persuade me to recant of what I had written, I would not. Someone from your day has put that first day very succinctly and accurately.

> The more Cajetan insisted upon the infallibility of the papacy the more Luther relied upon the authority of the

---

1 Brecht 1:250.

2 Brecht 1:240–41.

> Scriptures, and the more Cajetan argued that sacramental grace was conferred without faith, the more Luther stressed the importance of his "theology of the cross," although he still believed that his doctrines were in harmony with the church fathers and canon law.[3]

The second day, I told the cardinal that I was willing to prepare a written statement in response to the objections he had raised to what I had written. That statement could then be submitted to the theological faculties at the universities of Basel, Freiburg, and Louvain, or even Paris, for their opinions.

On the third day, I presented my written statement. The cardinal accepted it and said that he would send it to Rome, with his refutation, but he got so angry with me that he told me to recant or never again to see him. I chose the latter option.

Following that meeting with Cajetan, my gracious Father Staupitz, and my ecclesiastical superior, knowing that there was no turning back with me, released me from my monastic vows.[4]

Only two issues were at stake with Cajetan: the treasury of merits (from which the pope could make a withdrawal and apply those merits to another individual, even those in purgatory) and my contention that a person who receives the sacrament must have faith or he would receive it to his own damnation.

In Thesis 58 (*Explanations of the Ninety-five Theses*), I denied the existence of a "treasury of merits" for the pope's disbursal. I wrote, "Third, no saint has adequately fulfilled God's commandments in this life. Consequently the saints have done absolutely nothing which is superabundant. Therefore they have left nothing to be allocated through indulgences."[5] The "treasury of merit" fiction derived from a papal bull by Clement VI in the middle of the fourteenth century. The name of the bull, always derived from the first word in the bull, is *Unigenitus*. I sometimes referred to it as *Extravagante*[6] because it had never been entered into the official canons of the church. In *Extravagante*, Clement VI created an imaginary treasury of merits, something like a celestial bank account. The source of the merits were said to be the extra merits of the

---

3 LW 31:256.

4 Schwiebert, 354.

5 LW 31:213.

6 LW 31:261.

saints—more merits than needed to enter heaven—and the unlimited, infinite merits of Jesus. (No one seemed to ask why the extra merits of the saints were necessary since the merits of Jesus are unlimited.) Those banked merits could be withdrawn by the pope or those whom he designated and awarded to poor souls seeking to make satisfaction for their sins. Those merits were available as indulgences for sins and could be purchased from huckster indulgence salesmen.

In Thesis 7, I said that it is heresy to say that the sacrament (Lord's Supper) "gives justifying grace to those who place no obstacle in the way." I continued, "But it is impossible to proffer the sacrament in a salutary manner except to those who already believe and are just and worthy."[7] I should have added, "They are just and worthy who believe." I said that much later in 1529, when I wrote the short catechism: "But he is fully worthy and well prepared who has faith in these words, 'Given for you and poured out for the forgiveness of sins.'"

So, my meetings with Cajetan came to an end with no resolution. I returned to Wittenberg certain that an early death would be my lot.

I have no idea what I might say in my next letter, but I will continue. Until then, keep the faith.

---

7 LW 31:107.

Letter 27

I want to return to an issue that arose in late winter of 1518, long before I met with Cardinal Cajetan and even prior to my disputation in Heidelberg.

John Eck (his real name was John Maier, but because he was born in Eck, Swabia, his cognomen was Eck) was a very competent theologian and a professor at Ingolstadt. I considered him to be my friend and was told that he was sympathetic to my understanding of the Gospel. However, probably in February 1518, without notifying me in advance, he wrote a scathing attack on my Ninety-five Theses. He entitled the commentary *Obelisks*, which means "daggers." That was more than a title. A historian in your day has noted the significance of obelisks. "Obelisks were signs used in the critical study of ancient literature and the Bible to denote spurious portions of a text to be removed. In the Middle Ages they were used for marking false and heretical statements in texts."[1] In those *Obelisks*, Professor Eck not only attacked my theses—without properly understanding them—but he also attacked me personally. He called me a Bohemian (thereby identifying me with the heretic, according to Roman judgment, Jan Hus), a heretic, rebellious, presumptuous, and impudent. He further called me sleepy, simpleminded, unlearned, and a despiser of the pope. Only the last came closest to the truth, but at that early date I did not despise the pope.

I was not aware of the *Obelisks* until March, and by then I was preparing for my trip to Heidelberg. Not until May did I respond with my *Asterisks*, which means "little stars." The same historian whom I noted above has said of asterisks, "Asterisks were critical signs that marked the most valuable texts."[2] I sent the *Asterisks* to Eck but did not make them public. I hoped that the issue would then die and that my friendship with Dr. Eck could be mended and continued.

All may have been forgotten if it had not been for my colleague at Wittenberg Professor Andreas Karlstadt, who, without my knowledge, published some theses against Eck's *Obelisks* that he made public. By that action, the poison had spread, and there was no way out of the mess.

---

1 Brecht 1:211.

2 Brecht 1:211.

(I should introduce you briefly to Dr. Karlstadt. He was my senior at the University of Wittenberg, and it was he who conferred on me the degree of doctor of theology. Andreas had a better heart than head. He was captivated by the new understanding of the Holy Gospel, but rather than a reformer, he became a radical revolutionary. He became such a problem to the cause of reform that I had him removed from the faculty at Wittenberg in about 1522.)

The whole scene was a tragedy. I recall saying something like this: "May both sides regret this argument begun by the devil."[3]

I mention this scenario with Dr. Eck because about a year later I would be engaged in a fierce public debate with the learned doctor at the University of Leipzig. The debate would be in the summer of 1519. I'll tell you more about that later. Until then, keep the faith.

---

3 Brecht 1:213.

Letter 28

Return with me now to late 1518 following my meeting with Cardinal Cajetan in Augsburg. My prince, Frederick, had apparently received assurance from the cardinal that he would under no circumstances have me arrested. That was comforting, but I was quite certain that gracious gesture was only a temporary arrangement. My fate and future were still quite uncertain. At any moment, my prince could have surrendered me to Rome. Had that happened, I was prepared to eat the same flames that Hus and Savonarola were forced to eat.

Cajetan had written to Prince Frederick telling his side of our meeting (everybody has a bias in writing) and asked the prince to surrender me to Rome. It was nip and tuck, you might say, for me. I asked the faculty at Wittenberg to write a letter to the prince on my behalf. They graciously complied with my request.[1] (It was not publicly known for several centuries that I actually wrote the letter.[2]) That letter was very influential, although not the only factor, in Prince Frederick's final decision regarding my case with Rome.

To my great relief, on 8 December, Prince Frederick responded to Cardinal Cajetan saying, in effect, that I had complied with Rome's request to submit myself to the pope's legate, and therefore he would not surrender me to Rome. (The prince wrote much more delicately than I could ever write, but the letter saved my skin.)

The pope and his curia had not been sleeping while awaiting Prince Frederick's response. Even prior to my meeting with Cajetan, they apparently had a backup plan. In the curia, there was a minor bureaucrat, Karl von Miltitz, who was born and raised in Saxony. He was a distant relative of Prince Frederick. If I would not bend for an Italian cardinal, perhaps I would be more sympathetic to a fellow German. In addition, there was the Golden Rose, which the pope would award once annually to a "deserving" Christian king or prince. Would that honor, with the added privileges that accompanied the Golden Rose, move Frederick's sympathy to Rome's desired end—my arrest and submission to Rome?

---

1 Schwiebert, 364–65.

2 Schwiebert, 366.

Karl was promoted to papal nuncio, a rather heady title for a junior diplomat, and sent to my prince's court with a letter of excommunication, numerous letters for whatever occasion presented itself, and a variety of papal bulls for the same unknown circumstances. He was also given the Golden Rose to present to my sovereign, never explicitly stated, but quite understood, that the presentation was dependent on Frederick's action against me. However, Miltitz was not to engage me in discussion or debate and was to act only under the authority of Cardinal Cajetan in Augsburg. All three have earned doctor's degrees. (Nothing is true just because it is written by degreed people.)

As Miltitz traveled through the German lands, he discovered the support I had among the people. I dare not say that he changed his mind, but he was not a strong personality and was easily influenced. I have a suspicion that his knees were shaking a bit the closer he got to my sovereign's court.

Not until late in December, after Christmas, did Karl arrive at the court of Prince Frederick. By then he must have known of Fredericks's letter to Cajetan and his refusal to surrender me to Rome. I was instructed by my prince to meet with Miltitz. Spalatin, my friend and chaplain at Frederick's court, asked me to deal kindly with Miltitz. I did not like controversy, even though I had been thrust into it, and was pleased to deal kindly with Karl. (It is often easier to deal gently with those poor souls who have limited ability than with pompous asses who think they know everything.)

Karl and I met together at Altenburg, in Spalatin's house, on 4–5 January 1519. In spite of the pope's prohibition against Miltitz's discussion with me, we had a lively conversation that ended in agreement on several points. On the second day, those points were revised to two: (1) I would drop the indulgence issue providing the other side abided by the agreement, and (2) Miltitz would ask the pope to appoint a competent German bishop to examine my writings and cite in writing the errors from which I was to recant.[3] I honestly wanted to preserve the integrity and unity of the Roman Church, but I was not willing to recant anything unless I could be shown in writing where I had erred.

Even before our meeting, when walking through the German lands and finding the support that I had among the people, Miltitz began to change his tune and ascribe all the problems to the Dominican preacher

3 Schwiebert, 377.

Tetzel, the seller of indulgence letters. On his way back to Rome, Miltitz stopped in Leipzig, where he met with Tetzel and roundly chastised, or "rudely questioned and severely reprimanded," the "ailing old man," as one from your day has said.[4] My heart grieved for the poor fellow. I was certainly no fan of Tetzel, but I wrote to him and said that it was not he who "set the ball rolling. This child had quite another father."[5] Tetzel died in July 1519.

Another major event worked in my favor—no, not in my favor, in favor of the precious Gospel. Emperor Maximilian I died on 12 January 1519. Everything relating to my case was put on hold until a new emperor would be elected. My prince was one of seven electors. The pope wanted Francis I of France to become emperor, but to his chagrin his worst fears came to pass: Charles I of Spain was elected and became Charles V of the Holy Roman Empire.

I was not on vacation in early 1519. I took the brief respite to do some writing. I'll share something about that writing next time.

4 Schwiebert, 378.

5 Schwiebert, 378.

Letter 29

At the conclusion of my last letter, I mentioned that I had not been on vacation following my meeting with Miltitz and the death of Emperor Maximillian I. Frankly, I had never even heard of such a silly notion as a vacation.

Never forget, in addition to being a theological professor, I also had pastoral responsibilities at the town church. Theology was not an academic exercise for me as it had been for the Scholastics prior to my time and, as I understand, is all too frequent in your day. My protest against the sale of indulgences and the theology I presented in the Heidelberg Disputation were all for the sake of my dear congregation. They were being financially exploited and given empty promises by the sale of indulgence letters, and they were given false hope of life with God by performing religious exercises rather than relying on the free grace of God, received by faith alone in the sacrifice of Jesus Christ for their sins.

In the winter and spring of 1519, I gave myself to writing three practical items for Christian living: on marriage, meditation of Christ's suffering, and helpful comments on the Lord's Prayer.

Only four days after the emperor's death, I preached on the assigned text for the day, John 2:1–11, the marriage in Cana, in the province of Galilee. Someone took notes on the sermon and had it published. I did not like what had been written, so I set about revising my sermon and in May had it published as *A Sermon on the Estate of Marriage*.[1]

I said that there are three kinds of love. "False love is that which seeks its own. . . . Natural love is that between father and child. . . . But over and above all these is married love, that is, a bride's love, which glows like a fire and desires nothing but the husband."[2] I mean to say that married love wants not what the other has, but simply wants the other for who he or she is.

I agreed with the doctors of the church (the theologians) who have said that there are three useful things in marriage. First, marriage is a sacrament. That might surprise you, but in 1519 I still accepted marriage

---

1 LW 44:5–15.

2 LW 44:9.

as a sacrament. I commented on that by saying, "A sacrament is a sacred sign of something spiritual, holy, heavenly, and eternal."[3] For technical reasons, I later dropped calling marriage a sacrament, but, nevertheless, marriage is ordained by God and is something more than a mere "mating," as one in your day has written in reference to my *Sermon*,[4] that binds a man and women together as one.

Second, marriage is a "covenant of fidelity." I did not say it quite in these words, but words that you will understand. Marriage puts a limit on human lust. I, too, am a man and understand the sex drive of males. Therefore I said, "But, of course, a man has to control himself and not make a filthy sow's sty of his marriage."[5]

Third, I said, "Marriage produces offspring, for that is the end and chief purpose of marriage."[6] I was more passionate about this responsibility of marriage than the previous two. Therefore I had more to say about it. I wrote of the great responsibility of parents to raise their children to love and worship God. Perhaps my passion for raising children in a godly manner prompted me to exaggerate at bit. I said, "For bringing up their children properly is their shortest road to heaven."[7] I continued, "By the same token, hell is no more easily earned than with respect to one's own children."[8] I then wrote how that could happen. You can read the entire *Sermon*; it has been translated and is readily available in your language.

Marriage is such a holy estate that it grieves me to know how easily marriages are dissolved in your day. Even Christians seem to ignore the words of our Lord to the effect that marriages are for a lifetime, and the voluntary breaking of that bond is an expression of one's sin. Well, I guess that I can do nothing about that other than continue to grieve.

I had intended to tell you about what I had written on meditation of Christ's Passion and the Lord's Prayer. But I am so passionate about marriages and the proper raising of children that I am now exhausted. I'll have to tell you about those other two writings next time. Until then, keep the faith.

---

3 LW 44:10.

4 LW 44:5.

5 LW 44:11.

6 LW 44:12.

7 LW 44:12.

8 LW 44:12–13.

Letter 30

During the winter and spring of 1519, I was preparing for a disputation that I would have with Dr. Eck in Leipzig in the summer of that year. Eck was a resolute scholar, and I had to be prepared by studying the canons of the Church and the writings of the Church Fathers, not to mention the witness of the Holy Bible.

I wrote to my friend Spalatin at the court of Prince Frederick in mid-March:

> I am too busy to translate my explanation of the Lord's Prayer into Latin. Each evening I expound to children and ordinary folk the Commandments and the Lord's Prayer, I preach, and I am presently getting out Paul's Epistle to the Galatians; besides that, there are the *orationes ceremoniales* [ceremonial prayers] and the lectures. I really do not have enough time, not to speak of spare time. I am planning a treatise dealing with the meditation on Christ's passion. I do not know, however, whether I shall have enough leisure to write it out. Yet I will try hard.[1]

How wonderfully God provides. Only three weeks later, I was able to send a printed copy of *A Meditation on Christ's Passion* to Spalatin.[2]

I began by noting three improper ways to meditate on Christ's suffering: blaming the suffering on the Jews, seeking personal benefits by such contemplation, and simply feeling sorry that such an Innocent One had to endure such suffering. Of that last group I said, "Of what help is it to you that God is God, if he is not God to you?"[3] I emphasized that point by adding, "Of what benefit is it to you that food and drink are good and wholesome in themselves if they are not healthful for you?"[4]

Next, I spent some time writing about the proper way to contemplate Christ's suffering; it must be personalized. I began by saying, "They contemplate Christ's passion aright who view it with a terror-stricken heart

---

1 LW 48:113–14.

2 LW 42:3–14.

3 LW 42:8.

4 LW 42:8.

and a despairing conscience."[5] If that sounds harsh, I continued, "You must get this thought through your head and not doubt that you are the one who is torturing Christ thus, for your sins have surely wrought this."[6] And again, "For every nail that pierces Christ, more than one hundred thousand should in justice pierce you, yes, they should prick you forever and ever more painfully."[7] I hope that you can see how personal the suffering of Christ must be for you.

However, as crushing as the meditation must be, it must not lead you to or leave you in despair. Hear the blessed hope that accompanies proper meditation. "This meditation changes man's being and, almost like baptism, gives him a new birth."[8] I used a different image to contrast the personal torment of the contemplation with the sheer joy of knowing what Christ did for you thorough that suffering and death. "Until now we have sojourned in Passion Week and rightly celebrated Good Friday. Now we come to the resurrection of Christ, to the day of Easter. After man has thus become aware of his sin and is terrified in his heart, he must watch that sin does not remain in his conscience, for this would lead to sheer despair."[9] If that image is too abstract for you, let me say it differently. "If we allow sin to remain in our conscience and try to deal with it there, or if we look at sin in our heart, it will be much too strong for us and will live on forever. But if we behold it resting on Christ and [see it] overcome by his resurrection, and then boldly believe this, even it is dead and nullified."[10]

That's enough on that one, and it's as true in your day as in mine.

I thought that I could tell you about two writings in the spring of 1519, but what I want to say about the Lord's Prayer will make this letter too long. I fear that I will be exhausted if I continue. I will tell you about *An Exposition of the Lord's Prayer* in my next letter. Until then, keep the faith and meditate properly on the suffering of Jesus Christ for you.

---

5 LW 42:8.

6 LW 42:9.

7 LW 42:9.

8 LW 42:11.

9 LW 42:12.

10 LW 42:12.

Letter 31

I had given a series of sermons on the Lord's Prayer in 1517, months before I extended an invitation to scholars to debate my Ninety-five Theses. In the spring of 1519, I reworked those sermons, and in April I published *An Exposition of the Lord's Prayer for Simple Laymen*.[1] The little book had a wide circulation. I was amused to hear that a printer in Venice, clearly a Roman Catholic who did not know who wrote the book, had said, "Blessed are the hands that wrote this. Blessed are the eyes that see it. Blessed shall be the hearts that believe this book and cry to God."[2]

Even a summary of the book would be far too long for a brief letter. I will be content—as I hope you will be—with just a few comments that I made regarding the prayer.

> Our prayer must have few words, but be great and profound in content and meaning. The fewer the words, the better the prayer; the more words, the poorer the prayer. Few words and richness of meaning is Christian; many words and lack of meaning is pagan.[3]
>
> That does not mean that time in prayer should be short, only keep your words to a minimum.

On the opening of the prayer, "Our Father," I wrote,

> The name "Father" is part of our nature and is sweet by nature. That is why it is the most pleasing to God, and why no other name moves him so strongly to hear us. With this name we likewise confess that we are the children of God, which again stirs his heart mightily; for there is no lovelier sound than that of a child speaking to his father.[4]
>
> Among the seven petitions there is none greater for us to pray than, "Hallowed be thy name." . . . In this petition God becomes everything and man becomes nothing.[5]

---

1 LW42:17–81.

2 LW 42:17.

3 LW 42:19.

4 LW 42:22.

5 LW 42:27.

I concluded my comments on this petition by saying,

> Hence, since no one is without pride, and since everyone covets his own name and honor, there can be no one for whom this petition is not very necessary and useful.[6]

In writing about the second petition, "Thy Kingdom come," I made it very clear that there are two kingdoms, and they are mutually exclusive; nevertheless, believers live in both kingdoms simultaneously, while unbelievers live in only one kingdom.

"The first kingdom," I wrote, "is a kingdom of the devil." Then I added, "Now, all of us dwell in the devil's kingdom until the coming of the kingdom of God. However, there is a difference. To be sure, the godly are also in the devil's kingdom, but they daily and steadfastly contend against sins and resist the lusts of the flesh, the allurements of the world, the whisperings of the devil."[7] On the contrary, "The others dwell in this kingdom, enjoy it, and freely do the bidding of the flesh, the world, and the devil. If they could, they would always stay there."[8] "The other kingdom is that of God, namely, a kingdom of truth and righteousness."[9]

There is so much more to say about this petition, but you must read it all for yourself.

In the third petition, we pray for God's will to be done. I had a lot to say about this petition, but I summarized the whole petition by saying that in this petition, "God bids us to pray against ourselves. In that way he teaches us that we have no greater enemy than ourself."[10] I also made brief mention about a "free will." That may surprise you because a few years later, I wrote a very long treatise against Erasmus with the title *The Bondage of the Will.* I will tell you more about that in a subsequent letter. But in this *Exposition* I did not contradict what I would say later. A truly free will is the will that submits to God. I said, "A free will does not want its own way, but looks only to God's will for direction."[11] A hymn that is sometimes sung in your day accurately captures my thoughts on the issue of a free will. It begins, "Make me a captive, Lord, and then I shall be

---

6 LW 42:37.

7 LW 42:38.

8 LW 42:39.

9 LW 42:39.

10 LW 42:48.

11 LW 42:48.

free; force me to render up my sword, and I shall conqueror be." Think about that a bit.

When we pray "Give us this day our daily bread," my focus was on the true bread necessary for life, Jesus Christ. Christ is given in a twofold manner. "In the first place, outwardly, by persons, for instance, by priests or teachers."[12] Also, "In the sacrament Christ is received."[13] I certainly recognized that all have physical needs and those needs are satisfied only by a gracious heavenly Father. "But," I asked, "do we not also pray for our physical bread? Answer: Yes, this too may well be included in this petition. However, this petition refers principally to Christ, the spiritual bread of the soul."[14] When I wrote the Small Catechism ten years later, my brief comment on this petition referred only to our physical, material needs.

The fifth petition prays for forgiveness from God and offers forgiveness to those who sin against us. I'm getting weary of telling you what I wrote on each of these petitions. If you care enough, you can read it for yourself. You certainly know your need of forgiveness, and if you don't, nothing I say will convince you. Perhaps your biggest sin is not forgiving others. Don't expect God to forgive you if you are not willing to forgive others.

"Lead us not into temptation or trials." Temptation and trials will be your lot until you close your eyes in death. But here we pray that God will not lead us into such a state, and that when we encounter trials and temptations we pray, "Dear Father, help us so that we do not fall prey to them and yield to them, and thus be overcome and vanquished."[15] It was in this *Exposition* that I quoted from St. Jerome's *Lives of the Hermits*: "The aged hermit said to him, 'Dear brother, you cannot prevent the birds from flying over your head, but you can certainly keep them from building a nest in your hair.'"[16]

The last petition prays to be delivered from evil. I must have been getting tired because I wrote only three short paragraphs on this petition.

"Amen" is the word of complete assurance that God our heavenly Father hears our prayer and will surely honor and respond as any good

---

12 LW 42:57.

13 LW 42:57.

14 LW 42:61.

15 LW 42:71.

16 LW 42:73.

father would to his dear child. One from your day commented on what I had written and said, "Luther restored [Amen] to use by the congregation for the expression of a firm and hearty faith."[17] That sounds right to me because I did write, "Only that prayer is acceptable which breathes a firm confidence and trust that it will be heard (no matter how small and unworthy it may be in itself) because of the reliable pledge and promise of God."[18]

Throughout the spring of 1519, while writing several treatises, preparing and giving lectures at the university, attending to my pastoral responsibilities, and caring for my own spiritual needs through daily prayer and meditation on the writings in the Holy Scriptures, I was also preparing for a debate with Dr. Eck that would be held in Leipzig in July of that year. I hope to tell you about that very important debate in my next letter.

---

17 LW 42:76, n. 44.

18 LW 42:77.

Letter 32

By now you have discovered that I frequently change my mind and interject something that I had not intended when I wrote a previous letter. I will do that again today.

For some time, I have wanted to tell you about myself, but I find it difficult to speak objectively on that subject.

As I was reflecting on the Leipzig Debate, I remembered the formal proceedings prior to the actual debate. Part of the preliminary festivities included an address by Professor Petrus Mosellanus, professor of poetry at the University of Leipzig. In a separate writing, Professor Mosellanus gave a written description of both me and John Eck. I think I will simply write what the professor said about me. Remember, the description of me was in 1519 when I was a few months short of my thirty-sixth birthday.

> Martin is of medium height with a gaunt body that has been so exhausted by studies and worries that one can almost count the bones under his skin; yet he is manly and vigorous, with a high, clear voice. He is full of learning and has an excellent knowledge of the Scriptures, so that he can refer to facts as if they were at his fingers' tips. He knows enough Greek and Hebrew to enable him to pass judgments on interpretations. He is also not lacking in subject material and has a large store of words and ideas. In his life and behavior he is very courteous and friendly, and there is nothing of the stern stoic or grumpy fellow about him. He can adjust to all occasions. In a social gathering he is gay, witty, lively, ever full of joy, always has a bright and happy face, no matter how seriously his adversaries threaten him. One can see in him that God's strength is with him in his difficult undertaking. The only fault everyone criticizes in him is that he is somewhat too violent and cutting in his reprimands, in fact more than is proper for one seeking to find new trails in theology, and certainly also for a divine; this is probably a weakness of all those who have gained their leaning somewhat late.[1]

1 Brecht 1:313.

That is how another saw me. I think that he was as objective as anyone can be. I can confirm two things that he said: I was exhausted. I had spent many months preparing for a debate without any certainty that I would be allowed to participate. The debate had been officially scheduled between Dr. John Eck and my Wittenberg colleague Andreas Karlstadt. Nevertheless, I had written to Duke George several times asking for his permission to participate. The only response I got was that the duke would leave that decision to Dr. Eck. I wrote to Dr. Eck several times asking for his permission, but he never answered my letters. I think that was a deliberate ploy to keep me in suspense. With the uncertainty I still had to be prepared if I were to meet the most respected debater in Germany. Second, I can confirm that I was often "violent and cutting" as Professor Mosellanus noted. I wish that I could say that my speech became more tempered as I grew older, but alas, I fear that I may have become even more blunt and outspoken in later life.

Next time, I'll tell you about the debate with Dr. Eck at Leipzig. Until then, keep the faith.

LETTER 33

The debate at the University of Leipzig was scheduled between Dr. John Eck and my Wittenberg colleague Andreas Karlstadt, but there was no doubt that Eck wanted me as the contestant.

As early as 29 December 1518, Eck had published *Twelve Theses*, all of which were directed against what I had been teaching—penance, indulgences, good works, purgatory, and papal power. His only previous contention with Karlstadt had been over the freedom of the will and grace. The *Twelve Theses* mentioned nothing on those two issues. (The twelve theses later became thirteen, but the last thesis remained the same.) Eck, always a crafty fox, thought that he could squeeze me into a corner by noting that I had previously challenged the origin of the papacy. Consequently, his final thesis read, "We deny that the Roman Church was not over other churches before the time of Sylvester, but, on the contrary, we assert that he who possessed the seat and the faith of St. Peter was always regarded as the successor of Peter and the general Vicar of Christ."[1]

You will recall that when I met with Miltitz at Altenburg, I promised to keep silence provided the other side did the same. With Eck's *Twelve Theses*, I felt that the agreement had been breached. I was now free again to publicly defend the Holy Gospel. I responded to Eck by publishing my own thirteen theses in rebuttal to Eck's thirteen.[2] In my response to Eck's final thesis, I wrote, "The claim that the Roman Church stands above all others rests merely on the weak papal decretals of the last 400 years; while over against this claim there are 1,100 years of church history, the texts from the Holy Scriptures, and the decrees of the Sacred Council of Nicaea."[3]

When the debate opened on 27 June 1519, I was a mere spectator. Eck and Karlstadt were the only participants. Eck was fluent and engaging; Karlstadt was dull and laborious, reading long sections from books.

---

1 Schwiebert, 386.

2 LW 31:317–18.

3 Schwiebert, 387.

Finally, on 4 July, I was given the opportunity to replace Karlstadt. Eck and I debated all the issues that Eck had included in his *Twelve Theses*, but the heat was generated over the origin and the power of the papacy. Someone in your day has said that the significance of this debate was my challenge of the papacy, "which never before in the history of Christianity had occurred in this magnitude."[4] I was confident in my position; I had history on my side. But, you cannot imagine the weight that was on my shoulders contesting an office that was so widely and deeply entrenched in the mind-set and worldview of my day.

It was sometime during my preparation for this debate that I began to have doubts about purgatory and the pope. The teaching of the Roman Church was that all who enter purgatory would eventually gain heaven. I said that there is no biblical warrant for such certainty. In fact, I argued that purgatory and despair are the same thing.[5]

Because the pope had allowed the Holy Gospel to be replaced by church laws that became oppressive to people, I began to wonder whether the pope himself might be the Antichrist. In a letter to my friend George Spalatin in March 1519, I wrote, "And, confidentially, I do not know whether the pope is the Antichrist himself or whether he is his apostle, so miserably is Christ (that is, the truth) corrupted and crucified by the pope in the decretals."[6]

At one point, Eck charged me with being a Hussite. I denied being a Hussite, but I did myself no favor when I said that not all of the teachings of Hus were heretical. Of course, Eck jumped on that and insisted that I was no different than the "heretic" who had been burned at the stake at the Council of Constance in 1415, almost 104 years to the day before my contest with Eck. I still thought it quite probable that I would eat the same flames.

Who won the debate? Eck and I agreed that the faculties of the University of Paris and the University of Erfurt would render a verdict. I'll tell you more about that later.

When I returned to Wittenberg at the conclusion of the debate on 14 July, I was depressed. The whole debate had been a waste of time. The issues could have been resolved in two hours if Eck had been serious

---

4 Brecht 1:317.

5 Brecht 1:303.

6 LW 48:114.

about the issues. Truth seemed not to matter to him; the only objective was to win a debate by whatever means he deemed useful.

I am still confused by one in your day who said that this was "one of the greatest debates in European history."[7] The debate itself was a disaster. The only way it makes sense to call it a great debate or "the greatest debate" is to consider the later consequences of the debate. By the grace of God, and not by my debating skills, because, as you will learn later, Eck was declared the winner of the debate, the cause of the Gospel and the reform of the Holy Church was advanced. Again, I will use the words of one from your day. He summarized the results of the debate:

> But soon Eck was forced to acknowledge that his "victory" was not as impressive as it had seemed. Polemical pamphlets directed against him began to appear on all sides. The humanists turned away from him in droves. The council clerk Lazarus Spengler of Nuremberg came out in support of Luther. A satire called "The Dressed-Down Eck," most likely written by Willibald Pirckheimer, made a laughingstock of him. Johann Ökolampad (Oecolampadius), at that time a colleague of Erasmus and later a reformer in Basel, wrote against him. More and more students flocked to Wittenberg, among them subjects of Duke George. This included even the chief secretary at the disputation, the rector of the Thomas school in Leipzig, Johann Graumann (called Poliander).[8]

You might wonder what effect the Leipzig Debate had on me personally. I think I will answer that by telling you what two men who have studied me far more than I ever studied myself have said. Recall that I did a vast amount of study in preparation for this debate.

One has said,

> The Leipzig Debate greatly accelerated Luther's theological development. Since the beginning of his spiritual struggle in the monastery at Erfurt, Luther had been steadily drifting from the Catholic fold, but the change was so gradual that not even he was fully aware of the magnitude. . . . In the Leipzig Debate he came face to face with the orthodox Roman position on sin, grace, justification, the Church,

---

7 Schwiebert, 413.

8 Loewenich, 149.

> and papal power, and he began to realize how far he had really drifted.[9]

Because, as was said, I was unaware of the drift, I can only say that the comment may be close to accurate.

The other comment was shorter, but very close to the heart of the matter—the Word of God. He wrote, "The Leipzig Debate is of great significance in Luther's development as a reformer primarily because he on that occasion publicly stated his evangelical conception of the church in unmistakable terms and showed that in the last analysis his sole authority in matters of faith was the Word of God."[10] I liked that comment.

The primacy of the Word of God! That's a good place to stop writing.

---

9 Schwiebert, 416.

10 LW 31:311.

Letter 34

Following my debate with Eck in Leipzig, my name became known throughout Germany. I hesitate to use the word *fame* because fame should not be a part of the Christian vocabulary. Fame is dangerous; I never sought it, but, to my regret, fame found me. Don't misunderstand; fame was also accompanied by infamy. Perhaps more people loathed my name than admired it. I wanted neither. I wanted only the simplicity of life in the monastery, where I could live and pray with my brothers. I did not want to be a priest. I did not want to be a doctor of theology. All that was thrust upon me against my will. However, once I was in the position as a doctor of the church, I considered it my responsibility to contend for the truth of the Gospel.

Who won the debate? Did I tell you that four secretaries took notes on the debate? Eck and I agreed that one set of notes should be prepared, and only that which each of the four had transcribed should be included in the single set. Those notes were then submitted to the faculties of the Universities of Erfurt and Paris for their decision. Erfurt refused to give an opinion, and Paris took so long to respond, not until April 1521, that their response was outdated by subsequent events. When Paris did respond, they condemned my writings but made no mention of the Leipzig Debate. The condemnation was based on my writings that had been collected and published by Johann Froben in October 1518. (That was the first publication of my collected writings.[1])

Two other universities, Louvain and Cologne, without being asked for an opinion, condemned me as a heretic whose books should be burned.

Those condemnations did not bother me; I had the Word of God on my side. I do not recall thinking about it at the time, but later I found the words that the apostle Paul wrote to the Church in Rome to be so very true, "If God is for us, who can be against us?" You will find that in the eighth chapter of Romans. (The Bible was divided into chapters only about a hundred years before my birth, and verses were not added for more than a decade after my death.)

The preparation for the debate with Eck, and the condemnations I received following the debate, set me on fire. My mind raced, and my

1 Schwiebert, 427.

pen was ablaze. In nineteen months, from October 1519 until early April 1521, when I was required to stand before the emperor of the Holy Roman Empire at the Diet of Worms, I preached 116 sermons, wrote 16 (most lengthy) treatises, and completed a commentary on the Book of Galatians.[2] All that was in addition to my regular teaching assignment at the university. Fortunately, I had a good memory and the words flowed freely.

I think I will next tell you about some of the things that I wrote during that period between the Leipzig Debate and my appearance at the Diet of Worms in April 1521. Until then, keep the faith.

---

2 Schwiebert, 438–39.

Letter 35

I'm frustrated and bothered. You might think that where I now live in perfect harmony with God, the saints that preceded me, and those who have come after me, I would be free of frustration. I can't speak for all God's beloved who share this blessed estate, but I can speak for myself. The frustration is caused by the continued use of my name in your domain. I regret that I have become famous, a hero to some. I never wanted fame, and I despise hero worship. I have nothing in common with those who think of me as a hero! There is only one who must be the sole focus of every believer; especially do I care about those who use my name. The focus must be on Jesus.

I fear that you may think that when I stood against the pope and the whole Christian establishment of my day, and only about a year after my debate with Eck in Leipzig, I stood against the emperor of the Holy Roman Empire as a brave champion of the Gospel.

I did not; I was frightened in my boots. Don't jump to the wrong conclusion. I was not frightened about death; frankly, I expected it. Others before me who had opposed the tyranny of the pope met that fate. (Read again the opening of my Letter 26.) There was no reason for me to expect anything less. My fear was that if I was wrong, I would be leading many to hell. That weighed on me like a ton of bricks. Could I be right and all the others be wrong?

Perhaps I put that struggle with my conscience best when I wrote *The Misuse of the Mass* in the winter of 1521.

> I myself experience daily how extremely difficult it is to lay aside a conscience of long standing, one that has been fenced in by man-made ordinances. O with how much greater effort and labor, even on the basis of the Holy Scriptures, have I been barely able to justify my own conscience; so that I, one man alone, have dared to come forward against the pope, brand him as the Antichrist, the bishops as his apostles, and the universities as his brothels! How often did my heart quail, punish me, and reproach me with its single strongest argument: Are you the only wise man? Can it be that all the others are in error and have erred for so long a time? What if you are mistaken and

> lead so many people into error who might all be eternally damned?[1]

I hope that you can feel the weight that I carried during those early years. Only the most arrogant psychopath would relish such a terrifying conscience.

By God's grace, that engagement with Eck in Leipzig had a profound effect on me. After that encounter, I was more certain than ever that I was right. But that certitude was not the product of my own will or arrogance; it was the work of the Spirit of Christ. By the winter of 1521, I could write, "Finally, Christ with his clear, unmistakable Word strengthened and confirmed me, so that my heart no long quails, but resists the arguments of the papists, as a stony shore resists the waves, and laughs at their threats and storms!"[2]

Now that I have that off my chest, I can do what I promised in my last letter. I will tell you about some of the things that I wrote after I left Leipzig in July 1519.

---

1 LW 36:134.

2 LW 36:134.

LETTER 36

In the fall of 1519, I wrote three sermons on three sacraments: penance, Baptism, and the Lord's Supper. (At that time I still considered penance to be a sacrament. Only a year later I changed my mind about penance being a sacrament, not because I thought penance to be less important, but because it does not have the outward, visible sign that accompanies Baptism [water] and the Lord's Supper [bread and wine].)

Someone has called these three sermons the catechism of 1520 (although they were written in 1519).[1]

Now, five hundred years later, I want you to think of penance as repentance. I made that point in the very first of my Ninety-five Theses. There I wrote, "When our Lord and Master Jesus Christ said 'Repent' (the Roman Church translated that word 'do penance'), he willed the entire life of believers to be one of repentance." [See Letter 21.]

In my sermon *The Sacrament of Penance*,[2] I said that forgiveness is of two kinds: forgiveness of punishment and forgiveness of guilt. If the church imposes punishment, and I have no doubt that the church has that authority (and I grieve that in the church that bears my name in your day punishment for sin is seldom used), it also has the authority to remit that punishment. But, only God has the authority to remit the guilt of sin. The remission of guilt is immeasurably more important than the remission of punishment.

There are three parts to repentance. The first is absolution, in which the pastor, by virtue of the authority that Jesus gave to His Church (the words of Jesus in Matthew 16:19), announces and proclaims that your sins are forgiven. The second part of repentance is the gracious forgiveness of sins by which one's conscience is cleared and peace restored. The third element is faith that firmly believes the words of absolution spoken by the pastor as though they were the words of Jesus himself. You will not be surprised to hear me say that it all depends on faith because it is faith alone that makes the words of absolution come true.

---

1 Schwiebert, 444.

2 LW 35:3–22.

I was quite clear in saying that forgiveness is not dependent upon the words of a priest or pastor. Because it is the word of Jesus Christ that offers forgiveness, when a pastor or priest is not available, the same words of absolution spoken by any believer is a valid word of Jesus, and that word is to be firmly believed.

That's the main point of *The Sacrament of Penance*. I had more to say, but I can't reproduce the whole sermon for you.

That sermon was given in October, and I followed with *The Holy and Blessed Sacrament of Baptism*[3] in early November.

I rejoice that I had no contention with the pope on the Sacrament of Baptism. Indeed, I had no argument with anyone over this most basic of all Christian beliefs until some radicals came on the scene a few years later; they were called Anabaptists. They taught that infant Baptism was invalid because an infant cannot have faith. I didn't pay much attention to them when they first came to my attention, but when a couple of pastors asked for my advice on how to deal with them I wrote a very long letter to them, in the winter of 1527–28, in which I affirmed infant Baptism and said that those "rebaptizers" could not prove from Scripture that faith is lacking in an infant. (I think they put too much emphasis on the intellect rather than on simple trust as the basic element of faith.) In that letter, I said, "So no matter which way you look at it the Anabaptists are in error. They blaspheme and dishonor the order of God, calling baptism wrong on account of the wrongs and abuses of man, though even their claim of man's wrongs and abuses is unconvincing."[4]

In *The Holy and Blessed Sacrament of Baptism*, I made only three points. First is the sign of the sacrament in which an individual is immersed in water. I wrote, "Although in many places it is no longer customary to thrust and dip infants into the font, but only with the hand to pour the baptismal water upon them out of the font, nevertheless the former is what should be done."[5] Second, Baptism signifies (actualizes) the death of our old, human nature. That's why immersion is preferable: it carries out the symbolism of drowning—death—and resurrection to a new life as the one immersed is brought out of the water. Third, I wrote, "Yet only by lack of faith in its operation is baptism canceled out. Faith,

3 LW 35:23–43.

4 LW 40:248.

5 LW 35:29.

in turn, removes the hindrance to the operation of baptism. Thus everything depends on faith."[6]

I had a few other important things to say in that sermon, but those are the main points. I think that you would do well to find that sermon and read the whole thing. I've heard that Baptism is used as indiscriminately in your day as in mine; even more tragically, it is used without continued daily nurture.

In December 1519, my third sermon on the sacraments was published, *The Blessed Sacrament of the Holy and True Body of Christ and the Brotherhoods*.[7] I followed the same outline as I did on *Baptism*: the outward sign, the inward significance, and a living faith. Here, I said, is the relationship between all three. "These three parts must be found in every sacrament. The sacrament must be external and visible, having some material form or appearance. The significance must be internal and spiritual, within the spirit of the person. Faith must make both of them together operative and useful."[8]

In this sermon, I urged that the church would allow laypersons to receive both the blood of Christ as well as the body. I was not adamant about this and said that the desire for the cup was equivalent to receiving it.

In 1519, I did not yet object to transubstantiation, but I did not enthusiastically endorse it. I said, "The how and the where, we leave to him."[9]

I did object to the teaching that the sacrament works what it promises without faith in the receiver. There were a couple of technical terms that were used that are probably of no interest to you: *opus operatum* (the sacrament works by itself) and *opus operantis* (the sacrament requires faith to be effective). I concluded, "In short, such expressions as *opus operatum* and *opus operantis* are vain words of men, more of a hindrance than a help."[10]

---

6 LW 35:38.

7 LW 35:45–73.

8 LW 35:49.

9 LW 35:61.

10 LW 35:64.

Someone in your day has said that my understanding of the sacraments had not yet matured.[11] Perhaps he is right. Later, I had much more to say about this most precious identification of us sinners with our Lord and about the blessed assurance He gives us in this sacrament.

Now a word about the confraternities, or brotherhoods. In my day, they were similar to fraternal lodges in your day but with a religious bent. There were religious obligations, and the alleged benefits of those obligations flowed to all the members. Even after death, members benefited from the alleged "good works" of their fraternal brothers. There was one man in my city of Wittenberg who belonged to eight such brotherhoods. He had nothing to do but attend brotherhood meetings. What a waste of time! I wrote, "And the brotherhood is also supposed to be a special convocation of good works; instead it has become a collecting of money for beer."[12] I added, "If a sow were made the patron saint of such a brotherhood she would not consent."[13] Toward the end of the sermon, I wrote, "For such brotherhoods call themselves brotherhoods of the saints while they do the work of the devil."[14] You will understand that I wanted all brotherhoods abolished.

---

11 Schwiebert, 445ff.

12 LW 35:68.

13 LW 35:68.

14 LW 35:69.

Letter 37

One of the benefactors of our Augustinian monastery and the University of Wittenberg was suffering under the certainty of his own death. His death was not imminent, but it was certain. I knew the horror of that certainty because it was the fear of death and hell that drove me into the monastic life. Spalatin had asked me early in 1519 to prepare some help for this dear man. It was my pastoral privilege to help one dear soul face death with supreme confidence, but I did not have time to prepare a sermon on death until late in the year.

In November, *A Sermon on Preparing to Die*[1] was published and sent to our benefactor. In that sermon, I offered eighteen specific suggestions for that preparation.

I will not make lengthy comments on most of what I wrote, but because all who read this letter face the same fate, I will give a summary of the entire sermon.

You might be surprised that my first suggestion was quite practical. In terms of your day: prepare a last will and testament to prevent "squabbles, quarrels or other misunderstanding among his [your] surviving friends."[2]

Second, forgive all who have offended or sinned against you, and ask forgiveness from those whom you have offended or harmed.

Third, think of death as an entrance into the presence of God. I said, "Just as an infant is born with peril and pain from the small abode of its mother's womb into this immense heaven and earth, that is, into this world, so man departs this life through the narrow gate of death."[3] I then noted that the day of a saint's death is their "feast day." A "feast day" is like a birthday party, the celebration of new life.

The fourth preparation is sincere confession of all sins that weigh on one's conscience and the reception of the "holy and true body of Christ." I said, "The sacraments are nothing else than signs which help and incite us to faith, as we shall see. Without faith they serve no purpose."[4]

---

1 LW 42:95–115.

2 LW 42:99.

3 LW 42:99.

4 LW 42:100.

In the fifth suggestion, I again returned to the sacraments because they are God-given signs that give assurance to believers. (To unbelievers, the sacraments are nothing, entirely useless.)

What are the evils against which the sacraments provide strength? In the sixth preparation, I noted three: the terrifying image of death, the awesomely manifold image of sin, and the unbearable and unavoidable image of hell and eternal damnation. I also said, "We should familiarize ourselves with death during our lifetime, inviting death into our presence when it is still at a distance and not on the move."[5]

As one nears death, Satan will bring to mind one's sin and the dire consequences of hell. But, I said in the seventh item in preparation for death, "in the hour of death when our eyes should see only life, grace, and salvation, he [Satan] at once opens our eyes and frightens us with these untimely images so that we shall not see the true ones [life, grace, and salvation]."[6]

I continued in the eighth counsel with comments about how Satan turns one's attention to hell as death draws near; but in the ninth preparation I said that such thoughts must be dropped. There is a time to look seriously at death and hell, but that must be done earlier in life. But even then a believer must "see sin in the light of grace and hell in the light of heaven."[7]

The only death to consider when death raises its ugly head is the death of Christ, so I said in suggestion number ten. "Thus you must concern yourself solely with the death of Christ and then you will find life. But if you look at death in any other way, it will kill you with great anxiety and anguish."[8]

Look at grace, I said in number eleven. "The picture of grace is nothing else but that of Christ on the cross and of all his dear saints."[9] The grace of God, centered in the cross of Christ is every person's only certain hope.

I won't comment on my twelfth point because it relates to predestination about which, I think, very few in your day care much. That is

---

5 LW 42:101–2.

6 LW 42:102.

7 LW 42:103.

8 LW 42:104.

9 LW 42:104.

unfortunate, but at the time of death it certainly is not an issue on which to dwell. "Seek yourself only in Christ and not in yourself and you will find yourself in him eternally."[10]

Thirteen and fourteen are all about Jesus' death and how He faced it. He remained silent against all personal attacks that challenged His relationship to God, His heavenly Father. You must do the same and stay focused on what Jesus did for you.

The emphasis in preparations number fifteen, sixteen, and seventeen are all about the blessed sacraments that God has given to bring us comfort. I'll share with you just a few things that I said about the sacraments. "In the sacraments God himself grants you all the blessings we just mentioned in connection with Christ. God wants the sacraments to be a sign and testimony that Christ's life has taken your death, his obedience your sin, his love your hell, upon themselves and overcome them."[11] Still, it must be personalized. "What will it profit you to assume and to believe that sin, death, and hell are overcome in Christ for others, but not to believe that your sin, your death, and your hell are also vanquished and wiped out and that you are thus redeemed?"[12]

Finally, "The right use of the sacraments involves nothing more than believing that all will be as the sacraments promise and pledge through God's Word."[13] Ten years later, I noted what they promise: forgiveness of sin, life, and salvation.

The eighteenth preparation for a Christian is to firmly believe that one is not alone in the journey. "If God looks upon you, all the angels, saints, and all creatures will fix their eyes upon you. And if you remain in that faith, all of them will uphold you with their hands. And when your soul leaves your body, they will be on hand to receive it, and you cannot perish."[14]

Number nineteen is a reminder to never face death alone. "To this end he [you] must call upon the holy angels, particularly his [your] own angel, the Mother of God, and all the apostles and saints."[15]

---

10 LW 42:106.

11 LW 42:108.

12 LW 42:109.

13 LW 42:111.

14 LW 42:112.

15 LW 42:113.

Finally, number twenty, and the last preparation:

> Twentieth, what more should God do to persuade you to accept death willingly and not to dread but to overcome it? In Christ he offers you the image of life, of grace, and of salvation so that you may not be horrified by the images of sin, death, and hell. Furthermore, he lays your sin, your death, and your hell on his dearest Son, vanquishes them, and renders them harmless for you.[16]

I hope that this little sermon was helpful to the benefactor of my monastic order and university. (His name was Mark Schart.) I hope that they will also be helpful to you as you face a certain death.

16 LW 42:114.

Letter 38

There are two things I must do before I tell you about the momentous events of 1520 and the prodigious amount of writing I did in that year. I must return to the events that followed my debate with Eck in Leipzig in July 1519, but before I do that, I want to tell you about a sermon that I preached early that year.

Certainly you know that the Bible is abundantly clear that no one will enjoy the presence of God without being righteous, totally righteous, without blemish. You might ask, "Who can endure that requirement?" It appears that hell eagerly awaits the death of every sinner.

Because of that dismal end, and believe me, in my day that end was brought to our attention with regularity by the pope, bishops, and parish priests, I thought it necessary to preach a sermon on righteousness that would bring solace to forlorn sinners.

I could tell you again about my own agonizing experience with that frightening requirement of righteousness, but I need only refer you to Letter 14 wherein I told of those terrifying years before relief came to me when I discovered that the righteousness that God requires is the righteousness that God gives through faith in Jesus Christ

The title of the sermon that I preached early in 1519 is *Two Kinds of Righteousness*.[1] I made a clear distinction between what I called alien righteousness and proper righteousness. Do not jump to the invalid conclusion that alien righteousness is improper. Let me try to explain what I meant by those two kinds of righteousness.

I said, "The first is alien righteousness, that is the righteousness of another, instilled from without. This is the righteousness of Christ by which he justifies through faith."[2] (I wish that your language had the word "righteousification." In the Bible, the word for righteous and just is the same word. To justify is to make righteous.) The righteousness that gives you a standing before God is the righteousness of another, Jesus. That is why I called it an alien righteousness.

People who care will crave that righteousness, yearn for it, and ask how it may be obtained. I anticipated that yearning because it was my

1 LW 31:293–306.

2 LW 31:297.

own yearning when I entered the monastery. I said, "This righteousness, then, is given to men in baptism and whenever they are truly repentant."[3] Later I added, "Through faith in Christ, therefore, Christ's righteousness becomes our righteousness and all that he has becomes ours; rather, he himself becomes ours."[4] You see how intimately a believer is united with Christ; more intimately than the union between husband and wife.

About a year and a half later, I wrote a more extensive treatise, *The Freedom of a Christian*, in which I expressed the same thought in these words: "The soul is full of sins, death, and damnation. Now let faith come between them and sins, death, and damnation will be Christ's, while grace, life, and salvation will be the soul's; for if Christ is a bridegroom, he must take upon himself the things which are his bride's and bestow upon her the things that are his."[5] Some have called that "the happy exchange," and it certainly is.

Proper righteousness flows from alien righteousness. "The second kind of righteousness is our proper righteousness, not because we alone work it, but because we work with that first and alien righteousness."[6]

Proper righteousness is the fruits that grow on the tree of alien righteousness. That tree produces fruits (works) of kindness, goodness, faithfulness, peace, pardon, and other good works. For a believer, good works are as natural as apples that fall from an apple tree. Without first enjoying the gift of alien righteousness, no work is a good work in the presence of God. The prophet Isaiah put it in these words, "All our righteous deeds are like a polluted garment" (Isaiah 64:6).

I'll close this letter with a metaphor that I used: "Therefore through the first righteousness [alien] arises the voice of the bridegroom [Christ] who says to the soul, 'I am yours,' but through the second [proper] comes the voice of the bride [believer] who answers, 'I am yours.'"[7]

There is no distinction in heaven, earth, or hell that is more important than to understand that the righteousness that gives you a standing before God is not your own, but an alien righteousness that comes to you as a gift from God through Jesus Christ, and your righteous deeds, or good works, are the natural result of enjoying that alien righteousness.

---

3 LW 31:297.

4 LW 31:298.

5 LW 31:351.

6 LW 31:299.

7 LW 31:300.

Letter 39

Now, as I promised, I must tell you about some of the results of my contest with Dr. Eck at Leipzig.

Following Leipzig, I knew the split with Rome was irreconcilable. No longer was the debate limited to the value of indulgences. The greater issue was a contest between the authority of the Word of God and the authority of the pope, councils of the Church, and the opinions of the Church Fathers. Don't misunderstand; I always had, and still have, great admiration for the Early Church Fathers who formulated our understanding of the holy faith. But, I contended then and still contend that they were not without error. I always respected the office of the pope, but in my day those who occupied that office had sold their souls to a contest for political power among the sovereigns of Europe and the enjoyment of architectural and artistic beauty of the Renaissance. More than ever, I was committed to the Word of God as the only sure and safe source for Christian faith and life. My contest from Leipzig onward was between the authority of the pope and the Word of God.

Because of my uncompromising stand on the Word of God, I was branded a Hussite. I suppose that you know that Jan Hus, who lived about a century before me, took a strong stand on the Bible and opposed some of the teachings of the Roman Church. He was summoned to the Council of Constance in 1415 and promised safe conduct. Upon his arrival, he was imprisoned and subsequently tied to a stake and burned to death. I was never a true Hussite; Hus never really understood justification by faith alone, but I was so impressed with his stance on the Word of God that I recall saying sometime after the Leipzig Debate, "I agree now with more articles of Hus than I did at Leipzig."[1] Half a year later, I said, "We are all Hussites without knowing it."[2]

In spite of verdicts by the Universities of Louvain and Cologne, and subsequently Paris, all of which condemned me, many humanists became supporters of my cause. (I hesitate to call it "my cause" because it was the cause of the Gospel of Jesus Christ that I defended. But I take heart from the apostle Paul, who spoke of the same Gospel as "my gospel." Paul used

1 Bainton, 120.

2 Bainton, 120.

that phrase when he wrote to the Church in Rome (see Romans 2:16). Humanists were those who were fed up with Scholasticism [see Letter 17] and had a great appreciation for historical research of the original sources. They found my approach to the Word of God to be a refreshing breeze in the Christian Church.

I will share with you a bit of trivia that betrays my sinful nature in those days. Less than a year after the debate in Leipzig, where Eck was lauded the victor, the student population at the University of Leipzig had declined markedly. I noted that with sinful joy.

My beloved father in the faith, Johann von Staupitz, resigned his position as vicar of the Augustinian order in Germany in the spring of 1520. I fear that his love for me, and his disquiet over my actions, may have led to his resignation. I loved that man until my dying day. And even afterwards.

My debate with Eck in Leipzig was the occasion for a spat that developed between me and Jerome Emser, secretary to Duke George in Ducal Saxony. We exchanged some pretty strong words. I may tell you about that sometime. I may also include a contest with Jacobus Latomus, a professor at the University of Louvain. Until then, keep the faith.

Letter 40

I can't get my mind off of Augustine von Alveld, an intellectually incompetent Franciscan monk from Leipzig. In May, that minor league theologian attempted to be my teacher. Early in that month, he wrote a treatise against me trying to prove on the basis of the Bible that the papacy was divinely instituted. Fortunately, he wrote the treatise in Latin; few could read it. I thought it so inferior that I did not take the time to respond to it. I gave it to my *famulus* (I think you might call him an assistant or secretary), added a few suggested bits, and asked him to respond. He told Alveld that I had better things to do than to argue with an ass.

The response of Johann Lonicer, my *famulus*, did not quiet the ass from Leipzig. Against the advice of his superiors, who thought his scholarship to be inferior, he sent off another useless treatise. This time it was in German; laypeople could read that one. I knew that I must make a strong response. This was the time for me to present a complete statement on the nature of the church. Before the end of May, I had completed the treatise *On the Papacy in Rome against the Most Celebrated Romanist in Leipzig.*[1]

I put the issue squarely: "Whether the papacy in Rome, possessing the actual power over all of Christendom, as they say, is derived from divine or from human order; and, if so, whether it would be a Christian statement to say that all other Christians in the whole world are heretics and schismatics—even though they adhere to the same baptism, sacrament, gospel, and all articles of the faith in harmony with us . . . let themselves be aped and mocked like the Germans."[2]

Alveld thought that he had three strong arguments with which he could attack me. The arguments were as strong as stale German beer.

The first argument was simply calling me all the vilest names in his vocabulary—a heretic, a senseless blind fool, a snake, and a poisoned worm. I've been called worse by more competent people than that Franciscan ass. If it will please him, I will grant him the first argument; it means nothing to me.

The second argument is based on natural reason: every community must have a head under Jesus Christ. The single head of Christendom is

1 LW 39:49–104.

2 LW 39:57–58.

the pope, he argued. I responded that if the papacy is established by divine law, it seems ridiculous that it must be defended by human reason. Reason has its rightful place, but not in defense of divine revelation. I argued that the Bible speaks about the Church in only one way. It is the assembly of all people on earth who believe in Jesus Christ and who live by faith, hope, and love. Although separated by distance, there is only one body of believers. Yet within the physical body of Christendom, there are those who are not of the same spirit. They have excluded themselves from the true body of believers. "From this," I said, "it follows, and must follow, that, just as being under the Roman unity does not create Christians, so also being outside this unity does not make either heretics or non-Christians."[3]

Alveld did not understand, but I hope that you do; there is only one Church, but it must be understood in two ways. The first is the true Body of believers; I called that a "spiritual" church. The second is simply those who use the name Christian, but have neither faith, hope, nor love. I called that the "physical" church.

I used more than two-thirds of my response to instruct Alveld, and others who would be led astray by him, that the true head of Christendom cannot have an earthly head; the only head of the Church is Jesus Christ. When the Romanists use the words of Jesus in Matthew 16:18–19, "You are Peter, and on this rock I will build My church," to affirm that the pope, as successor of Peter, is the head of the Church and that divine authority is given to him alone, I counter with the words of the same Jesus in Matthew 18:18, "Whatever you bind on earth shall be bound in heaven, and whatever you loose on earth shall be loosed in heaven." Those words are not given to Peter alone, but to all believers.

I had much more to say to Alveld, but I will add only two additional things that I said toward the end of 1520 in my reply to him. "I do not want anyone to oppose the pope. . . . I fight for only two things: First, I will not tolerate it that men establish new articles of faith and scold, slander, and judge as heretics, schismatics, and unbelievers all other Christians in the whole world only because they are not under the pope."[4] The second thing that I said was "I shall accept whatever the pope establishes and does, on condition that I judge it first on the basis of Holy Scripture. For my part he must remain under Christ and let himself be judged by Holy Scripture."[5]

That's a good place to end this letter. Perhaps next time, I will get to Emser.

---

3 LW 39:67.

4 LW 39:101.

5 LW 39:101.

Letter 41

When the gracious Gospel of my Lord Jesus Christ had finally captured me, every day of my life was filled with passion for that great liberating Gospel. But as I look back on my life, I must say that the years 1520 and 1521 were probably the most eventful years of my life, both in terms of events over which I had no control and in regard to what I wrote.

Rome had discovered that I could not be persuaded to be an obedient son of the church, as Rome understood such obedience, either by quiet diplomacy, pious persuasion, or threat. I was no longer considered merely a drunken German monk, but a threat to the church. (Really, the "threat to the church" was not so much over theological teachings, but my Gospel had dried up funds that flowed to Rome because of the sale of indulgences.) I had no doubt that I would eventually receive the same fate as Jan Hus had a century earlier—death by burning at the stake. In June of 1520, Pope Leo considered me enough of a threat to write a papal bull demanding that I desist from my teaching on pain of excommunication. I did not receive that warning until December of that year. I will tell you the whole story about that event in a later letter.

I did not abandon my teaching and writing. My personal life is not of much importance; I will tell you mostly about what I wrote. But remember that all my writing that others printed, often without my approval, was done in my spare time. My primary occupation was as a professor of Bible at the University of Wittenberg. It was from that occupation that I received my bread. In addition to my teaching, I was often the preacher at the Castle Church at the university and also at the city church. Writing letters occupied a good deal of my time. As the movement for the Gospel spread throughout the German lands, I was constantly called to give advice and support, thus my "spare time."

I intended to tell you about something I wrote about confession, but I got carried away with other things of less importance.

You will recall that [in Letter 36] I told you about my treatise *The Sacrament of Penance*. In that treatise, and on other occasions, I wrote and spoke about the misuse of the sacrament of penance. My friend George Spalatin, court chaplain for my protector, Prince Frederick, asked me to expand on how confession should be made. I wrote a letter to him with my comments. Somehow, it got into the hands of a printer and was published. A friend from Augsburg told me about the published copy and asked me to revise it. When I saw what had been written, I agreed. What one writes to a friend and what is to be published are frequently not the same. In the spring of 1520, I wrote *A Discussion on How Confession Should Be Made*.[1]

In my day, confession of sin to a priest, as part of the sacrament of penance, was a requirement, not a privilege. There was even a church law, promulgated by Pope Gregory about two hundred years before my time, that a Christian must make confession of all his sins at least once a year.[2] That, I said, "either is a diabolical and murderous doctrine or is in dire need of a loose interpretation."[3] I am convinced that many people came to confession more because they feared the church law rather than because they feared God. I think that many still preferred their former way of living.

Confession should first be made to God; only then to the priest to hear the gracious words of forgiveness.

I feared that the requirement to make confession to a priest caused people to manufacture fictitious sins but neglect the more serious sins against the commands of God. I wrote, "No one calls an adulterer a heretic; fornication is a light sin; even schisms and discords, inspired, preserved, and increased by the authority and in the name of the church, are merits; but to eat meat on Friday is the greatest of all heresies."[4] Again, the requirement gave people a false sense of security taking comfort in their confession rather than in the promise of God. I put it more clearly in 1520 than I can today.

> That is why it is necessary, above all, that he who confesses should not put his trust in the confession he is about to make or has made. Rather, he should put his trust in the most merciful promise of God alone, with complete faith and with the certainty that he who promised the forgiveness of sins to the person about to confess them will most faithfully fulfill his promise.[5]

---

1 LW 39:23–47.

2 LW 39:35, n. 10.

3 LW 39:35.

4 LW 39:40.

5 LW 39:28.

What sins should be confessed? All sins of which a person is aware should be confessed to God. But to a priest I think that it is not necessary to confess hidden sins of the heart. I put it clearly and succinctly, "I am content with the fact that not all sins of the heart have to be confessed."[6] Such a requirement serves only to satisfy nosey priests.

I still believe that confession should be made to a pastor. (In 1520, I continued to think in terms of priests, but later I thought more in terms of pastors.) I regret that in your day this practice has been largely discontinued. If that is the case, you have lost a great treasure of the Church that came from the earliest days of our holy faith. Somewhat in conclusion I said that after making confession to God and receiving God's forgiveness for the guilt of the sin one should go to the priest to be absolved from the penalty. I put it in these words, "Thus, absolved in the court of God and from the guilt of conscience and from sins, he should be sent to the court of the church to be absolved from the penalty."[7]

The essence of confession is not in the confession itself, but in the forgiveness of sin by a gracious God. "For this is [God's] total glory," I said, "that we trust his mercy with all our heart."[8]

I can think of no better theme on which to stop writing.

Keep the faith!

---

6 LW 39:33.

7 LW 39:42.

8 LW 39:41.

LETTER 42

I may have failed to tell you that in 1515 I was called to be the pastor of the town church in Wittenberg. That was an additional duty to my teaching responsibilities at the university. Most of what I wrote was for the benefit of my congregation and other laypeople. One of those writings was *Fourteen Consolations*.[1] The occasion for that writing was a grave illness suffered by my prince, Frederick the Wise.

In 1519, upon his return from the Diet in which Charles I of Spain was elected emperor of the Holy Roman Empire (he was Charles V of the Empire), my prince was so ill that many thought that he would not survive. My friend Spalatin asked me to write some words of comfort for his majesty. Although Frederick was not a member of the Wittenberg congregation, he had been so gracious in protecting me that I agreed to send him words to console him as he approached death. (I should mention that Frederick did not die of that illness.)

I used a legend that was popular in my day to structure my comments. The legend was of a shepherd who in 1446 had a vision of the Christ Child surrounded by fourteen saints. I offered my prince seven evils, followed by seven blessings, that God gives to believers for his contemplation, thus the *Fourteen Consolations*.

Before I share with you the fourteen consolations, you might like to know how I addressed my sovereign. Prior to the body of my writing, I attached a letter of dedication to my prince. This is how I began: "To the Most Illustrious Prince and Lord, Frederick, duke of Saxony, archmarshal and elector of the Holy Roman Empire, landgrave of Thuringia, margrave of Meissen, His Most Gracious Lord."[2]

I began by presenting "the seven images of evil . . . which will make the troubles of the present lighter."[3]

The first image is the evil within us. To contemplate this evil is worse than any other suffering because it leads to hell and, indeed, is hell itself.

The second is the future evils that may be our lot. These evils lead to

1 LW 42:117–66.

2 LW 42:121.

3 LW 42:123.

fear. Please note that the future evil that you fear may not be your lot. If you are spared those evils, give thanks to God, but whatever you fear in the future is an evil. No one fears a future joyous or happy occasion.

The third is past evil. I said, "Never does a man feel the hand of God more closely upon him than when he remembers the years of his past life."[4] You may know the evil of regret. You may lie awake at night wishing that you could change the past, but to no avail. This is another evil worse than any physical pain.

The fourth is the evil beneath us, infernal evil. "I ask you, what are all the sufferings life can bring compared with eternal punishment?"[5] The certainty that a believer need not fear this horrible "evil beneath us" surely makes any other suffering bearable.

The fifth is the evil on our left hand. These are the evils that could have happened to us by wicked people. I noted, "The higher a man's position in life and the broader his rule, the more he is exposed to such persecutions, intrigues, slander, and plots of his enemies."[6] To seek fame, fortune, or power is to invite these evils. My sovereign and I understood this evil better than most of you.

The sixth is evil on the right hand. These are the evils suffered by our friends. I think of all the saints who have gone before us and the suffering they experienced simply because they believed the blessed Gospel. Reflecting on their innocent suffering and death because of their witness to Jesus Christ makes our suffering more bearable.

The seventh and final evil is the evil above us. This is the evil suffered by our Lord Jesus Christ. I said, "Here is Jesus Christ, the Crucified, head of all the saints, the prince of all sufferers."[7] Because of Jesus' suffering and death, I said, "In death we are all like all other men: the outward mode of our dying is not unlike others, except the thing itself is different, since for us death is dead." There is our ultimate consolation.

I then added seven blessings of consolation for my sovereign to contemplate.

The first is the blessing within us. There is a little song from your day that I wish I had known in my day; I would have included it for my prince.

---

4 LW 42:130.

5 LW 42:134.

6 LW 42:135.

7 LW 42:141.

Part of the song includes these words, "Count your blessings, name them one by one; count your blessings, see what God has done." I did write, "And if, by the grace of God, you enjoy the use of these excellent gifts for ten, twenty, or thirty years, and in that time suffer for a few days now and then, how bad is that?"[8]

The second is the blessing before us. This blessing is the gift of hope given to believers. Our greatest blessing is in the future. Cynics will call this great hope "pie in the sky by and by." (That's another phrase that I learned about cynics in your day.) But to whom God has given this gift of hope it is more certain than sunrise. "However," I said, "these are attained only through suffering and death."[9] I added, "It is a great thing that death, which to others is the greatest of evils, is made the greatest gain for us."[10] I wish that you could read all that I had to say about the death of a believer, but I must limit my comments to one other that I made to console my prince. I said, "For the believer death is already dead and behind its cloak and mask it holds no terrors. Like a slain serpent, death still has its former terrifying appearance, but now this is only a mask, for it is now a dead and harmless evil."[11]

The third is the blessings behind us. This is the easiest of all. Only a numbskull will fail to count all the blessings that have been his from youth, childhood, adolescent years, and adulthood. I need not enumerate, nor can I, for each must reflect on his own past blessings.

The fourth is the blessing beneath us. I called it "the infernal blessing." You ask, how can anything infernal be a blessing? It is the blessing of God that He destroys evil and those who resist the call of God to repentance. Consider: would you like an eternity filled with all the evils that you have experienced in this life? I think not. Give thanks to God for the blessing of hell that swallows evil and evildoers.

The fifth is the blessing on our left hand. Those blessings are the adversaries in this life. They are hard even for believers to understand. It is the blessing of trials that confront us from the evil and evildoers of this world. I wrote to my prince, "Thus it is good for us always to be oppressed with some trouble, lest in our weakness we succumb to the offenses of

---

8 LW 42:144.

9 LW 42:148.

10 LW 42:149.

11 LW 42:150.

the world and fall into sin."[12] I did not think of it at the time, but Paul's words now come to mind: "Give thanks in all circumstances; for this is the will of God in Christ Jesus for you" (1 Thessalonians 5:18).

The sixth are the blessings on our right hand. "This is the church of the saints, the new creation of God, our brothers and our friends, in whom we see nothing but blessing and nothing but consolation." In addition to that great blessing, God also provides abundant material wealth to many believers. God gives this for our comfort, but also to share with others. Nevertheless, these blessings are, I said, "only shadows and signs of their real blessings, which are faith, hope, love, and other gifts and graces, which are shared with all through love."[13]

The seventh is the supernal blessing or the blessing above us. This is "Jesus Christ, the King of glory, rising from the dead, just as in his suffering, death, and burial he formed the seventh image of evils."[14] No greater consolation and hope can a believer have than his Lord Jesus Christ bringing victory over death in His glorious resurrection.

Well, dear reader, those are the words of consolation that I shared with my sovereign, Prince Frederick, in an hour of grave illness. You also will experience the same, and one day face the ultimate enemy, death. When your hour comes, remember the seven evils from which you have been spared by the grace of God and the seven blessing that have been yours from the day of your birth.

I signed my letter "Brother Martin Luther, Augustinian at Wittenberg."

---

12 LW 42:159.

13 LW 42:161.

14 LW 42:163.

Letter 43

I have now lived for more than five hundred years, and I still cannot fathom the ignorance of some believers; they have heard the good news of the forgiveness of sins and justification (having been made righteous before God) by faith alone and consequently think that good works are irrelevant to Christian living. Apparently, it is no different in your day than in mine.

A scholar in your day has written, "Luther had been accused by his enemies that his stress on justification by faith alone had led—and indeed would increasingly lead—to a total neglect of good works and a concomitant rise of lawlessness, license, and immorality."[1] I seldom agreed with my enemies, but in this case, regrettably, they were right. Of course, that did not mean to retreat from the blessed Gospel of forgiveness of sins by faith alone; it simply meant that I had to remind believers that good works are the natural result of God's gracious forgiveness.

An additional problem was the way that faith was understood in my day; perhaps it is still the same in your day. Faith was understood to be simply accepting as true some propositions regarding God, a mere intellectual activity. There was a second, supposedly more advanced understating of faith, namely, a faith "adorned by good works by which men make themselves acceptable in the sight of God and win his favor."[2] I hope that you see how such an understanding robs God of the gift of grace and puts everything back in the hands of humans.

I knew that I had to write something for the dear members of my congregation. I had no stomach for it, but I knew that it must be done. In 1520, I finally completed what was to be a sermon but got so long that it became a treatise. It was simply entitled *Treatise on Good Works*.[3]

Before I tell you about the treatise, I will share with you what a scholar from your day has said about it. "Both in spirit and in style Luther reached a lofty height in the *Sermon on Good Works* unsurpassed in

1 LW 44:17.

2 LW 44:18.

3 LW 44:15–115.

his whole literary career."[4] I care nothing about what scholars think; I wrote only for the sake of my dear people in Wittenberg, certainly not for scholars who spend their time fussing about me and my writings. In my introductory comments, I wrote, "If we cannot all be writers, then we all want to be critics! I will most gladly leave to anybody else the glory of greater things. I will not be ashamed in the slightest to preach to the uneducated layman and write for him in German."[5]

I structured the treatise around the Ten Commandments.

My very first words were seminal to the whole treatise, "The first thing to know is that there are no good works except those works God has commanded, just as there is no sin except that which God has forbidden."[6] To set the stage and make it abundantly clear that faith in Jesus Christ is foundational to everything that a believer does, I said, "The first, highest, and most precious of all good works is faith in Christ."[7] I then referenced Jesus' words in John 6:28–29.

In my day, the Roman Church created a great dichotomy between the sacred and the secular. Good works were what the church said they were: fasting on prescribed days, pilgrimages to Rome or other religious shrines, certain prescribed prayers, going to Mass, or any other activity prescribed by a priest as satisfaction for one's sins.

I totally rejected that fiction. Good works are what the occasion requires; no one knows "the occasion" in advance. I said, "A Christian man living in this faith has no need of a teacher of good works, but he does whatever the occasion calls for."[8] To emphasize the fact that good works do not gain any merit before God, I wrote, "Thus a Christian man who lives in this confidence toward God knows all things, can do all things, venture everything that needs to be done, and does everything gladly and willingly, not that he may gather merits and good works, but because it is a pleasure for him to please God in doing these things."[9]

A living faith in God, honoring Him by simply trusting His Word, fulfills the First Commandment, "You shall have no gods other than Me."

---

4 Schwiebert, 445.

5 LW 44:22.

6 LW 44:23.

7 LW 44:23.

8 LW 44:26.

9 LW 44:27.

The second good work is to honor God's name, as God commanded, "You shall not take the name of the Lord your God in vain."

Honoring the holy name is done in three ways. "After faith we can do no greater work than to praise, preach, sing and in every way laud and magnify God's glory, honor, and name,"[10] I wrote. The second way to honor God's name is to disdain honor for ourselves. I said, "Therefore, the second work of this commandment is to be on one's guard, to flee from and to avoid all temporal honor and praise, and never to seek a name for oneself, or fame and a great reputation, so that everyone may sing your praises and talk about you."[11] "The third work of this commandment is to call upon God's name in every need."[12] God is honored when we recognize our need for him.

The Third Commandment tells us to keep holy the holy day. You may note that I did not maintain a legalistic commitment to a particular day of the week, the seventh or Sabbath. The holy day for believers is the day on which God raised Jesus from the dead and thereby opened heaven to us. Sunday is our holy day.

There is so much more to say about this commandment, but I will write all night if I continue. You must get a book and read the whole thing.

I will mention only briefly what I said about the Fourth Commandment. You will then have to be on your own to discover what I said about the rest of the Commandments.

Honor your parents. This is God's command, not merely a social or familial expectation. This seems so natural, but it is not always the case. Of the last seven commandments, all relating to how we are to live in relation to other people, the first is to honor parents. I have watched over the past five centuries how children naturally love and honor their parents when they are very young, but frequently rebel against them during adolescent years. Sometimes, that respect returns in later years, but not always. Sometimes, things get worse in later life. I wrote, "But the matter becomes still worse when the child in turn has children of his own. Then love for them increases, while the love and honor due to the parents declines."[13] I had a good deal to say about parental responsibility in this

---

10 LW 44:39.

11 LW 44:42.

12 LW 44:46.

13 LW 44:82.

context also. I must limit it to only one statement. "On the other hand," I said, "parents cannot earn hell more easily than by neglecting their own children in their own home and by not teaching them the things spoken of above ('to train and teach himself and his child to honor God properly')."[14]

There is so much more to say about good works, even about the Fourth Commandment, but I am getting tired. Remember, this is only a letter, not a book. Find a book with the entire treatise. The whole treatise is only about ninety pages long in the books published in your day. You will note that I covered the last six commandments briefly, in only fourteen pages.

I will close the letter with a comment made by a theologian from your day. He said, "Luther never fails to relate every good work to the source from whence it issues and whither it returns: faith in Christ alone."[15] He's got that right. Then he added, "Without such faith good works not only avail nothing, they are nothing. With this single treatise Luther obliterated the distinction between the 'religious' and the 'secular,' and altered the whole system of Christian ethics."[16] I think that he is right, and I couldn't be happier for that observation.

---

14 LW 44:86.

15 LW 44:19.

16 LW 44:19–20.

Letter 44

In June 1520, the pope finally took action against me. A group of about forty Roman theologians and church officials (believe me, there is a difference) agreed on a bull that would give me sixty days to change my teachings and submit to Rome. I had heard some vague rumors about being excommunicated but knew no specifics. I did not receive the bull for several months. I will tell you more about the bull later. (It was not a bull of excommunication.)

As for my work, I continued my pastoral responsibilities to my dear people in Wittenberg—in addition to my professorial responsibilities at the university.

The laity had been deceived in their understanding of the Mass. (Perhaps I should clarify something about the Mass. You think of the Mass as an entire worship service. In one sense, you are correct, but when I wrote about the Mass, I was thinking primarily of the sacrament of the Lord's Supper, which is the high point of the Mass.) The Mass was understood by the Romanists, and taught to the congregations, to be an offering that the priest presents to God on behalf of the congregation. The Mass then becomes a good work that people give to God rather than a gift that God gives to His people. That grievous error had to be corrected for the comfort of my congregation. Consequently, I wrote *A Treatise on the New Testament, That Is, the Holy Mass*.[1]

I will make this letter brief because I dealt more thoroughly with the matter a few months later when I wrote *The Babylonian Captivity of the Church*.

In the first third of the treatise, I focused on the word "testament." You know something about a last will and testament; it takes effect upon death. So the "new testament" is a gift that God gives to His faithful, and it took effect when Christ died. I wrote, "For if God is to make a testament, as he promises, then he must die; and if he is to die, then he must be a man. And so that little word 'testament' is a short summary of all God's wonders and grace, fulfilled in Christ."[2] I hope that you

1 LW 35:75–111.

2 LW 35:84.

understand, as my dear people in Wittenberg understood, that the Mass (sacrament) is no work that you do, or any priest does, but entirely God's work, a gift that God gives to you. If you think you are unworthy of so great a gift from God, you are absolutely correct. Because so many feel that way, I concluded the first half of the treatise by writing, "For this is precisely what makes it a divine testament, that it brings blessings so great to people so unworthy."[3]

In the second third of the treatise, I denied that the sacrament is a sacrifice. That is related to what I mentioned above about the priest making an offering to God. I will say more about that when I share what I wrote in *The Babylonian Captivity*.

In the last third, I decried several misuses of the Mass. Masses for the dead (in purgatory) were a common practice. In mid-summer, I still did not deny the place of purgatory, but I could find no scriptural bases for masses on behalf of those poor souls.

I was much more concerned about the manner in which the Mass was presented to the congregation. I said, "I fear that the holy words of the testament are read so secretly, and kept so hidden from the laity."[4] I had no need to clarify those words for the people to whom I first wrote, but you may not understand. A theologian from your day clarified the statement. "The canon of the mass, the invariable part of the liturgy of the mass in which the elements were consecrated, was read in a whisper by the priest."[5] How can people believe if they cannot hear? Note what Paul said in Romans 10:14: "And how are they to believe in Him of whom they have never heard?" The words of Christ spoken when He instituted the sacrament must be heard so that they may be believed!

The Romanists abused the sacrament by withholding the cup from the laity. In this treatise, I said, "This does not matter much, since the word is more important than the sign."[6] Nevertheless, I said, "Not that I should like to cause turmoil over this issue, for I regard the word as mightier than the sign; still I cannot stand for such an outrage."[7] I took a stronger stand when I wrote *The Babylonian Captivity of the Church*.

---

3 LW 35:90.

4 LW 35:106.

5 LW 35:95, n. 26.

6 LW 35:106.

7 LW 35:107.

Finally, I objected to the different values that were ascribed to various masses. I said, "Furthermore they have now made one mass better than another. One is valued as useful for this, another for that. Thus they have made seven 'golden masses.' The 'mass of the holy cross' has come to have a different virtue from the 'mass of Our Lady.'"[8] I claimed all that fiction was done for mere money.

That was more than I intended to write, but it is not the first time that I got carried away with words.

8 LW 35:107–8.

Letter 45

After I responded to the Franciscan nitwit Augustine von Alveld [see Letter 40], a more competent, but equally deluded, counselor to Pope Leo, Prierias, picked up where Alveld left off. Someone has found a copy of the letter in which I responded to Prierias. In that letter, I said, "And now farewell, unhappy, hopeless, blasphemous Rome!"[1] I had more to say, and the words were much stronger, but those introductory words let you know where I stood in relation to Rome in late spring of 1520.

As I concluded my response to Alveld, I had said, "Moreover, I would certainly let kings, princes, and all the nobles try to keep the knaves of Rome from their streets."[2]

By the end of late June, I had written another treatise in which I more clearly called upon the nobility to take action against Rome. The treatise was addressed *To the Christian Nobility of the German Nation Concerning the Reform of the Christian Estate*.[3] These were my introductory words: "To His Most Illustrious, Most Mighty, and Imperial Majesty, and to the Christian Nobility of the German Nation, from Doctor Martin Luther."[4]

I told His Imperial Majesty and the other nobles, "The Romanists have very cleverly built three walls around themselves. Hitherto they have protected themselves by these walls in such a way that no one has been able to reform them. As a result, the whole of Christendom has fallen abominably."[5]

The first wall was their contention that secular power had no authority over them, and that spiritual power (which they assumed to themselves) is superior to secular power.

I attacked that first wall by denying that there is a division between the secular and the spiritual. "All Christians," I said, "are truly of the spiritual estate, and there is no difference among them except that of

---

1 LW 44:118.

2 LW 39:102.

3 LW 44:115–217.

4 LW 44:124.

5 LW 44:126.

office."[6] I then quoted what Paul wrote in 1 Corinthians 12:12–13 in which he taught that all Christians are of one body. In my challenge to Rome's claim, I affirmed as strongly as any other place in all my writings, if I recall correctly, the great truth of "the priesthood of all believers." In our Baptism, we are made priests before God. Don't misunderstand and think that because God has made you a priest you have the right to function in that capacity within a community. That function is a matter of office and can be filled only when called to that office by a community of believers. I said, "A cobbler, a smith, a peasant—each has the work and office of his trade, and yet they are all alike consecrated priests and bishops."[7] I concluded, demolishing the first wall, by saying, "For these reasons the temporal Christian authority ought to exercise its office without hindrance, regardless of whether it is pope, bishop, or priest whom it affects."[8]

The second wall of Rome is that when confronted with Scripture they claim that only the pope has the right to interpret Scripture.

What a stupid claim! I pointed out, "And if what they claim were true, why have Holy Scripture at all? Of what use is Scripture? Let us burn the Scripture and be satisfied with the unlearned gentlemen at Rome who possess the Holy Spirit!"[9] I should add, "At least they believed that they alone possessed the Holy Spirit." I had more to say about this fiction but concluded, "Therefore, their claim that only the pope may interpret Scripture is an outrageous fancied fable."[10]

The third wall is that when the claims of Rome are threatened by a council of the whole church (an "ecumenical" council composed of all bishops of the church), they claim that only a pope can convoke a council. What nonsense! I said that there is no such authority granted by the Scriptures, and additionally, Emperor Constantine convoked the very first council of the Church at Nicaea. Subsequent councils were also convoked by emperors, not by popes.

---

6 LW 44:127.

7 LW 44:130.

8 LW 44:131.

9 LW 44:134.

10 LW 44:134.

I concluded the first part of this treatise by saying, "With this I hope that all this wicked and lying terror with which the Romanists have long intimidated and dulled our conscience has been overcome."[11]

In the second part, I shared what I thought should be considered by a church council. These were issues pertinent to my day. I need not take you down that path. If you are interested, find the treatise and read what I had to say.

I began the third part by saying, "Now, although I am too insignificant a man to make propositions for the improvement of this dreadful state of affairs, nevertheless I shall sing my fool's song through to the end and say, as far as I am able, what could and should be done, either by the temporal authority or by a general council."[12] Again, these were issues of my day. Find them and read them, if you choose.

---

11 LW 44:138–39.

12 LW 44:156.

Letter 46

My mind was racing and my pen burning. For many months, I knew that I had to write against the sacramental system of the Roman Church, a system by which the church held the faithful in bondage from birth until death—the sacrament of Baptism at birth and the alleged sacrament of extreme unction at the point of death. "Where," you may ask, "is the bondage?" Failure to adhere to the teachings of the Roman Church could result in excommunication (the withholding of the sacraments from an individual, thereby depriving him of a primary means by which God's grace is received) or by an interdict (the withholding of the sacraments from an entire nation for failure of its sovereign to submit to Rome). Don't misunderstand. My contention was not with the blessed sacraments, but the Roman sacramental system that held people captive in fear.

As early as December 1519, I wrote to my friend Spalatin and said, "But there is no reason why you or any man should expect from me any sermon on the other sacraments [holy orders, marriage, confirmation and extreme unction] until I learn by what text I can prove that they are sacraments. I esteem none of the others a sacrament, for that is not a sacrament, save what is expressly given by divine promise exercising our faith."[1] You see, at that time I accepted only Baptism, the Lord's Supper, and penance as sacraments. Within a year, I rejected penance as a sacrament.

In the fall of 1520, the time had come to launch the attack. At the conclusion of my treatise *To the Christian Nobility of the German Nation*, I wrote, "Well, I know another little song about Rome and the Romanists. If their ears are itching to hear it, I will sing that one to them, too—and pitch it in the highest key. You understand what I mean, dear Rome."[2]

By early October, I had completed *The Babylonian Captivity of the Church*.[3] I spent nearly half the treatise on the two sacraments—Baptism and the Lord's Supper. The remaining five alleged sacraments got shorter treatment.

---

1 Smith 1:263–64.

2 LW 44:217.

3 LW 36:3–126.

I began by saying, "Yet, if I were to speak according to the usage of the Scriptures, I should have only one single sacrament [Christ], but with three sacramental signs."[4] (Not long ago I met a Roman Catholic theologian from your day. I was delighted to learn that he had written a book, *Christ, the Sacrament of the Encounter with God*.[5] He was not a "Lutheran" as you might say, but a Roman Catholic theologian. I was delighted know that his thought paralleled mine.)

I began my fire with the Lord's Supper; I called it "the sacrament of bread."

The first disgrace (I called it the first captivity) of the Lord's Supper was withholding the cup from the laity. The reception of only the bread did not make the sacrament invalid because, as I have said so often, it is God's word of promise that creates the validity. I objected because, as I said, "The sacrament does not belong to the priests, but to all men."[6] I brought this disgrace to an end with these words, "I conclude, then, that it is wicked and despotic to deny both kinds [bread and wine] to the laity, and that this is not within the power of any angel, much less of any pope or council."[7]

The second captivity is less serious; it is the doctrine of transubstantiation. You need not understand that term; most laypeople, and many clergy, do not. It is mere speculation of how Christ becomes really present in the bread and wine. Believe it if you choose; your faith will not be affected by it. But it has no basis in the Scriptures. I put it in these words, "For what is asserted without the Scriptures or proven revelation may be held as an opinion, but need not be believed."[8]

"*The third captivity of this sacrament* is by far the most wicked abuse of all . . . that the mass is a good work and a sacrifice."[9] I addressed this fable in *A Treatise on the New Testament* [see Letter 44]. I said there, and I will say it again, this sacrament is a testament given by God "signed when our Redeemer died, Sealed when He was glorified."[10] That last phrase I learned from a hymn that was written about two hundred years

---

4 LW 36:18.

5 Schillebeeckx.

6 LW 36:27.

7 LW 36:27.

8 LW 36:29.

9 LW 36:35.

10 *The Lutheran Hymnal* 149:4.

before your day; it captures my thought completely. I wrote, "But the priests have strayed into godless ways; out of the sacrament and testament of God, which ought to be a good gift received, they have made for themselves a good deed performed, which they then give to others and offer up to God."[11] The Romanists taught that people could "participate" in a mass even though they were not present, and could obtain the benefits of the "good works" of the masses said, merely by participating in one of the brotherhoods [see Letter 36].[12] It is not difficult to learn from whence those fictions arose; it was for money. I said, "On these the priests and monks depend for their entire livelihood."[13]

In addition, Rome taught that the sacrament works by itself with no reference to the faith or unbelief of the recipient. I denied that vigorously. I said, "Therefore, let this irrefutable truth stand fast: Where there is a divine promise, there every one must stand on his own feet; his own personal faith is demanded, he will give an account for himself and bear his own load [Gal. 6:5]."[14] Furthermore, I said, "Now there is yet a second stumbling block that must be removed, and this is much greater and the most dangerous of all. It is the common belief that the mass is a sacrifice, which is offered to God."[15] I hope that you see how Rome inverted the direction of the blessed sacrament. A sacrifice is directed from humanity to God; the blessed sacrament is a gift from God to believers. I used these words: "So it is a contradiction in terms to call the mass a sacrifice, for the former [testament] is something that we receive and the latter is something that we give."[16]

This letter is getting to be far too long, and my blood is boiling as I recall the tragic distortion of the holy Mass in my day. I better quit before I say something that I might regret. In the past five hundred years, I have learned a bit about holding my tongue.

In my next letter, I will share with you my comments on the sacrament of Baptism and the other five alleged sacraments. Until then, keep the faith.

---

11 LW 36:49.

12 LW 36:35, nn. 79, 80.

13 LW 36:36.

14 LW 36:49.

15 LW 36:51.

16 LW 36:52.

LETTER 47

In my last letter in which I told you about my treatise *The Babylonian Captivity of the Church*, I took so much time telling you about the distorted understanding, misuse, and mere speculation regarding the sacrament of the Lord's Supper that I was too exhausted to tell you about the holy sacrament of Baptism, and I did not write about the other five alleged sacraments of the Roman Church. In this letter, I will complete that task.

I had no quarrel with the Romans on the sacrament of Baptism. I said, "Blessed be God and the Father of our Lord Jesus Christ, who . . . has preserved in his church this sacrament at least, untouched and untainted by the ordinances of men, and has . . . not permitted it to be oppressed by the filthy and godless monsters of greed and superstition."[1] I wrote almost half as much about Baptism as I did about the Lord's Supper, but I had no issues with Rome about that sacrament. I had so many wonderful things to say about God's grace, and assurance for the salvation, given to believers in Baptism; I wish that you could read all that I wrote. I must share with you only a few comments that I made. "But we must so consider it [Baptism] as to exercise our faith in it, and have no doubt whatever that, once we have been baptized, we are saved."[2] Some lump heads will then charge me with giving license to sin because Baptism saves believers. No true believer will even think to suggest such foolishness. Sin does not belong to a believer; it must be confessed daily, and repentance must follow. I said something like that when I wrote, "Therefore, when we rise from our sins or repent, we are merely returning to the power and faith of baptism from which we fell, and finding our way back to the promise then made to us, which we deserted when we sinned."[3] Oh, how great is this sacrament; here we are united with our Lord Jesus!

When I began this treatise, I said that penance was one of three sacraments. By the time I began to write about penance, I had changed my mind. I said, "The first and chief abuse of this sacrament is that they

---

1 LW 36:57.

2 LW 36:59.

3 LW 36:59.

have completely abolished it. Not a vestige of the sacrament remains."[4] I noted that the Roman Church had divided penance into three parts: contrition, confession, and satisfaction. I affirmed the necessity of being sorry for one's sins before making confession. And of confession I said, "As to the current practice of private confession, I am heartily in favor of it, even though it cannot be proved from the Scriptures. It is useful, even necessary, and I would not have it abolished."[5] I grieve that it has been abolished in most congregations that bear my name. I objected that confession had to be made only to a priest, as though only a priest has the authority to forgive sin. I wrote, "For Christ has given to every one of his believers the power to absolve even open sins."[6] But satisfaction was another matter. I began by saying, "How unworthily they have dealt with *satisfaction*."[7] I continued, "They have taught it in such a manner that the people have never had the slightest understanding what satisfaction really is, namely, the renewal of a man's life."[8] Rather, they have people running hither and yon performing good works in an attempt to make satisfaction for their sin without any reference to faith in the satisfaction that Christ has made for their sin.

When I wrote about the remaining four alleged sacraments (confirmation, marriage, ordination, and extreme unction), I said, "I do not say this because I condemn the seven sacraments, but because I deny that they can be proved from the Scriptures."[9] All are useful practices in the church; I only deny that they are sacraments. As for confirmation, I said, "For this reason it is sufficient to regard confirmation as a certain churchly rite or sacramental ceremony, similar to other ceremonies, such as the blessing of water and the like."[10] (The Roman Church distinguished between *sacraments*, which convey grace directly, and *sacramentals*, which do not.)

I never denied that marriage is a sacred act given by God, but to be a sacrament there must be a promise from God and a sign to accompany that promise. I said, "There is not even a divinely instituted sign in

---

4 LW 36:81.

5 LW 36:86.

6 LW 36:88.

7 LW 36:89.

8 LW 36:89.

9 LW 36:91.

10 LW 36:92.

marriage, nor do we read anywhere that marriage was instituted by God to be a sign of anything."[11] We can endure some things in the church that are not found in the Scriptures "so long as they do not conflict with the faith and the Holy Scriptures."[12] I would not split the church over this issue or the remaining three alleged sacraments. Regrettably, people in your day have split the Body of Christ over issues far less substantial than the sacramental character of these last four alleged sacraments. What did I think about divorce? You may be surprised. I said, "As to divorce, it is still a question for debate whether it is allowable. For my part I so greatly detest divorce that I should prefer bigamy to it; but whether it is allowable, I do not venture to decide."[13] Believe me, I am not now recommending bigamy; I got myself and the reform movement into deep trouble several years later when I suggested bigamy for a neighboring prince. I may tell you about that later.

As for ordination, I said, "Of this sacrament the church of Christ knows nothing; it is an invention of the church of the pope."[14] Nevertheless I said, "I do not hold that this rite, which has been observed for so many centuries, should be condemned; but in sacred things I am opposed to the invention of human fictions."[15] In one of my previous letters, I have now forgotten which one, I said that all the baptized are priests. I said it again in this treatise. "Therefore we are all priests, as many of us as are Christians. But the priests, as we call them, are ministers chosen from among us. All that they do is done in our name; the priesthood is nothing but a ministry."[16] I thought that ordination ought not to be abolished. I gave this reason: "The sacrament of ordination can be nothing else than a certain rite by which the church chooses its preachers."[17]

In my day, extreme unction (*extreme* means "the end"; *unction* means "to anoint") was an alleged sacrament that was administered only once in life—at the point of death. In your day, it has become the anointing of the sick and can be administered as frequently as seems useful. That is a great and welcome reform in the Roman Church. The Romanists throw

---

11 LW 36:96.

12 LW 36:96.

13 LW 36:105.

14 LW 36:106.

15 LW 36:107.

16 LW 36:113.

17 LW 36:113.

in my face James 5:14–15 to claim this unction as a sacrament. I noted, "But here they are able to cast in my teeth that, in the case of this sacrament, there are on the authority of the apostle James both promise and sign, which, as I have maintained all along, do constitute a sacrament."[18] I am not certain that James the apostle wrote the epistle, but I added, "But even if the apostle James did write it, I still would say, that no apostle has the right on his own authority to institute a sacrament, that is, to give a divine promise with a sign attached. For this belongs to Christ alone."[19] I certainly didn't mean to suggest that this rite of the church should be abandoned, any more than confirmation, sacred marriage, or ordination. I just deny that they are sacraments. I added, "We do not deny, therefore, that forgiveness and peace are granted through extreme unction; not because it is a sacrament divinely instituted, but because he who receives it believes that these blessings are granted to him."[20] You see, again, it all has to do with faith in God's promise.

After about 114 pages, I concluded the treatise by saying, "*Herewith I conclude this prelude.*"[21] If all that precedes has been only a prelude, where, you might wonder, is the main thing? Wait until my next letter. I'll tell you.

---

18 LW 36:118.

19 LW 36:118.

20 LW 36:122.

21 LW 36:125.

Letter 48

My mind was fresh and my conscience clear. I had dropped a very heavy load on Rome in my two treatises *To the Christian Nobility of the German Nation* and *The Babylonian Captivity of the Church*. My pen had been ablaze, and I used some very harsh words against those pretenders to power and usurpers of the blessed Gospel of our Lord Jesus Christ.

Before I had even completed *The Babylonian Captivity* in October, Karl von Miltitz [see Letter 28] met with my dear father confessor, Johann von Staupitz, and his successor as vicar general of the Augustinian monks in Germany, Wenceslaus Link, and asked them to persuade me to write a nice letter to Pope Leo X assuring him that my attacks had not been directed against him personally. I was pleased to accommodate them. I even agreed to add a devotional writing that would accompany the letter. By early November, I had completed the "devotional writing," *Martin Luther's Treatise on Christian Liberty*. It has come to be known as *The Freedom of a Christian*.[1]

In my letter to Leo, I retracted nothing that I had written, but I did call Leo "most blessed father."[2] I said, "If men do not perceive that I am your friend and your most humble subject in this matter, there is One who understands and judges [John 8:50]."[3] My contention was with the Roman curia and the whole Roman system of operation. I did not hesitate to say to Leo, "All this is clearer than day to all, and the Roman church, once the holiest of all, has become the most licentious den of thieves [Matt. 21:13], the most shameless of all brothels, the kingdom of sin, death, and hell. It is so bad that even Antichrist himself, if he should come, could think of nothing to add to its wickedness."[4] I ended my letter with these kind words, "Finally, that I may not approach you empty-handed, blessed father, I am sending you this little treatise dedicated to you as a token of peace and good hope."[5] I said of the treatise, "Unless I am mistaken, however, it contains the whole of Christian life in a brief form, provided you grasp its meaning."[6]

---

1 LW 31:327–77.

2 LW 31:334.

3 LW 31:343.

4 LW 31:336.

5 LW 31:343.

6 LW 31:344.

I'll share with you a bit of what I wrote in *The Freedom of a Christian*. I began by saying,

"A Christian is a perfectly free lord of all, subject to none. A Christian is a perfectly dutiful servant of all, subject to all."[7]

I said, "Man has a twofold nature, a spiritual and a bodily one."[8] I called the spiritual nature the "inner man," and the bodily nature I called the "outer man." In relation to God, believers are free. (In this context, I am speaking about the "inner man.") Faith, and nothing but faith in God's promises, sets them free from all judgment and damnation. Sin no longer has authority over them. I noted that Scripture is divided into two parts: commandments and promise. I said, "For the commandments show us what we ought to do but do not give us the power to do it."[9] But the promise of God is quite different. I said, "Thus the promises of God give what the commandments of God demand and fulfill what the law prescribes so that all things may be God's alone, both the commandments and the fulfilling of the commandments."[10] Oh, the benefits of faith—how rich they are! One of the benefits, I said, is that "it unites the soul with Christ as a bride is united with her bridegroom."[11] Someone, perhaps it was I, I do not recall, has called this unification of the soul with Christ "the happy exchange." I wrote, "The soul is full of sins, death, and damnation. Now let faith come between them and sins, death, and damnation will be Christ's, while grace, life, and salvation will be the soul's; for if Christ is a bridegroom, he must take upon himself the things which are his bride's and bestow upon her the things that are his."[12] That union with Christ makes all believers priests, just as Christ himself is a priest. To make it short: what Christ is, believers are. This treatise is so rich that I hope you will find it and read all of it. I cannot say more about the absolute freedom of the "inner man" that stands innocent before God simply by faith in Jesus Christ.

The "outer man" stands not in relation to God, but to his neighbor. I wrote, "Here we shall answer all those who, offended by the word 'faith' and by all that has been said, now ask, 'If faith does all things and is

---

7 LW 31:344.

8 LW 31:344.

9 LW 31:348.

10 LW 31:349.

11 LW 31:351.

12 LW 31:351.

alone sufficient unto righteousness, why then are good works commanded? We will take our ease and do no works and be content with faith. '"[13] No believer ever speaks like that. I added, "Insofar as he is free he does no works, but insofar as he is a servant he does all kinds of works."[14] One cannot have the benefits of union with Christ—freedom from sin, death, and damnation—without also having the joyous privilege of being a servant to others as Christ Himself was the supreme servant who gave His life for the sins of the world. United with Christ, all of what Christ is, believers are—priests and servants. The "outer man," I said, "should be guided in all his works by this thought and contemplate this one thing alone, that he may serve and benefit others in all that he does, considering nothing except the need and the advantage of his neighbor."[15] Toward the close of the treatise, I said, "He [a believer] lives in Christ through faith, in his neighbor through love. By faith he is caught up beyond himself into God. By love he descends beneath himself into his neighbor."[16]

At one point, I said that all of my writings should be burned and only the catechism and my writing against Erasmus, *The Bondage of the Will*, should be kept. I might change my mind. This treatise on Christian freedom and responsibility is so rich that I think it would be beneficial to all who bear my name in your day. It might be beneficial to others also, but if you bear my name, pay attention to what I say.

---

13 LW 31:358.

14 LW 31:358.

15 LW 31:365.

16 LW 31:371.

Letter 49

The folks in Rome had not been sleeping while I was pouring out page after page in one treatise after another during, especially, the latter half of 1520. In early June, I had heard a rumor from the German knight Ulrich von Hutten that Rome was preparing articles of excommunication against me. I expected nothing less. Frankly, I did not think that I would be excommunicated; I expected execution. Excommunication caused me not the slightest strife. Hutten had offered me the protection of the German knights in February and now repeated that offer, again assuring me that the offer had the support of the leading German knight Franz von Sickingen. I appreciated their offer, but I was not interested in that protection. I had One, and only One, on whom I relied for protection

Opinion in Rome was divided as to how the pope should deal with me. Finally, it was agreed that I should not be immediately excommunicated, but articles defining my errors should be prepared and sent to me, calling me to recant within sixty days or face excommunication. The sixty days were to begin when the papal bull containing the charges against me were published in Rome and in the three bishoprics of Germany: Brandenburg, Meissen, and Merseburg. That was finally completed when the bull was published in Brandenburg on 29 September.

Perhaps I should tell you what a papal bull is. The word bull comes from *bulla*, a lead seal. That seal was applied to a papal document just as in your day a notary's seal authenticates the signature of one who signs a document.

Two papal nuncios (representatives) were to carry the bull to Germany. John Eck, you will remember him from the Leipzig Debate, and Jerome Aleander, a well-educated papal librarian, were the reluctant nuncios. Eck was to deliver the bull to bishops and universities, and Aleander was to deliver it to the emperor and secular princes. Neither nuncio relished his assignment. One historian in your day said that each undertook their task "at the risk of his life."[1] The delivery did not go well. Eck was received well in the three bishoprics named above, but in other sees he had difficulty obtaining the full support of the bishops. He also said, "At Leipzig, Eck had to hide for his life in a cloister. At Erfurt, when

---

1 Bainton, 157.

he had the bull reprinted, the students dubbed it a 'balloon' and threw all the copies into the river to see if they would float. At Torgau, it was torn down and besmeared [with filth]."[2] Excuses and delays frustrated his deliveries and postings. In many places princes and bishops simply would not allow the publication because they feared an uprising by the laity. I did not know it at the time, but your historian is correct. Poor Aleander suffered an even worse reception. When the bull was posted, the procedure was to include the burning of my books. (They had been burned in Rome when the bull was posted there in July.) In some places, students threw Scholastic books into the fire; in other places, the bull was torn from its posting; in other places, there was a refusal to even post the bull; and in Mainz, Aleander was pelted with stones and feared for his life. Finally on 10 October, I received the threatening document. Dr. Eck did not have the courage to bring the bull to Wittenberg and deliver it to me in person. From Leipzig, he had the militia deliver the bull to a citizen of Wittenberg, who in turn gave it to the Wittenberg rector, Peter Burkhard, who then gave it to me. Peter said that the bull was delivered "in a thieving manner and with villainous cunning."[3]

Forgive me. I got carried away telling you how the bull was executed and delivered to me without telling you anything about the bull. I must tell you a bit about it.

You may know that all papal bulls bear the title of the first words of the body of the bull. The bull threatening my excommunication is entitled *Exsurge Domine* (Arise, O Lord). I will share with you a few of the opening words. "Arise, O Lord, and judge thy cause. A wild boar has invaded thy vineyard. Arise, O Peter, and consider the case of the Holy Roman Church, the mother of all churches, consecrated by thy blood. Arise, O Paul, who by thy teaching and death hast and dost illumine the Church."[4] You may guess who the wild boar was.

The bull then added forty-one errors taken from my writings. It must have been written by an apprentice. The substance of my teaching was ignored. One historian from your day wrote, "The contemporary observer notes the omission of an explicit statement of Luther's fundamental positions, such as the teaching of justification or his conception of faith."[5]

---

2 Bainton, 158.

3 Brecht 1:402.

4 Bainton, 147.

5 Brecht 1:391.

Another said, "The forty-one articles were not pronounced uniformly heretical but were condemned as 'heretical, or scandalous, or false, or offensive to pious ears, or seductive of simple minds, or repugnant to catholic truth, respectively.'"[6] It was a hodgepodge of statements taken from my writings without consideration of the context or thrust of the entire writing.

I lost no sleep over that bull. But I could not remain silent. What might you expect me to do? Of course, write something in reply. I did, but I did more. Two months after I received the bull in October, on 10 December, I invited faculty and staff to gather outside the city gate for my reaction to the burning of my books throughout Germany. When all had gathered, a fire was lit. I threw into the fire five or six books that the Romans prized so highly, and then I threw in the *corpus juris canonici* (the body of canon law by which the Roman Church was governed). I don't recall whether I had planned it or just acted on an impulse; I took from my gown a copy of *Exsurge Domine* and threw it into the fire. Someone noted that as I threw the bull into the flames, I said, "Because thou hast destroyed the truth of God, may the Lord consume thee in these flames."[7]

Later that morning, I wrote to my friend George Spalatin and said, "This was done so that the incendiary papists may see that it doesn't take much to burn books they cannot refute."[8]

Of course, I had to respond to the bull as well. I wrote a couple of pieces: *Why the Books of the Pope and His Disciples Were Burned by Doctor Martin Luther*[9] and *Against the Execrable Bull of Antichrist*. I need not bore you with those writings; my actions spoke as clearly as any words.

---

6 Bainton, 147.

7 Schwiebert, 491.

8 LW 48:187.

9 LW 31:383.

LETTER 50

It didn't take the canon lawyers in the Roman curia long to write the formal bull of excommunication. On 3 January 1521, Pope Leo signed the papal bull *Decet Romanum Pontificem* ("It is fitting for the Roman Pontiff"). By virtue of that bull, I was officially excommunicated from the Church of Rome. I didn't pay much attention to it because I knew that I had been faithful to the Word of God. In less than four months, I would stand before the emperor of the Holy Roman Empire and make that confession.

I'll share just a bit of the bull with you.

> Nevertheless Martin himself—and it gives us grievous sorrow and perplexity to say this—the slave of a depraved mind, has scorned to revoke his errors within the prescribed interval and to send us word of such revocation, or to come to us himself; nay, like a stone of stumbling, he has feared not to write and preach worse things than before against us and this Holy See and the Catholic faith, and to lead others on to do the same.[1]

So that you who, regrettably, bear my name know that you are also included in this excommunication note the following words:

> Our purpose is that such men should rightfully be ranked with Martin and other accursed heretics and excommunicates, and that even as they have ranged themselves with the obstinacy in sinning of the said Martin, they shall likewise share his punishments and his name, by bearing with them everywhere the title "Lutheran" and the punishments it incurs.[2]

Shortly thereafter the bull continues, "Our decrees which follow are passed against Martin and others who follow him in the obstinacy of his depraved and damnable purpose."[3]

You may already be bored with these words of condemnation, but I will bore you with only one more.

---

1 Papal Encyclicals Online. *Decet Romanum Pontificem.* Papalencyclicals.net (accessed October 25, 2018).

2 Papal Encyclicals Online. *Decet Romanum Pontificem.* Papalencyclicals.net (accessed October 25, 2018).

3 Papal Encyclicals Online. *Decet Romanum Pontificem.* Papalencyclicals.net (accessed October 25, 2018).

> On all these we decree the sentences of excommunication, of anathema, of our perpetual condemnation and interdict; of privation of dignities, honours and property on them and their descendants, and of declared unfitness for such possessions; of the confiscation of their goods and of the crime of treason; and these and the other sentences, censures and punishments which are inflicted by canon law on heretics and are set out in our aforesaid missive, we decree to have fallen on all these men to their damnation.[4]

You will understand that many of you share the excommunication with me, even to the confiscation of your property.

I would have been a dead man within weeks or months had it not been for my prince and the angry revolt of the German people. Prince Frederick did some heavy negotiating with the imperial counselor and even with the emperor himself to postpone any action against me. A diet was to be held in Worms during the winter of 1520–21. My prince persuaded the emperor to grant me a hearing at that diet.

In early February, Aleander had written to a cardinal in Rome, "The whole of Germany is in full revolt."[5] Sometime during these tumultuous days, Aleander had written another letter to Rome saying, "Nine tenths of the Germans cried, 'Luther,' while . . . the other tenth 'Death to the pope.'"[6] That is clearly an exaggeration but suggests the attitude of many in the German lands.

I hope you understand that the "hidden God" uses common, historical events and people to accomplish His purposes. Because of the intervention of my prince and the German people, I was permitted to continue to teach and write.

Before I close this letter, I want to make two points. I take excommunication by the church very seriously. It is a last resort that the church must use to dismiss from its fellowship those who ignore the Word of God and remain impenitent. But a distinction must be made between ignoring the Word of God and ignoring ecclesiastical bureaucrats. Excommunication belongs to a Christian congregation, not to ecclesiastics far removed from the fellowship of believers. Additionally, it must be used with the greatest care and discrimination.

---

4 Papal Encyclicals Online. *Decet Romanum Pontificem*. Papalencyclicals.net (accessed October 25, 2018).

5 Gritsch, 39.

6 Bainton, 168.

Second, I did not leave the Roman Church; I was dismissed from it. Note also that my contention with the Roman Church was not over moral issues—believe me, there were plenty of moral issues that I could have addressed—but those issues vary from culture to culture and from time to time; it was over basic theological issues that I had a grievance against Rome, and for that I was excommunicated.

I grieve when I see how tragically the Body of Christ has been torn apart after my time. I am especially grieved to witness people who use my name splitting from one another because each group thinks they are as infallible as the pope in my day in interpreting the Scriptures. I still pray to God every day that where believers have created division, and even hostility, the Holy Spirit of God will re-create holy harmony. May God's peace rest on the entire Church redeemed by the precious blood of our common Lord, who is Jesus Christ.

Keep the faith. Remember to be faithful to Jesus Christ, not to Martinus.

Letter 51

A leader has a responsibility for those he leads. I have said previously that I had no desire to be a leader; I wanted only to be a simple monk. I was thrust into a leadership position against my will, and once in the position, I could not abdicate my responsibility.

Following my formal excommunication from the Church of Rome, I still expected death. That troubled me not the least, but I cared deeply for those who had read what I wrote, heard what I preached, and believed what I taught. The bull *Exsurge Domine* threatened those who read, published, or defended my books with the same consequences that I would receive if I did not submit to Rome. I'll share with you part of the bull that prescribes the consequences.

> We forbid each and every one of the faithful of either sex, in virtue of holy obedience and under the above penalties [major excommunication] to be incurred automatically, to read, assert, preach, praise, print, publish, or defend [Luther's writings]. They will incur theses penalties if they presume to uphold them in any way, personally or through another or others, directly or indirectly, tacitly or explicitly, publicly or occultly, either in their own homes or in other public or private places. Indeed immediately after the publication of this letter these works, wherever they may be, shall be sought out carefully by the ordinaries and others [ecclesiastics and regulars], and under each and every one of the above penalties shall be burned publicly and solemnly in the presence of the clerics and people.[1]

The threat was fearful in itself, but what should my dear people have done when they went to confession, and the priest asked them about having or having read any of my books. What were they to do? I would never ask them to lie. Spalatin asked me to write something that would be helpful to those dear souls. I knew that I must. In February 1521, I completed writing *An Instruction to Penitents Concerning the Forbidden Books of Dr. M. Luther*.[2]

---

1 Papal Encyclicals Online. *Exsurge Domine*. Papalencyclicals.net (accessed October 25, 2018).

2 LW 44:219–31.

One option, of course, would be to tell them to not go to confession. That was unthinkable. I so treasured confession that I even called it a sacrament. I wrote, "Do not make the holy sacrament of confession the occasion for a quarrel."[3]

I suggested that all penitents must be respectful, but when asked about having or having read my books, they might respond something like this. "My dear sir, I beg you, cease from hounding me into dangerous snares. I have come to confession not to be trapped but to be absolved."[4] If necessary, they might say, "My dear sir, you are a father-confessor, not an officer. I am obliged to confess what my conscience prompts me to confess. It is not your duty to force me to confess; neither is it your duty to probe the secrets of my heart."[5] If the priest continues to refuse absolution, I said, "In those cases where he still will not grant remission I would just let him keep his absolution. I would go away from him as from one who, together with Lucifer, goes beyond his duty and authority and usurps the jurisdiction of God by probing into the secrets of the heart. . . . Where man does not absolve, there God absolves."[6]

I loved the privilege of private confession and to hear the blessed words that my sins are forgiven for Jesus' sake. I regret that privilege has been denied many of the faithful in your day. It seems that pastors and bishops in your day think that if something is not required, it is not necessary. I concluded my little "instruction" by saying, "For although private confession is one of the most salutary of practices, we know perfectly well that the authority on which it is based is quite shaky."[7]

This little instruction may not be of much value to you, but it certainly was to the troubled consciences of my day. As for you, if you are deprived of the privilege of private confession, remember to confess your sins to God every day. Know that in that confession you can be certain of God's absolution. Look at the cross; remember that Jesus Christ died for you. Then receive the sacrament of Christ's body and blood as the guarantee that your sins are forgiven.

---

3 LW 44:224.

4 LW 44:224.

5 LW 44:224.

6 LW 44:225.

7 LW 44:229.

Letter 52

I told you about the papal bull *Exsurge Domine* that threatened me with excommunication [Letter 49]. I responded to that bull, but not the way the pope had intended. Rather than recant, I published four responses. [Two are mentioned in Letter 49.] There is no need for me to tell you about all of the four; I will share with you only the last one because I think it is the best of the four. And then I will share with you only a brief part of my response because you are not familiar with the charges made against me; you would have to read *Exsurge* to know them. Responses make no sense without knowing the charges. I began to write *Defense and Explanation of All the Articles of Dr. Martin Luther Which Were Unjustly Condemned by the Roman Bull*[1] shortly after I received the bull on 10 December 1520.

You will recall that *Exsurge Domine* leveled forty-one specific charges against me. I responded directly to each of the charges. This letter would be far too long if I were to tell you my response to each of the articles. A historian from your day has summarized my responses quite well. He said, "Once again he gave a defense of his teaching on anthropology [human nature], repentance, and justification. This time he dealt extensively with the earlier Heidelberg thesis that stated that man's free will after the fall was nothing but an empty title."[2]

Nevertheless, I will share with you a few things that I said. I began by talking about the church in my day. I said, "This true church has been hidden so long beneath sacred vestments, ritual, works, and similar outward pretensions and man-made laws that we have finally been taught that we can be saved through the contribution of money rather than through faith."[3] Please note that I did not deny that the true Church existed within the Church of Rome, only that it was so hidden that few enjoyed its blessings.

I was accused of claiming to be everybody's teacher. I denied that again, saying that it was not my personality to put myself forward. I said, "I am always inclined to crawl into a corner."[4] Nevertheless, I did say,

1 LW 32:3–99.

2 Brecht 1:413.

3 LW 32:7.

4 LW 32:8.

"Who knows? God may have called me and raised me up [to be everybody's teacher]. They ought to be afraid lest they despise God in me."[5] I also said, "I do not claim to be a prophet, but I do say that the more they scorn me and the higher they regard themselves, the more reason they have to fear that I may be a prophet."[6]

I then began my response to each of the forty-one charges. I will give you only two samples of what I wrote; one is the greatest treasure of the blessed Gospel, while the other is filled with ridicule and scorn.

In a previous letter [19], I told you about the treasury of merits claimed by the Roman Church. Those alleged merits were available to those who "purchased" letters of indulgence. (The Roman Church would never admit there was any purchase involved.) The seventeenth article of *Exsurge* charged me with teaching, "The treasury of the Church, from which the pope grants indulgences, are not the merits of Christ and of the saints."[7] Part of my response was this, "No Christian is so naive as not to know that Christ's merits and suffering take away our sins and save us."[8] With that assurance, we need no further indulgences from the pope or anyone else. Christ alone is enough for every believer.

In Article 18 of *Exsurge Domine*, I was charged with teaching, "Indulgences are pious frauds of the faithful, and remissions of good works; and they are among the number of those things which are allowed, and not of the number of those which are advantageous."[9] My response was this, "But now that the holy father pope orders me to recant, and condemns this article, I will be obedient and say, 'I confess my error; this article is not true.' And this is the reason: The indulgences are not a pious fraud, but an infernal, diabolical, antichristian fraud, larceny and robbery, whereby the Roman Nimrod [Gen. 10:9] and teacher of sin peddles sin and hell to the whole world and sucks and entices away everybody's money as the price of this unspeakable harm."[10]

That's more than enough from my response to *Exsurge Domine*. If you care to know more, you must do your own research. But you must first read the bull in order to understand my responses.

---

5 LW 32:8.

6 LW 32:9.

7 Papal Encyclicals Online. *Exsurge Domine*. Papalencyclicals.net (accessed October 25, 2018).

8 LW 32:63

9 Papal Encyclicals Online. *Exsurge Domine*. Papalencyclicals.net (accessed October 25, 2018).

10 LW 32:64.

Letter 53

In early 1521, I preached two sermons that I want to share with you. I give them to you because I think that they are as pertinent in your day as in mine. The first bears the title *Sermon on the Worthy Reception of the Sacrament*,[1] and the second is *A Sermon on the Three Kinds of Good Life for the Instruction of Consciences*.[2]

In my day, many people received the Lord's Supper because they felt obligated by the church; it was a requirement. In your day, many may do the same because it is an expectation, or even only a habit; others may refrain from receiving the sacrament because they feel unworthy. The worthy reception is in constant need of clarification. From what I have heard, I fear that clergy in your day fail in this pastoral duty. I have even heard that some who bear my name offer the holy body and blood of our Lord to the unbaptized. What a scandal! Even the Roman Church in your day would not think of such an outrage. Well, I need not preach to you. Let me tell you something about *The Worthy Reception*.

Believe me, there are some who should not receive this sacrament. I began by saying, "First, those who openly live in sin or who willfully harbor evil thoughts, such as of hatred, of uncleanness, and the like, shall not receive the sacrament. Until they shun these sins, the church's precept is not meant for them."[3] There is another group who should not come to the Lord's Table. "Second," I said, "those who find that that they are prompted to partake of it merely because of the order of the church or from habit, who, if wholly free to choose, would not come to it with good will and longing, also must not partake of the sacrament."[4]

The other side of the coin, to use an expression from your day, is those who fear to come for this holy meal because they feel unworthy. Those poor souls have been deluded by priests and bishops who warn the people that they must be righteous and pure before they come to the supper. Therefore, they come with fear. But I said, "If you do not want to

---

1 LW 42:166–77.

2 LW 44:231–42.

3 LW 42:171.

4 LW 42:171.

come to the sacrament until you are perfectly clean and whole, it would be better for you to remain away entirely."[5] I think I put it better about seven years later in a sermon in which I said, "Don't say: I am not fit today, I will wait a while. This is a trick of the devil. What will you do if you are not fit when death comes? Who will make you fit then? Say rather: Neither preacher, prince, pope, nor emperor compels me, but my great need and, beyond this, the benefit."[6]

Listen for those blessed words "Come, for all is ready" or "Our Lord invites you to His Table" or "To all who are baptized and live by faith and daily repentance, our Lord invites you to His Table." Come with joy and receive the benefits of heaven: Jesus Christ in you for the forgiveness of your sins.

A reformation does not happen overnight or even in several months. People may indeed change their minds about what is to be believed, but when taught from youth that certain prescribed religious activities are necessary for salvation, those activities do not die easily. A priest or pastor must deal gently with people as they move from error to truth, from relying on their religious activities to relying on what God has done for them in Jesus Christ. One in your day who read my *Sermon on the Three Kinds of Good Life* said that I wrote it for those "who were confused by the steady proclamation of justification by faith alone."[7] He said, "They found it extremely difficult, if not impossible, to disengage themselves from old ideas and ways. They were accustomed to ceremonies, fast days, holy days, and to the kind of good works taught by the church."[8] I don't recall saying that, but he might be right.

If you read my *Sermon*, you might wonder why I said that there are three kinds of good life. Perhaps I should have called the sermon *Three Kinds of Religious Life*. There is only one kind of good life as I showed in my *Sermon*.

The first kind of religious life is all tied up with religious activities and duties. I said, "The laity think the same, that all they have to do is to keep their fasts and feasts. As if our God were bothered in the slightest whether you drink beer or water, whether you eat fish or meat, whether

---

5 LW 42:175–76.

6 LW 51:192–93.

7 LW 44:233.

8 LW 44:233.

you keep the feasts or fasts!"[9] (I called those who find some hope in these activities "churchyard saints.") I continued by saying, "This means that their holiness is circumscribed by their five senses and their bodily existence. And yet, this very holiness shines brighter in the eyes of the world than does real holiness."[10]

The second kind of religious life engages in really good works. "These are humility, meekness, gentleness, peace, fidelity, love, propriety, purity, and the like."[11] No one can argue against such a life. (I called this kind of religion "the nave," using the churchyard and the church structure for the outline of my sermon.) I said, "He who takes this course is traveling on the right road to heaven."[12] But traveling is not arriving.

The third kind, and this is the only really "good life," is a life that relies on Christ alone for holiness, righteousness, and salvation. (To continue my symbolic outline, I said these are they who live in the "holy of holies.") I said, "Here he has set Christ before us and promised that he who believes in him and calls on his name shall at once receive the Holy Spirit. . . . He who calls on Christ in faith, however, possesses his name, and the Holy Spirit most certainly comes to him."[13]

I concluded by saying that in the church the nave and the sanctuary belong together, so also faith and good works belong together. Faith without works cannot endure.

This sermon is just as fresh and relevant in your day as in mine.

Keep the faith!

---

9 LW 44:237.

10 LW 44:238.

11 LW 44:239.

12 LW 44:239.

13 LW 44:241.

Letter 54

I now look back and laugh at how God works to accomplish His purpose in history through politicians, secular and ecclesiastical, who think they are "making history." It was no laughing matter at the time. I had been condemned as a heretic and excommunicated from the Roman Church. That caused me no great anxiety. Those who excommunicated me had no authority over the Gospel of Jesus Christ, which had set me free; nor did they have authority over the blessed sacraments that kept me united with my Lord Jesus.

After my condemnation by the church, I had to face the threat of the secular government. Remember, in my day the church and the secular government worked like hand in glove, to use another phrase from your day. There was frequently great tension between the hand and the glove, but like a bad marriage, there was never any question about the interrelationship. What action would the imperial government take against me?

The emperor, Charles V, was a resolute Roman Catholic, and his empire had been invaded by a new understanding of the Christian faith. That could not be allowed. What could he or would he do? There were some limitations. The emperor was not a dictator; he was a constitutional monarch. When he was chosen to be the emperor of the Holy Roman Empire of the German Nation on 28 June 1519, there were two stipulations in the constitution that he was bound to observe. No German could be taken to trial outside of the German lands, and no one could be condemned without a just cause and given a fair hearing.[1] There was a second political reality with which the emperor had to contend. A large number of Germans gave me their ardent support. (I expect that many did not understand the issues at stake, but they saw me as an opponent of an oppressive Roman Church.)

How strong was that support? It's hard to say, but, as I mentioned in a previous letter, when Aleander the papal nuncio [representative] came to oppose me at Worms, he was greeted with contempt, and with plenty of Roman money he could secure only a small unheated room for his

1 Bainton, 167.

lodging.[2] He wrote back to Rome, saying, "Nine tenths of the people are shouting 'Luther' and the other tenth, 'Death to the pope.'"[3] I have no doubt that was a gross exaggeration, but it gives you a sense of the sentiments of the German people.

My prince was an honorable and fair person. He called upon Erasmus, the most highly respected intellect of my day, and asked for his opinion about me and the cause that I represented. Erasmus responded, "Luther sinned in two respects; namely, that he knocked off the crown of the Pope and attacked the bellies of the monks."[4] That gave my prince some ease in protecting me.

A diet was to be held in Worms in the spring of 1521. There would be an opportunity for a hearing before the emperor and the lords, princes, and estates of the German nation. My protector and prince, Frederick the Wise, had been in Worms since 5 January 1521. I was never told, but I have no doubt that he intervened with the emperor on my behalf. (He may have had some success because Frederick was the uncle of Charles.)

As early as 28 November of the previous year, Charles had written, "Beloved Uncle Frederick: We are desirous that you should bring the above mentioned Luther to the Diet at Worms."[5]

I learned later that Aleander, upset by the invitation, wrote to the emperor, "As for myself, I would gladly confront this Satan, but the authority of the Holy See should not be prejudiced by subjection of the judgment of the laity."[6] And further, "The laity, including the emperor, are not in a position to review the case. The only competent judge is the pope."[7] Aleander had more to say, but whatever he said was enough to sway the emperor. The invitation to Worms was revoked on 17 December.

A good deal of political maneuvering followed. Finally, on 6 March, Charles was forced to reverse himself again and issued the summons for me to appear at the diet. The invitation included a promise of safe travel. On 2 April, three companions and I left Wittenberg for the journey to Worms. On 16 April, we arrived at Worms and were welcomed by one

---

2 Schwiebert, 495.

3 Bainton, 168.

4 Schwiebert, 488.

5 Schwiebert, 172.

6 Schwiebert, 172.

7 Schwiebert, 172.

hundred horsemen who provided a triumphal entry into the city. That kind of reception for a convicted, excommunicated heretic? Unbelievable!

Next I will tell you about the trial, if indeed it can be called a trial.

As for you, keep the faith!

Letter 55

When the Diet of Worms opened on 28 January 1521, I was not even on the agenda. The new emperor had been crowned in Germany only three months earlier. But to follow precedent, he must go to Rome to be crowned by the pope. Like any politician, the emperor would not go alone; he must have a large contingent to accompany him. How to pay for that journey was on the agenda, along with the many grievances of the German nation against the Roman curia. But the diet was haunted by what was called "the Luther issue." So contentious was that issue that at one point, two of the electors, my prince, Frederick, and the elector of Brandenburg, nearly came to blows before they were separated. Consequently, against the protestation of Aleander and the desire of the emperor himself, the political realities forced the emperor to summon me to appear before the diet.

Thankfully, I did not have to wait long for my appearance before that illustrious assembly. On the day after my arrival in Worms, I was told to appear at 4:00 p.m. As I was being escorted to the diet, the streets were so crowded with spectators that my escorts brought me into the diet through a side door.

There I stood, a humble monk before the collected power of the German nation, much larger than the Germany you know in your day. I did not count, but apparently someone did, and noted, "The whole of Germany was there: six electoral princes (only the King of Bohemia was absent), the Archduke Ferdinand, the Emperor's brother, two landgraves, five margraves, twenty-seven dukes, numerous counts and prelates, counsellors, lawyers and some guards; and, on a canopied seat, the Emperor."[1] Was I frightened? Would you be? I am no different than you. My life was at stake. Even though I had been promised safety, I could not forget that the same safety had been promised to Jan Hus the previous century when he was summoned to the Council at Constance. He was later burned to death because "no promise had to be kept to a heretic." All alone, I had no support other than the support of my Lord Jesus Christ. That was enough. I would stand firm on His precious Gospel. My life counted for nothing.

---

1 Olivier, 161.

A stack of books was on a table. A simple question was posed: "Martin Luther! His Imperial Majesty has caused you to appear to put two questions to you: Do you recognize these books published under your name as yours? Are you prepared to disavow them, as a whole or in part?"[2]

I did not hesitate to acknowledge the books to be mine. The second question related to the salvation and the priority of the Word of God. Those were momentous issues. I asked for time to consider my response. I was given twenty-four hours and then I must answer orally without any written notes.

The following day, I was asked the same two questions. I said that my books were of three different kinds. The first dealt with faith and morals; the second was directed against the papacy that extorted money from the faithful and burdened them with guilty consciences; the third was directed against individuals who defended the Roman tyranny. I then said, "I therefore beg Your Majesty, your distinguished lordships and whoever else can, from the greatest to the smallest, to debate, to convince me of my errors, to refute me by the writings of the prophets and the Gospel. If I could thus be better instructed, none would be more eager than I to retract whatever errors there are. I would be the first to throw my books on the fire."[3]

I had spoken in German; I asked if I should repeat my comments in Latin.

There was a brief recess as the nobility discussed my response. Apparently they thought that it was too ambiguous. They must have a clear response.

Upon resumption of the meetings, I was asked point blank, "Reply honestly and sincerely, without evasion: do you wish to retract your books and all the errors which they contain? Yes or No?"

My final response: "Since Your Majesty and your lordships desire a simple reply, I will answer without horns and without teeth. Unless I am convicted by Scripture and plain reason—I do not accept the authority of popes or councils, for they have contradicted each other—my conscience is captive to the Word of God. I cannot and I will not recant anything, for to go against conscience is neither right nor safe. God help me. Amen."

---

2 Olivier, 162.

3 Olivier, 165.

I returned to my quarters, exhausted, but with a free conscience. I had been faithful to my Lord and to the precious Gospel.

Even the memory of that experience exhausts me. I can write no more.

Next I will tell you about an ingenious plan of Elector Frederick.

P.S. I should tell you that both Aleander and I left a written report of my appearance at the diet. People have taken it upon themselves to collect my writings, and some have been translated into English. You can find both reports in *Luther's Works*, American Edition, volume 32.

Letter 56

I remained in Worms for about ten days after my defense of the Gospel before the German Diet. During those days, there were private attempts to meet with me to resolve the differences that separated me from the Roman Church. Many with whom I met were good and well-intended men. But the breach was too great; reconciliation was impossible without compromising my conscience-bound commitment to the Word of God. I remained ready to be instructed, but I insisted that the basis of the instruction must be the Scriptures. All attempts met with failure.

It was time to return to my home in Wittenberg. I was a heretic, and soon I would be a criminal, subject to arrest or even death by anyone.

Prior to my leaving, Prince Frederick decided to take matters into his own hands. Through Spalatin, his private secretary, my prince informed me that he had arranged for me to be taken to a safe place of hiding. He gave me no details and said that the arrangement must be keep secret. On 24 April, I wrote to Lucas Cranach and said, "I shall submit to being 'imprisoned' and hidden away though as yet I do not know where."[1] My colleague and traveling companion, Amsdorf, knew something was up. I recall writing to Spalatin about a month later, "Amsdorf knew, of course, that I was to be captured by somebody, but does not know the place of my captivity."[2] I think that Frederick himself chose not to know all the details; he could then honestly say that he did not know where Luther could be found.

On 26 April, I left Worms with my traveling companions. I made a brief stop in Möhra to visit relatives. On 3 May, some of my companions separated from us and went home by a different route. Only Amsdorf and another monk were left with me. The three of us continued our journey on 4 May. As we made our way through the Thuringian forest, about nightfall we were suddenly surrounded by four knights on horseback. I was roughly snatched from the wagon, my arms were tied, and I was dragged along behind the horses until we rounded a corner and were no longer visible to Amsdorf and the driver. (The other monk who was

1 Brecht 1:470.

2 Smith 2:28–29.

accompanying us had scampered away, frightened, into the forest.) I was then dressed as a knight and given a horse to ride. We finally arrived at the Wartburg castle about eleven o'clock in the evening. I was exhausted and thrown into a small room as a criminal so that the guard would not suspect my identity. I was then known as Junker Jörg and was confined to my room until my tonsure had grown out and I had raised a good beard. To further protect my identity, I was taught the ways and vocabulary of knighthood. Meals were brought to me twice a day.

I was now a captive. What was I to do? Fortunately, when I was captured, I was able to secure my Hebrew and Greek Bibles. I could feast on the Word of God. But what about my students in Wittenberg? What about all of my friends who perhaps thought me dead? I had too much time on my hands. Inactivity drove me crazy. But I was not alone; my Lord was with me every minute of my captivity. There I could spend additional time in prayer.

It did not take me long to engage in productive activity. I'll tell you about that another time.

Letter 57

When I left Worms, my spirit was buoyed because I knew that the Spirit of God had sustained me, and I had been faithful to my Lord and to the Holy Gospel. At the same time, I knew, without a doubt, that the diet would formally condemn me as a criminal. I have told you that I had earlier been convicted as a heretic by the Roman Church. In my day, a conviction by the church had almost the same force as a conviction by the secular government.

The formal condemnation was prepared for the emperor by my nemesis, the papal representative, Aleander, and presented for his signature on 8 May. I know that because the *Edict of Worms* is dated 8 May 1521. But the edict was not published until about 26 May. I wondered why the delay. A historian from your day provided the answer. He wrote, "Aleander brought the edict to the emperor for his signature. He took up the pen. 'Then,' says Aleander, 'I haven't the ghost of a notion why, he laid it down and said he must submit the edict to the diet.'"[1]

The emperor could have issued the edict on his own authority, but he was a wise politician. He wanted the princes, dukes, and representative of the various estates to have some ownership in the edict. They would then feel a greater compulsion to enforce it in their respective territories.

The diet concluded the day before the edict was published. However, my sovereign, Prince Frederick, had left the diet two days earlier because he was suffering from gout. Therefore he could plead that he was not a party to the edict.

I did not know until I learned that one of your historians had done some research and discovered that Prince Frederick had requested exemption from enforcing the edict. He wrote, "One of the most peculiar episodes in this context is Frederick the Wise's request to Charles V that he be exempted from serving Luther with the mandate against him. Surprisingly, the emperor, despite his earlier assertion that he would proceed energetically against Luther, seems to have complied with the request."[2] Frankly, there were so many other pressing political issues on

---

1 Bainton, 189.

2 Brecht 1:474.

the emperor that he had no time to pursue one single monk. The other German nobles did not seem overly anxious to push the issue. But I was, nevertheless, a convicted criminal.

I understand that you have what are called terrorists in your day. You know what is expected of anyone who knows the location of a terrorist. To fail to notify the authorities amounts to complicity with the terrorist. I was the "terrorist" of the Holy Roman Empire in my day. No one was allowed to give me food or shelter but must capture me and turn me over to the authorities. Anyone who supported me or my cause was equally as guilty as I. Anyone who read what I wrote, or gave to another to read, was equally guilty.

I will give you just a sample of the words from the edict:

Punishment

> For the crime of *lèse majesté* [high treason] and for very serious offense and indignation against the prince.
>
> Item. Confiscation and loss of body and belongings and all goods, fixed and movable, half of which will go to the Lord (they did not mean Lord Jesus, but the secular lord) and the other half to the accusers and denouncers. With other punishments as given more fully in the present edict and mandate.[3]

I'm not sure why I even bothered to write this letter; it is really a bunch of irrelevant chatter. I suppose that I wrote it so that you will have record of my formal conviction as a criminal.

Next time, I'll tell you something more important—my activity during the rather lengthy stay at the Wartburg castle.

3 The Voice: Biblical and Theological Resources for Growing Christians. "The Edict of Worms (1521)." accessed January 3, 2019, Crivoice.org./creededictworms.html.

Letter 58

The first few days at the Wartburg castle gave my body time to recover; I was exhausted. But my mind kept racing. I was concerned about my colleagues, my students, my teaching responsibilities. Those dear friends must have thought that I had been killed, although Amsdorf knew something about my condition.

My mind never stopped racing. I had only my Greek and Hebrew Bibles with me. I had wanted to translate the Bible into my native language so that the laity could read it. I made a start, but was hindered because I was without the books that I needed for the translation. There were other writings that I had begun before going to Worms. I wanted to complete those works also.

About ten days after my arrival, I wrote a letter to my friend Spalatin. I said, "I am sitting here all day, drunk with leisure. I am reading the Bible in Greek and Hebrew. I shall write a German tract on the freedom of auricular confession. I shall also continue working on the Psalms and the *Postil* as soon as I have received the necessary things from Wittenberg—among which I also expect the unfinished *Magnificat*."[1]

On 26 May, I was interrupted by a book written against me by a theologian from the University of Louvain, Latomus (his real name was Jacobus Masson). I hated to be distracted from my translation by this incompetent, half-witted professor. But he challenged some very central teachings of the Bible that I had highlighted and promoted. I knew that I had to respond. In less than a month, I had completed more than 120 pages of response: *Against Latomus*.[2]

I can't summarize more than one hundred pages in a short letter, but I will tell you briefly what I confirmed about my teaching in contradiction to Latomus. The issue was all about sin and grace; the basic article of justification; how sinners are made righteous before God.

I affirmed again that all people are sinners from birth to death. Even Baptism into Jesus Christ does not free one from sin, repentance does not free one from sin, and above all, religious activity does not free one

1 LW 48:225.

2 LW 32:133–260.

from sin. Sin clings to each person, believer and unbeliever alike, to the point of death.

What then is the difference between the baptized believer and the baptized or unbaptized unbeliever? The forgiveness of sin by the great, unmerited mercy of God belongs to the believer. Sin always condemns—believer and unbeliever alike. The difference is, to paraphrase the words of the apostle Paul, the believer is wrapped in the righteousness of Jesus (Galatians 3:27). Or, as Paul says in another place, "There is therefore now no condemnation for those who are in Christ Jesus" (Romans 8:1). In Christ, to use a phrase favored by Paul, sinners are freed not from sin, but from the consequences of sin. That makes all the difference in the world. It is the difference between heaven and hell.

To put the matter very simply, I said that Christians are simultaneously saints and sinners.

Some historian in your day said my response to Latomus was "one of Luther's most significant theological works . . . this effort resulted in one of Luther's most systematic statements of his teachings on justification and the principles of scriptural interpretation."[3] I'm not sure that he is right, but he has probably researched what I wrote more thoroughly than I have. Frankly, I'm not too interested in what I wrote. I would prefer that those scholars read the Bible rather than spending their time nosing around in my writings.

---

3 Loewenich, 206.

Letter 59

At the Wartburg, my thoughts were always with my students and colleagues in Wittenberg, but I had no anxiety about the cause of reform that had begun there. The reform was not mine; it was from God and was sustained by the Spirit of God. But God almost always works through human agents. I was confident that God had capable, Spirit-filled people who could provide leadership in my absence.

I had the highest confidence in and respect for my young colleague Philip Melanchthon. He was only twenty-four years old when the weight of leadership was unexpectedly cast upon him. His German name was Philip Schwartzerd. As a student, and like many humanists in my day, Philip chose the Greek equivalent of Schwartzerd—Melanchthon. The English equivalent of both names is black earth.

Melanchthon was fourteen years my junior but my closest colleague in the university faculty. He came to us in 1518 as a twenty-one-year-old humanist to teach Greek. At that tender age, his great-uncle John Reuchlin, himself a great humanist scholar, called Philip the best Greek scholar in Europe with the exception of the famous Erasmus.

Melanchthon was a child prodigy. He entered the University of Heidelberg at age 12, got his bachelor's degree at age 15, and his master's degree at age 17.

Melanchthon did not study as a theologian, but we formed a mutual bond almost immediately. Two days after Philip's inaugural address, I wrote to Spalatin and said, "I certainly do not wish to have a different Greek instructor as long as he is alive."[1] John Lang told me that Philip had written to him and said, "If there is anything on earth I love, it is Martin and his pious writing; but, above everything else, I love Martin himself."[2]

With Philipp's assistance we revised the curriculum of the theological faculty. No longer were students immersed in philosophy and Scholastic theology; it was back to the Bible and the Church Fathers. Almost immediately, our university became the leading university in Germany.

---

1 LW 48:78.

2 Schwiebert, 299.

On one occasion, George Spalatin visited our school and noted that I had four hundred students who attended my lecture; Melanchthon had six hundred attendees.

Philip was such a great teacher that he became known as *praeceptor Germaniae* (teacher of the Germans).

That great teacher was also a great student. Shortly after his arrival in Wittenberg, he became a student of theology. Within one year, he was already giving lectures on theology. I recall writing to John Lang in December 1519, "I am only sorry that I cannot send all the friars (brother monks) into Philip's theological lectures on Matthew at six o'clock in the morning. That little Greek scholar outdoes me even in theology itself."[3]

Melanchthon was not only a godsend to our university, but he was also a great asset in the cause of theological reform. Within three years of his arrival in Wittenberg, he published the first systematic theology of what some call the "Wittenberg Theology." His book was called *Loci communes rerum theologicarum* (common places in the nature of theology). Most often it is simply called the *Loci* or *Loci communes*. Within that short period, only three years, Philip accomplished something that I was never able to complete—a comprehensive, systematic writing of the Christian faith.

The elector thought so highly of Melanchthon's brilliant mind that when the German nobles prepared to present their common Protestant faith to the emperor in 1530, he asked Melanchthon, along with a few others, to prepare a written statement that would represent that faith. For all practical purposes, Melanchthon was the author of the Augsburg Confession, which was presented to the emperor and the German Diet on 25 June 1530. Perhaps I'll tell you more about that at another time.

As much as I loved that dear man, Philip's temperament and mine were quite the opposite. There wasn't a gene in my body, not a chromosome, that would allow me to compromise on issues of the faith. Philip was a conciliator, certainly more gracious and perhaps more willing to understand the opposition's point of view than I. I was anxious to speak and write against the foe; Philip was more willing to listen.

The hardest lesson for me to learn, and I never did learn it prior to my death, is that there is a time to be adamant, unrelenting, and uncompromising and a time for patient listening to the other side of an argument. No, I should say that the patient listening must precede any

---

3 LW 48:135–36.

strong, uncompromising stance. The greatest Spirit-directed wisdom is needed to know what to do and when to do it; what to say and when to say it.

A major problem erupted in Wittenberg about six or seven months after my absence from the city. I cannot tell you about it now but will later. Philip was not strong enough to handle the problem. I returned for about a week or two, in opposition to the elector's will, to address the problem.

Letter 60

Jerome Emser was secretary to Duke George in Albertine Saxony and served as the court chaplain, but he was a weasel. Several weeks after my debate with Dr. Eck in Leipzig in early July 1518, I was invited to preach in Dresden. Following that sermon, Jerome begged my attendance at a banquet. I never turned down a good meal. During the course of that meal, I and a fellow invitee engaged in a rather heated debate on indulgences and other matters. I did not learn until later that a Dominican monk had been standing behind a door to eavesdrop on our conversation. (That's when I learned that Emser was a weasel, never again to be trusted.) The whole banquet was a setup to catch me in private conversation making comments that could be used to embarrass me in public. (You know that people, you included, say in private what you would never say in public or put into writing.)

About a year later, Emser defended my orthodoxy against the claim that I was no different than Jan Hus, the convicted heretic, from Bohemia. I was not impressed with his defense; it was only anther ploy to trap me.

I did not want to waste precious time responding to this minor-league theologian. I waited almost two and a half years before his incessant lies and misrepresentation of my teaching compelled me to answer. Failure to answer may have authenticated his lies with some people.

One from your day, a student of the Reformation and also a professor, said that I wrote four treatises against Emser.[1] I count only one treatise.

My first reply, *To the Goat in Leipzig*,[2] was only a short letter, about four pages long. I should explain my use of the term "goat" in reference to Emser. The picture of a goat was on Emser's coat of arms, and he displayed it on the title page of his writings. The reply is nothing more than an excoriation of Emser's lies and misrepresentation of my teaching. Believe me, you would waste your time reading it. I'll give you just two samples of what I wrote. "I certainly know that it is not easy to deal with

1 LW 39:110.

2 LW 39:105–15.

a shameless slanderer and liar, for according to the proverb, 'This I know for sure: if I fight against filth, I shall not remain pure, whether I win or lose.'"[3] I called Emser to attention by saying, "Every day you can see that I am not afraid of those who have more skill and intelligence in one hair than you have in your whole body and soul together, and yet you dare defy me and try to scare me! Thus you really prove that you confuse stupidity with reason and have changed from a man into a goat."[4]

There was no more of substance than that in my first letter to Emser.

Emser responded immediately, but not to me personally. A friend living in the territory of Duke George either received or intercepted the reply and forwarded it to me. That sniveling goat who cared nothing for the truth chastised me for a comment that I had made at the Leipzig Debate that Emser said offended so many people. My comment had been this: "This matter did not begin in God's name, and it will not end in God's name either."[5]

That comment by itself could be understood to refer to the reform movement and make me look like an arrogant jerk. I had reference only to the Leipzig Debate, which from beginning to end had been stacked against me. I told Emser, "My words, therefore, did not refer to me but to Eck, Emser, and the Leipzig theologians."[6]

I had to respond again. I wrote *Concerning the Answer of the Goat in Leipzig*.[7] I had to let Emser know that his willful distortion of my words was characteristic of his deception. I said, "But if I knew that my teaching were injurious to any single man (which cannot be, since it is the gospel itself), I would rather suffer ten deaths than allow such teaching to go forth or let it go unrecanted."[8]

The only other comment I made worth noting related to Emser's attack on me personally. The attack did not bother me; I have a thick skin, and I had been rendered a devil by more competent people than he. I said, "But I refuse to debate very much about whether I am a proud man, since this concerns not my teaching but my person. I have said more than once that anyone may attack my person in any way he pleases. I do

3 LW 39:114–15.

4 LW 39:111.

5 LW 39:122.

6 LW 39:123.

7 LW 39:117–35.

8 LW 39:125.

not pretend to be an angel. But I let no one attack my teaching without a counterattack, since I know that it is not mine but God's."[9]

This slightly longer letter to Emser—it amounted to only fifteen pages—is no more worthy of your time reading than is *To the Goat in Leipzig*.

Next time, I'll tell you about a full treatise that I wrote against the Leipzig goat. That one will be worth your time to read.

Recalling the interchanges with that purveyor of lies, distortions, and deceit fatigues me even now. I must return to my rest. As for you, keep the faith.

---

9 LW 39:125.

Letter 61

Jerome Emser had been a thorn in my side since July 1518, shortly after my debate with Dr. Eck in Leipzig [see Letter 33]. I have previously told you about two letters that I wrote to him, castigating him for his lies, deception, and misrepresentation of my teaching.

After I had written *To the Christian Nobility of the German Nation* [see Letter 45], Emser, apparently trying to impress his sovereign, Duke George, wrote *Against the Un-Christian Book of the Augustinian Martin Luther, Addressed to the German Nobility*. I had no stomach to respond to this pest from Leipzig. I wrote to Spalatin, "Emser is vomiting his poison at length to please Duke George. I am obliged to answer the man only on account of his most impure lies."[1]

Two letters of chastisement had not put a stop to this villain. I had to respond with a full-length treatise based on Holy Scripture and clear thinking to undress this liar. In February, I had completed *Answer to the Hyper-Christian, Hyper-Spiritual, and Hyper-Learned Book by Goat Emser in Leipzig—Including Some Thoughts Regarding His Companion, the Fool Murner*.

In response to Emser, I made only two major points: the right understanding of priesthood, that is to say, that all believers are priests; and the correct way to understand and use the Bible. I'll tell you about Murner later.

I could not help myself; I spent seven pages chastising Emser for misrepresenting my teaching. Then I got to work.

I have heard that in your day you use the phrase "priesthood of all believers" and attribute that phrase to me. I do not recall ever using the phrase, but it is exactly what I taught and exactly what I tried to pound into that numbskull from Leipzig. However, the universal priesthood of all believers is not my teaching; it is the clear teaching of the Bible. When I quoted 1 Peter 2:9, "You are . . . a royal priesthood," Emser wanted to call that a spiritual priesthood and separate it from those consecrated by bishops as priests for a specific function within the church.

---

1 Smith 1:465.

I had to give Emser a lesson in vocabulary. I told him that Scripture never refers to those set aside for a special function in the church as priests; they are always designated in terms other than priest: ministry, servitude, and other similar terms. "Nowhere is it called 'priesthood' [*sacerdocium*] or 'spiritual' [*spiritualis*]."[2]

Dear fellow believer, in a short letter I cannot tell you all that I said to Emser, but your status as a priest before God is so important that I urge you to find a copy of my treatise and read it. I seldom encourage people to read what I wrote, but this is an exception.

I must clarify one point. It is one thing to be a priest, quite another to exercise that priesthood within a community of believers. I said to Emser, "You also lie that I have made all laymen bishops, priests, and spiritual in such a way that they may exercise the office without a call. But, as godly as you are, you conceal the fact that I added that no one should undertake this office without a call unless it be an extreme emergency."[3]

I made another comment, only distantly related to the priesthood of all believers that I think is even more important in your day than it was in mine. I wrote, "His [Emser's] first lie is that I intend to cut off the head of the church [pope] and then heal the body."[4] I had no such intention. Further along, I said, "If that had been my intention at the time, why should I have suggested that the papacy be reformed? This suggestion proved that I wanted to retain and hold on to it; otherwise, I would have had to say that one should destroy it instead of reforming it."[5]

Consider yourself fortunate to live in a day when it appears that God is reforming the papacy. Julius II and Leo X from my day would not have recognized Pope John XXIII from sixty years ago or Francis, who now serves in the papal office. Give thanks to God for a new day of hope and reconciliation in the Holy Christian Church. (I need not mention my grief over the fracture of the church in the New World that bears my name.)

I must share briefly some comments that I made regarding the right interpretation of Scripture. When Emser, like many in your day, doesn't like what the clear word of Scripture says, he quotes Paul, "The letter kills, but the Spirit gives life" (2 Corinthians 3:6). Emser wants to give

---

2 LW 39:154.

3 LW 39:174.

4 LW 39:172.

5 LW 39:172.

the Scripture a double meaning: "an external one and a hidden one, and he calls these two meanings 'literal' and 'spiritual.'"[6] He then puts his own twist on what the "spiritual" meaning should be.

I insisted that the literal meaning, and only the literal meaning, must be maintained. I said, "The Holy Spirit is the simplest writer and adviser in heaven and on earth. That is why his words could have no more than the one simplest meaning which we call the written one, or the literal meaning of the tongue."[7]

Because of a fourfold interpretation of Scripture that developed long before my day, but was still in use in my day, one meaning of which was the literal meaning, I thought best to clarify the issue further by saying, "Thus 'literal meaning' is not a good term. . . . Those who call it 'grammatical, historical meaning' do better."[8]

I had some important things to say about God's Law and Gospel, but I cannot put everything into one letter.

When I referred to Thomas Murner as a fool, I used a play on words. The word for fool in the German of my day was *Marnarr*. Thus, *Marnarr Murner*.

I had little time to respond to his several writings against me. I was overly busy with my other duties, especially making preparation for my appearance before the German Diet in Worms. I hastily completed this treatise on 29 March and was on my way to Worms in early April.

I will only repeat what a scholar from your day said about the final part of the treatise. "Thus Luther limited his reply to the two principal points Murner attacked: that the church is a spiritual, 'Platonic' community and that the primacy of the pope cannot be derived from Matt. 16:18."[9]

Emser responded to my lengthy treatise but simply reiterated his previous prejudice that 1 Peter 2:9, "you are . . . a royal priesthood," has a double meaning.

Again, I did not want to reply but was pressed into it by others. While at the Wartburg, I penned my "surrender." The title I chose was *Dr. Luther's Retraction of the Error Forced upon Him by the Most Highly Learned*

---

6 LW 39:175.

7 LW 39:178.

8 LW 39:181.

9 LW 39:141.

Priest of God, Sir Jerome Emser, Vicar in Meissen.[10] Emser did not get the irony of the title and concluded that he had won the battle.

I cannot say more than I have already said. This was my final comment on the issue. "If you ask how this can be I will tell you: in all my writings I never wanted more than that all Christians should be priests; yet not all should be consecrated by bishops, not all should preach, celebrate mass, and exercise the priestly office unless they have been appointed and called to do so. This was my final intention."[11]

I did add one more item. I said, "Well then, this is finished. But it still has one major fault. I shall be glad to humble myself and hear women and children preach."[12]

There is so much more to be said on these crucial issues, but I must stop now.

10 LW 39:225–38.

11 LW 39:233.

12 LW 39:234.

Letter 62

Confinement, voluntary or involuntary, cannot keep one from thinking. At the Wartburg, I had only my Greek and Hebrew Bibles. I could work on translating the Bible into readable German. I'll tell you about that some other time. I also had the leisure to prepare sermons on the appointed Epistle and Gospel for the Sundays of the Church Year. Good sermon preparation takes time for reflection and thought on the biblical texts. In confinement, I had that time.

I had begun the task of writing those sermons while in Wittenberg prior to being summoned to appear before the German Diet. I had completed eight sermons for the Sundays in Advent. Shortly after arriving at the Wartburg, I asked that those Advent sermons be sent to me. While I waited, I worked on eight sermons for the Christmas season. The Advent sermons never did arrive, so I set myself to rewrite those sermons in German. The first set written in Wittenberg I had written in Latin.

These series of sermons were called the *Church Postil*, or sometimes the *Wartburg Postil*. Somebody translated the *Christmas Postil* into English. It's available if you want to read any of the sermons.[1]

A scholar from your day has said, "But the two most valuable contributions he made during his time at the Wartburg were the German church postils (homiletical expositions) and the German translation of the New Testament."[2]

I can hardly deny the valuation. Another writer of your day evidently found a letter I had written to a friend in 1527. In that letter, I had called the *Wartburg Postil* my best book.[3]

You may know that on another occasion I said that all of my books should be burned except the Small Catechism and *The Bondage of the Will*. Call me inconsistent if you will, but please learn to read all that I wrote or said in the context in which it was delivered.

I can't possibly tell you all that I wrote in those sermons, but I do want to share with you a few things that I wrote in an introduction to the postils. The introduction had the title *A Brief Instruction on What to Look*

---

1 LW 52.

2 Loewenich, 208.

3 Bornkamm, 33.

for and Expect in the Gospels.[4]

I summarized the Gospel by saying, "For at its briefest, the gospel is a discourse about Christ, that he is the Son of God and became man for us, that he died and was raised, that he has been established as a Lord over all things."[5]

Be careful not to think of Jesus as merely a moral example of a God-centered life. I wrote, "In short this mode [of understanding Christ as simply an example] does not make Christians but only hypocrites."[6]

When you have been captured by God's grace to recognize Jesus as your Savior from the consequences of your sin, then, and only then, can you look to Him as an example for living.

This is how I put it in the Introduction: "Now when you have Christ as the foundation and chief blessing of your salvation, then the other part follows: that you take him as your example, giving yourself in service to your neighbor just as you see that Christ has given himself for you."[7]

That is the substance of what I wrote in that Introduction. The Gospel is so very simple. I'm a bit embarrassed that it took me nine pages to present such a simple case. However—am I now justifying my lengthy writing?—the Gospel has to be said over and over again in a variety of ways, never wandering from the central truth that Jesus Christ is God's gift to you for your salvation, until the Spirit of God implants that gift in your heart and the heart responds in faith.

I did make one other comment worth noting. I said, "And the gospel should really not be something written, but a spoken word which brought forth the Scriptures, as Christ and the apostles have done. This is why Christ himself did not write anything but only spoke. He called his teaching not Scripture but gospel, meaning good news or a proclamation that is spread not by pen but by word of mouth."[8]

If you are aware of all the writing that I did, you might think me to be violating that principle. Believe me, I did speak the Gospel thousands of times, in addition to writing it. My final comment in this Introduction was to the point that I would prefer not to write but only speak the Gospel. I wrote, "O would to God that among Christians the pure gospel were known and that most speedily there would be neither use nor need for this work of mine."[9]

---

4 LW 35:113–24.

5 LW 35:118.

6 LW 35:119.

7 LW 35:120.

8 LW 35:123.

9 LW 35:123–24.

Letter 63

A friend asked me when I first saw a Bible. The question seemed quite trivial, but I suppose because the Bible became my dearest treasure, the question was important to my friend. I assure you that I did not see a Bible in my parents' home. During my youth and early adulthood, the few Bibles available were in Latin, totally incomprehensible to my parents and their peers.

The question was raised during some casual conversation with friends around the dinner table, if I remember correctly. Several of those friends took notes on what I said on a variety of subjects—as you might say, off the cuff remarks. Later, those remarks were collected and published as *Luther's Table Talks*. I must warn you not to take too seriously what you read in those collected conversations. They were mere notes taken and later expanded as best the recorder could recall the comments.

One who took notes recorded me as saying, "When I was twenty years old I had not yet seen a Bible."[1] I do not recall saying that, and I do not think it is an accurate statement. To the best of my recollection, I think I first saw a Bible when I was a student at Magdeburg. I was then about fourteen years of age. In Magdeburg [see Letter 4], I was introduced to the Brethren of the Common Life. They put great emphasis on reading the Bible and living a pious life. That community of believers left a lasting impression on me.

When I first saw a Bible is of trivial concern; the impression upon my first reading of the Bible is of profound concern. I fell in love with the Bible; it became the guiding light throughout my life. I wanted all my dear German people to have the same privilege of reading the Word of God in their own native language that I had when I first read it in Latin.

In Wittenberg, I had done some minimal translating of parts of the Bible, only a few psalms and the beautiful Magnificat of the blessed Virgin Mary. At the Wartburg, I had more leisure to devote myself to translating the entire New Testament.

In June 1521, I wrote to Spalatin, "I am studying Hebrew and Greek."[2] I had learned a bit of Greek in Wittenberg thanks to John Lang and Phil-

1 Schwiebert, 121.

2 LW 48:255.

ip Melanchthon, but I did not begin that study until after age 30, hardly the best age to begin studying a language. By December, I began translating the New Testament. I used the recently published Greek New Testament prepared by Erasmus. He used the oldest and best manuscripts available in my day to produce that gem.

My translation was not the first German translation of the New Testament. A scholar from your day has noted that there were fourteen high German translations dating from 1462.[3] I found that interesting. I knew of previous editions, but I did not know the number.

How was my translation different from previous editions? Another scholar noted that mine differed in two ways: my translation was based on the original Greek text (not on the inaccurate Latin Vulgate), and I used common ordinary words that people could understand.[4] That same scholar found a comment that I had made, recorded in the *Table Talks*. Apparently I said, "The language used was the language of the Saxon chancellery, used by every prince and king in Germany, and so it was the German language common to everyone."[5] Whether I actually said that I cannot confirm, but it sounds right.

I completed the translation of the entire New Testament in eleven weeks. The completed work was contained in 222 folio pages. It was published in September 1522. Someone has estimated that five thousand copies were sold within two months.[6]

I was rewarded greatly for that task, not with ducats or gulden, but with the sheer joy of seeing my most precious treasure in hands of my beloved people.

On that note of joy, I return to my rest.

P.S. I should tell you that with the help of some friends in Wittenberg, more proficient in Greek and Hebrew than I, the entire Bible, including the Old Testament, was finally published in 1534.

---

3 Schwiebert, 527.

4 Loewenich, 210.

5 Loewenich, 210.

6 Schwiebert, 531.

Letter 64

In June 1521, while at the Wartburg, I learned that Karlstadt proposed a disputation on celibacy. He argued that priests ought to be forced to marry, and no one should be allowed to become a monk prior to age 60. He based his argument on a couple of verses in Timothy. I agreed with much of his conclusions but objected to forced marriage as being an abridgement of evangelical freedom. I was also convinced that he did a poor job of interpreting the scriptural passages that he cited (1 Timothy 3:2; 5:9). I wrote to Spalatin and said, "How I wish that Karlstadt had tried to refute celibacy with more fitting Scripture passages!"[1]

I may have let the issue die, but I learned that three monks had taken wives. I approved of the freedom to marry but was concerned about the motives. The flesh is weak and temptations are subtle.

By November, I knew those actions were the result of my evangelical teaching. On 1 November, I wrote to a friend and said, "For Philip [Melanchthon] and I have a powerful conspiracy concerning the vows of monks and priests; they have to be abolished and made void."[2]

I had previously made a comment about the irrationality of these vows. When I wrote *To the Christian Nobility of the German Nation*, I said, regarding celibacy, "The pope has as little power to command this as he has to forbid eating, drinking, the natural movement of the bowels, or growing fat."[3]

I began writing *The Judgment of Martin Luther on Monastic Vows* on 11 November and completed the 150 pages (in your edition) in ten days.

While I was writing this treatise, I learned that more than a dozen had left the monastery in Wittenberg. By the time I returned to Wittenberg in March 1522, all the monks had left the monastery with the exception of the prior, Helt.

It is quite impossible to summarize 150 pages in a short letter, but I hope to give you the substance of what I said. In five sections, I gave five reasons why monastic vows must be eliminated.

---

1 LW 48:293.

2 LW 48:321.

3 LW 44:178.

1. "[Monastic] Vows Do Not Rest on the Word of God: They Run Counter to the Word of God."[4]

Contrary to the Word of God, "they divide the Christian life into a state of perfection and a state of imperfection. To the common people, they ascribe a life of imperfection; to themselves, a life of perfection."[5] Have the monks not read that the apostle Paul wrote that "all have sinned and fall short of the glory of God" (Romans 3:23)? Do the monks exclude themselves from "all" humanity, or do they think of themselves above and beyond humanity? Either conclusion is absurd.

2. "Vows Are Against Faith"[6]

I had a great deal to say about this issue, but perhaps I can summarize my comments with these words: "Vows and the works of vows are but law and works. They are not faith, nor do they issue from faith, for what else is a vow but some kind of law? In their own words they say, 'What was a matter of choice before the vow, is a matter of obligation after the vow.'"[7] If monastic vows did not promise some benefit before God, no one would make those vows. If they would only tell the truth that faith in Jesus Christ saves, and that vows contribute nothing to one's eternal salvation, monasteries would empty in a week.

3. "Vows Are Against Evangelical Freedom"[8]

I noted above that I had written a whole treatise on Christian freedom. Vows bind people; Christ sets people free. Those simple truths should make it abundantly clear that vows and Christian freedom cannot live together. It should also be clear that Christian freedom allows vows. I'll say more about that later.

4. "Vows Are Contrary to the Commandments of God"[9]

I began by saying, "Proof that [the monastic institution] has no divine authority lies in the fact that monasticism has no testimony from

---

4 LW 44:252.

5 LW 44:262.

6 LW 44:273.

7 LW 44:280.

8 LW 44:295.

9 LW 44:317.

Scripture."[10] Further, I said, "After faith in God there is nothing greater than obedience to parents."[11] That statement was very personal to me because I became a monk against the will of my father. When I wrote this treatise on monastic vows, I sent a copy to my father with an accompanying letter.[12] I told my father, "For my vow was not worth a fig, since by taking it I withdrew myself from the authority and guidance of the parent [to whom I was subject] by God's commandment."[13]

5. "Monasticism Is Contrary to Common Sense and Reason"[14]

Some numbskull who has memorized one line of what I wrote, but knows nothing more, will remind me that at one time I had said that reason is the devil's whore,[15] and now I am using reason to destroy monasticism. Yes, and I also called natural reason an anointed idol[16] and Madam Jezebel.[17] But I made those comments about reason only as reason relates to human relationships to God and to the holy faith. Reason is a gift of God to be used in human affairs.

I showed the irrationality of both celibacy and poverty (the irrationality of poverty does not argue for the rationality of wealth). If two out of three monastic requirements fall to irrationality, the third falls because, as a requirement, [obedience to a vow] destroys evangelical freedom. The Gospel is then lost, and Jesus is no longer necessary. All that is needed is a prior to enforce vows, and a monk's salvation is assured. What diabolical nonsense!

In all that I said, you must understand that I do not oppose vows as long as they are taken voluntarily, promise no spiritual rewards, and may be revoked without guilt by the maker. I said that clearly in these words, "Faith remains unhurt only when a vow is regarded as a matter of free choice and not as necessary to attain righteousness and salvation,"[18] or again, "Sometimes vows are made through Christ working in us in

---

10 LW 44:317.

11 LW 44:326.

12 LW 48:330–36.

13 LW 48:332.

14 LW 44:336.

15 LW 40:175.

16 LW 52:107.

17 LW 52:149.

18 LW 44:296.

the spirit of freedom, provided that they are taken and kept voluntarily, when neither satisfaction for sins is claimed by them, nor righteousness and salvation sought through them."[19]

Next time, I'll tell you about some work I did as a gift to my lord, Duke John Frederick. Until then, keep the faith.

19 LW 44:303.

Letter 65

Before I was summoned to appear before the German Diet in Worms, I had begun a commentary on the beautiful song of the blessed Virgin Mary, the song attributed to her by Luke upon being told that she would be the mother of the Savior. I wanted to present the commentary as a gift to Duke John Frederick, nephew of my sovereign, Frederick the Wise. John Frederick would become my sovereign in 1532.

Even in your day, that most beautiful song from the heart is still called the Magnificat. The word is taken from the first Latin words in the song recorded in Luke chapter 1: *magnificat anima mea Dominum* (my soul magnifies the Lord).

I was intimately familiar with the words because, as I told the Duke, "It is a fine custom, too, that this canticle is sung in all churches daily at vespers."[1] It is a great tragedy that most congregations that use my name no longer have daily worship services: no matins, no vespers; only one worship service each week. They feed their bellies three times a day, but their spirits only once a week. Where did such insanity develop that leads to spiritual malnutrition? But that's a subject for some other time.

I was pleased that Joseph Klug included this beautiful song in the hymnbook he prepared in 1533. Some scholar in your day has said that it is "quite likely" that I "pointed the canticle, possibly also providing the following preface."[2] Why should it matter what I did? It's Mary's song that is important. Anything beyond the song is merely a distraction.

At the Wartburg, I had time to finish my offering to the duke.

The song of Mary is so rich and beautiful that it is better to read it than to read about it. Nevertheless, I will share with you a few things that I said in my tribute to the duke.

In her opening words, "My spirit rejoices in God, my Savior," "she teaches us to love and praise God for Himself alone."[3] I said, "That is the true bride of Christ, who says to Him, 'I seek not Thine, but Thee; Thou are to me no dearer when it goes well with me, nor any less dear when it goes ill.'"[4]

---

1 LW 21:298.

2 LW 53:176.

3 LW 21:309.

4 LW 21:311.

I commented on all parts of Mary's song, but I want to share with you only a few thoughts. First I said that not everyone can praise God. Who are they? "First, there are those who will not praise Him unless He does well to them."[5] They are not the worst; others err to the opposite extreme. "They magnify themselves by reason of the good gifts of God and do not ascribe them to His goodness alone."[6] Both kinds are self-centered clods.

Mary contraposes those whom God opposes—the wise, mighty, and rich—with those whom He honors—the poor in spirit, the oppressed, and those who lack the necessities of life. Later in my treatise, I graded the three whom God opposes. "For the rich are the least His enemies; the mighty are much more hostile; but those smart alecks are the worst of all because of their influence on others."[7]

God hasn't changed. Your wealth, dangerous as it may be, need not condemn you. It all depends on how you use it. If for your own comforts and aggrandizements, it is fatal; if for the poor in spirit, the oppressed, and those lacking bodily necessities, then your life is aligned with that of Jesus and your wealth is a blessing. If God has given you a position of political power, use that power for those who have no power of their own. If you are in a position where you teach, or in some other way influence others, you are in the most dangerous position of all. You handle the truth, more precious than riches or power. Regarding the wise ones, I said, "But these wise ones utterly extinguish the truth itself and replace it with other things, the imagination of their own heart, so that the truth cannot come into its own again."[8] There may be hope for "the wise ones," but it will come only by walking down the never-ending, difficult path of humility.

I concluded my comments on Mary's song by writing about six works of God that I took from that song: mercy, breaking spiritual pride, putting down the mighty, exalting the lowly, filling the hungry, and sending the rich away empty.[9]

It is one thing to read or sing Mary's beautiful song, but quite another thing to live it. Go now and live it.

---

5 LW 21:307.

6 LW 21:308.

7 LW 21:343.

8 LW 21:343.

9 LW 21:332–55.

I included a warning against too great a devotion to Mary. I wrote, "Hence all those who heap such great praise and honor upon her head are not far from making an idol of her, as though she were concerned that men should honor her and look to her for good things, when in truth she thrusts this from her and would have us honor God in her and come through her to a good confidence in His grace."[10]

Next time, I will tell you about my departure from the Wartburg castle.

10 LW 21:322.

Letter 66

In November, I was mad, first-class mad. Three things raised my ire. I had sent three manuscripts to Spalatin and asked him to forward them to Melanchthon for publication. The three were *On Monastic Vows*, *On the Abrogation of Private Masses*, and *Against the Idol in Halle*. They had not been published. In early November, I had received a letter from Spalatin saying that the elector did not want the treatises published because they might disturb the peace. I responded immediately on 11 November and said, "Your idea about not disturbing the public peace is beautiful, but will you allow the eternal peace of God to be disturbed by the wicked and sacrilegious actions of that son of perdition [Albrecht]? Not so, Spalatin! Not so, Elector!"[1] Second, I learned that there had been some unrest in Wittenberg relating to how the sacrament of the Mass should be celebrated. A professor from your day has noted that in the Augustinian monastery, "Zwilling delivered impassioned pleas to the brothers to refuse to celebrate unless the Mass was reformed. The prior responded that he would rather have no mass than to have it mutilated."[2] "The Elector was disturbed," noted the same professor. "As a prince he was responsible for the public peace. As a Christian he was concerned for the true faith."[3] Neither a committee nor the university faculty nor the Augustinian monastery could decide what do. "What a mess we are in," said Spalatin, "with everybody doing something else."[4] Third, and this boiled my blood more than the other issues, Albrecht, the archbishop of Mainz, was at the old business of selling indulgences to raise money. I had written to him twice telling him to put a stop to the idolatry. In my third letter, on 1 December, I threatened to release another treatise against the selling of indulgences that I had already written, *Against the Idol in Halle*. I gave the archbishop two weeks to reply. He did not reply; therefore, I insisted that the treatise be published.

The anger, frustration, and concern for the reform in Wittenberg prompted me to visit the city. On 2 December, I took leave from the

---

1 LW 48:326.

2 Bainton, 203.

3 Bainton, 203.

4 Bainton, 204

Wartburg and arrived in Wittenberg on 4 December. I did not go to my brothers at the Augustinian monastery lest I be recognized. (I had long curly hair and a large beard. I stayed with my friend Melanchthon and saw very few folks.) I learned that Spalatin had not forwarded my manuscripts to Melanchthon. I excoriated him for his failure and threatened to write even more damning material if he did not forward them immediately. He did forward two, but with my grudging reluctance he withheld *Against the Idol in Halle*.

The day prior to my arrival in Wittenberg there had been an unfortunate event in the Town Church. In the dark of early morning on 3 December, some students and burghers prevented the priests from entering the Town Church for the reading of Mass. When some priests managed to gain entry and began to chant the Magnificat (the Office of Mary), those gathered outside began to pelt them with stones. In spite of that incident, I left Wittenberg quite pleased with how the reform movement was progressing. After about six days in Wittenberg, I returned to the Wartburg castle and arrived there on 11 December.

While I was still in Wittenberg, Melanchthon and Amsdorf wanted to play a joke on the famous painter Lucas Cranach. "They invited him to come and paint a picture of a famous visiting knight,"[5] noted another from your day. Because of that painting, you have my picture as Junker Jörg.

My visit was short but quite satisfying. Within a month of my return, Wittenberg experienced a world of confusion and disarray. I'll tell you about that next time. Until then, keep the faith.

---

5 Kittelson, 173.

Letter 67

Soon after my return to Wittenberg, I received a happy surprise. Archbishop Albrecht responded to my letter of 1 December. "My dear doctor," he began, "I have received your letter, and I take it in good part and graciously, and will see to it that the thing that so moves you be done away, and I will act, God willing, as becomes a pious, spiritual and Christian prince."[1] The sale of indulgences in Halle was stopped. Even bishops can sometimes be moved by the Spirit of God. Twenty years later, I learned that Albrecht was again up to his old tricks of selling indulgence letters. By then the game was over; everyone knew that indulgence letters were bogus and worthless. Someone noted, "This time his (my) mood rang with the liberating laughter of a winner. Now he no longer had to view the indulgence game as posing a serious threat to souls."[2]

After my return, I was not content for long. Two incidents caused me concern. Three men came to Wittenberg from Zwickau. They claimed to have received direct revelation from God. Because of this immediate revelation from God they had no need for the Bible. Melanchthon didn't know how to handle the situation. I was not deeply concerned; I thought the best was to simply put the three in jail. The issue proved to be more serious than I first thought.

The second issue was more serious. Initially it seemed innocuous, but it caused a great disaster. On Christmas Day 1521, Karlstadt officiated at the Castle Church worship service without wearing the normal priestly vestments, told the people that there was no need to fast or make confession before receiving the sacrament, and distributed the sacrament in "both kinds." Karlstadt did not know how to lead a reform. Excessive enthusiasm is dangerous. People need to be educated before making structural changes. On 11 January, the monks in the Augustinian monastery, under the leading of Gabriel Zwilling, but with the backing of Karlstadt, "led an iconoclastic riot, overturning altars and smashing images and pictures of the saints."[3] "Coupled with this attack on art in religion," says one of your professors, "went an attack also on music in religion. 'Relegate organs, trumpets, and flutes to the theater,' said Carlstadt."[4]

---

1 Smith 2:80.

2 Bornkamm, 43.

3 Bainton, 207.

4 Bainton, 208.

The Elector Frederick forbade Karlstadt from preaching, and Zwilling left Wittenberg.

I knew that I had to return. I had previously planned to return before Easter, but when I learned of the riot and the disturbance created by the Zwickau self-proclaimed prophets, I knew that I must return as soon as possible.

The Town Council in Wittenberg had a strong preference for the reform movement, although I think that they did not understand the full significance of what was at stake in that reform. The confusion created great consternation within the Council, and even the elector did not know what to do.

Frederick dismissed the idea that I should return. Nevertheless, as noted by one of your own, "The council knew nowhere to look for leadership save to the Wartburg, and without consulting or even informing the elector invited Luther to return."[5]

On 5 March, I wrote to the elector and told him, respectfully, that I was returning to Wittenberg. The substance of what I said is contained in these short words,

> I have written this so Your Electoral Grace might know that I am going to Wittenberg under a far higher protection than the Elector's. I have no intention of asking Your Electoral Grace for protection. Indeed I think I shall protect Your Electoral Grace more than you are able to protect me. And if I thought that Your Electoral Grace could and would protect me, I should not go. The sword ought not and cannot help a matter of this kind.[6]

On 6 March, I returned to Wittenberg.

I knew that my return created a problem for my sovereign. Remember, I was an outlaw by virtue of the Edict of Worms and a heretic by virtue of my excommunication from the Roman Church. Frederick was a Roman Catholic prince and was expected to honor both the excommunication by the church and the edict of the Empire. A day after my return, His Electoral Grace sent a letter to Jerome Schurff, professor of law at our university, instructing him to tell me to prepare a letter addressed to the sovereign explaining why I had returned. I will share with you just

---

5 Bainton, 210.

6 LW 48:391.

two sentences of his letter that will show his intent to protect himself from the emperor and the Roman Church. The last words of the first sentence show his benevolence toward me.

> But inasmuch as the doctor is now in Wittenberg without our previous knowledge, it is our desire that on the authority of this letter you give him our gracious greeting and this oral message. He is to send us a letter in which he sets forth the reasons for his return to Wittenberg and the fact that it is without our permission; he is also to exercise some self-restraint and say that he does not wish to give anyone any trouble, and the letter is to be so formulated that we can show it to some of our friends, the princes, in order to maintain our honor.[7]

I responded immediately and complied with my gracious lord's request.

---

7 Smith 2:96.

Letter 68

The reform movement gave birth to some very ugly children, some even malformed. In my previous letter, I mentioned three young men who came to Wittenberg from Zwickau when I was still at the Wartburg castle. One of the three men, Marcus Thomae, had been a student at the University of Wittenberg; Melanchthon remembered him from his student days. Everyone called Thomae "Stübner," because his father owned a bathhouse. In my native language, a bathhouse is called a *Badstube*. The other two were Nicholas Storch and Thomas Drechsel, both unlearned weavers by trade.

When the three came to Wittenberg, Melanchthon was at first impressed by their knowledge of the Bible and their certainty that God had spoken to them apart from the Scriptures. Their religious fervor captivated Melanchthon. Give him credit, however, because he became suspicious when the three objected to infant Baptism. They argued that Luther had said that faith is necessary for the sacraments to accomplish their work. They said that infants could not have faith.

Please think kindly of Melanchthon. Although he was a brilliant young man, he was, nevertheless, a young man, only about twenty-four years old, when the three came from Zwickau. Additionally, Philip was primarily a humanist, teaching classical languages. Yes, he was a fast learner and was not only studying theology but, by 1521, he was already lecturing in the department of theology. But he was of different temperament than I and always ready to listen to another point of view. All those factors contributed to his confusion when the three, sometimes called "heavenly prophets," arrived in town. Not knowing how to handle the situation, he asked Prince Frederick to have me returned from the Wartburg to the university. As always, Frederick did not act just because another thought a situation to be critical.

The man behind the scenes, and responsible for the fanatical claims of the three, was their pastor in Zwickau, Thomas Münzer. Thomas had become a very dangerous man; he was overwhelmed by enthusiasm, but that enthusiasm was ignited by a malignant spirit. Another of your historians has correctly noted, "He [Münzer] also encouraged Storch to conduct secret meetings in order to teach others the steps of mystical immersion: amazement, disengagement, contemplation, endurance, and so on, down to 'the very righteousness of God.'"[1] Imagine! Teaching people "how to." That reduces the Christian faith to a technique to be taught, like teaching a person how to play a musical instrument. Those misguided folks who talk so much about the work of the Holy Spirit now seize the teaching from the Holy Spirit and put it into their own hands. I get angry thinking about the mess that Münzer instigated. I will tell you more about him in a later letter.

The three "heavenly prophets" did not stay long in Wittenberg. They blew through like a tornado, did their damage, and left. I don't think Storch and Drechsel were in Wittenberg more than a few days. Tornados do great damage in a short time. Stübner remained and continued his prophesying.

One of the results of their presence was a disaster for my Augustinian monastery. Another of your historians wrote, "When in November, 1521, the Zwickau prophets stirred up the student body of the University of Wittenberg, thirteen Augustinian monks joined the movement, departing from the monastery amid considerable commotion."[2] Be alert, dear friends, disorder and commotion do not come from the Spirit of God.

The fantastic claims made by Stübner earned him the humorous disdain of the students. Melanchthon protected the poor soul by taking him into his own home. I do not remember whether Philip ever told me about the incident, but one from your day, who does a lot of research, said, "But Melanchthon himself must have laughed when, one day at table, Thomae (Stübner) awoke from a brief nap and announced that now he was John Chrysostom—with a sad face of one in purgatory."[3] (John Chrysostom was a famous fourth-century preacher and bishop.) That story was news to me, but it fits the Stübner I knew.

In April 1522, Stübner returned to Wittenberg, accompanied by another friend, and tried to convince me of his prophetic powers. I listened to them with skepticism the first day. After meeting with the two a second day, I had heard more than enough. I said, "I have spoken with the devil incarnate."[4] One of your historians said of me, "He dismissed those

---

1 Bornkamm, 57.

2 Schwiebert, 225–26.

3 Bornkamm, 60.

4 Bornkamm, 77.

two fickle spirits with the scorn worthy of an Old Testament prophet: I forbid your god to perform any miracles contrary to the will of my God."[5]

That's enough to tell you about the three who spent so little time in Wittenberg but did untold damage to the cause of the reform of the church.

Enthusiasm for the Christian faith should be encouraged, but enthusiasm without a firm grounding in the Word of God can become malignant. The benefit and tragedy of enthusiasm is that it can affect so many people. Enthusiasm for worship, enthusiasm for sharing the faith, and enthusiasm for serving other people all need the greatest encouragement. But unbridled enthusiasm—what I called "Schwärmerei" (which suggests the swarming of insects)—can destroy not only people's faith but their lives and property as well.

Beware of well-read, talented orators in your day who know nothing about the Gospel but preach hatred and spread division among believers.

---

5 Bornkamm, 77.

Letter 69

In November 1521, while still at the Wartburg, I wrote a little piece that I called a pamphlet, but you may call it an open letter. I entitled it *A Sincere Admonition by Martin Luther to All Christians to Guard against Insurrection and Rebellion.*[1]

I thought seriously about omitting mention of this little piece, but I decided to include a brief comment on it because I know that you are experiencing insurrection in your day, even in the New World.

The opening sentence will make it clear that there was no specific addressee: "May God grant grace and peace to all Christians who read this pamphlet or hear it read."[2]

I did not want to incite undue fear; therefore, I said near the beginning, "I think—indeed I am sure and have no fear whatsoever on this score—that there will not be any insurrection or rebellion, at least none that would be general and affect the entire pack."[3]

Some might remember that only about three or four months later, in a letter to the elector, one of the reasons that I gave for returning to Wittenberg, in spite of his objection, was my certainty that there would be rebellion in the German lands. I said to the elector, "The third reason [for my return]: I am rather afraid (and I worry that unfortunately I may be only too right) that there will be a real rebellion in the German territories, by which God will punish the German nation."[4]

Why the sudden change in tone? Events can and do change the course of history, sometimes within minutes. You have your Pearl Harbor and the attack on the Twin Towers. Between my open letter and the letter to the elector, unexpected events occurred. Karlstadt and Zwilling incited destruction in Wittenberg in late December. The self-proclaimed Zwickau prophets, enflamed by that evil-spirited Thomas Münzer, created conflict in the city. I had heard of Münzer's antics in Zwickau but expected that it was only a local matter. When he sent those three young

1 LW 45:49–75.

2 LW 45:57.

3 LW 45:58.

4 LW 48:396.

men to Wittenberg, I could smell rebellion moving beyond that small community. I was right, and in a subsequent letter, I will tell you more about the rebellion that smoldered for a year or two before it broke out in full insurrection and rebellion.

There was much in the open letter that pertained only to my day, but I will share with you a few sentences that are foundational to the whole letter, and pertain to you as much as they did to believers in my day. "Hence, no insurrection is ever right, no matter how right the cause it seeks to promote."[5] "If you start anything on your own hook you are already in the wrong, and are much worse than your opponents. I am and always will be on the side of those against whom insurrection is directed, no matter how unjust their cause; I am opposed to those who rise in insurrection, no matter how just their cause; because there can be no insurrection without hurting the innocent and shedding their blood."[6] Finally, I said, "Now insurrection is nothing else than being one's own judge and avenger, and that is something God cannot tolerate. Therefore, insurrection cannot help but make matters much worse, because it is contrary to God; God is not on the side of insurrection."[7]

Let God be God and bring judgment on whom He pleases, when He pleases. As for you, live in peace with all people.

---

5 LW 45:63.

6 LW 45:63.

7 LW 45:63.

Letter 70

After ten months of near seclusion in the Wartburg castle, I was thrilled to be back in Wittenberg with my colleagues, friends, and students. One from your day has said, "During the ten months at the Wartburg, all alone with his God, Luther the Reformer of later years was born."[1] I'm not certain that he was accurate in that assessment. Of course, every event in life prepares one for succeeding years. In that sense he was correct, but also rather banal. Second, the comment sounds as though all I did was pray and meditate all day long while secluded. Prayer was a very important part of my life, but not more so at the Wartburg than in Wittenberg. I was as busy writing at the Wartburg as I was back at the university.

Another from your day has said, "For Luther a fortunate year was unfolding. [It was 1522, and] peace had been restored in Wittenberg."[2] That professor was correct; 1522 was a good year. That same professor noted that on 10 May, I had written to Spalatin and said, "Here there is nothing but love and friendship."[3] That was quite different from five months earlier.

By now you have noted that I am not a historian. It has not been my intention to present you with a history of the whole Reformation movement. My intention has been only to share with you a bit about my life and introduce you to some of the things that I wrote. Occasionally, I have mentioned individuals, movements, or events that might help you understand my actions and writings, but those comments need further elaboration than I can provide in these short letters. There are many excellent books on the history of the reform movement. You will not be able to understand how the reform movement succeeded without consulting those books. They will tell you about all the political, economic, and philosophical forces at play prior to and during the Reformation Era. You will understand better what I wrote and why I wrote when you know what was going on in Europe at that time.

---

1 Schwiebert, 520.

2 Bornkamm, 89.

3 Bornkamm, 89.

Three days after my arrival in Wittenberg, I was back in the pulpit. It was *Invocavit* Sunday. Regrettably, most people in your day have forgotten the ancient names for the Sundays of the Church Year. *Invocavit* Sunday is the first Sunday in Lent.

From *Invocavit* Sunday to *Reminiscere* Sunday, I preached eight consecutive days. Someone who wrote an introduction to those sermons said, "This remarkable series of sermons, which are powerful, inspired preaching of the gospel, had the effect of restoring tranquility and order almost at once."[4]

Someone has said that I preached almost two thousand sermons. I have no idea; I never counted. I do want to give you just a sample of my preaching. In my next letter, I intend to share with you a bit of what I said during those eight days in March 1522. In order to understand those sermons, you must remember the context in which they were preached: I had just returned from ten months away from my congregation, and Wittenberg had recently been convulsed by some strange self-proclaimed prophets.

This has been a brief interlude letter. I wanted to give you a little respite before I share with you some of my other writings during succeeding years. Believe me, I did slow down in publishing and spent more time promoting the reform movement in surrounding communities and preparing material for the same.

---

4 LW 51:69–70.

Letter 71

The eight sermons that I preached from *Invocavit* Sunday through *Reminiscere* Sunday, immediately following my return to Wittenberg from the Wartburg castle, must be understood against the violent acts that had taken place in Wittenberg around Christmas Day 1521 and the weeks following. Under the leadership of Professor Andreas Karlstadt and the Augustinian monk Gabriel Zwilling, sacred images had been torn from churches, priests stoned, altars desecrated, folks were told to come to Communion without making confession of their sin, and almost forced to receive the sacrament in both kinds—bread and wine (contrary to the practice of many centuries of laypeople receiving only the bread). Chaos was replacing reform.

The main themes in my eight sermons were these: Reform is accomplished by the Word of God alone, not by simply changing practices. Practices can and should be changed after the freedom given to us by the Gospel is clearly perceived. Second, a clear distinction must be made between what is required of a Christian and wherein freedom lies. Only that which is commanded by God is a "must." In all other matters, Christians are free, with the understanding that Christian freedom requires restraint out of consideration for one's neighbor.

While still at the Wartburg, I had written *Faithful Exhortation for All Christians to Shun Riot and Rebellion*. About a hundred years before your day, a scholar wrote an introduction to my *Eight Sermons* and said of the content of that treatise, "He emphasizes the principles reiterated in the Eight Sermons, the sufficiency of the Word and the duty of dealing gently with the weak."[1] I want to share with you a few of the things that I said in those sermons.

In the first sermon, I began with four fundamental themes of our faith. First, we must all die alone. I said,

> The summons of death comes to us all, and no one can die for another. Every one must fight his own battle with death by himself, alone. We can shout into another's ears, but every one must himself be prepared for the time of death, for I will not be with you then, nor you with me.[2]

---

1 PE 2:389.

2 LW 51:70.

> Secondly, that God has sent us his only-begotten Son that we may believe in him and that whoever trusts in him shall be free from sin and a child of God. . . .
>
> Thirdly, we must also have love and through love we must do to one another as God has done to us through faith. . . .
>
> Fourthly, we also need patience."[3]

Karlstadt, Zwilling, and the other rioters in Wittenberg did not recognize the difference between reform and revolution. Reform takes time and patience; revolution takes matters out of God's hands and forces immediate change.

With that setting, I continued for eight successive days preaching the need for reform, but refusing to force reform. On Monday, I said, "In short, I will preach it, teach it, write it, but I will constrain no man by force, for faith must come freely without compulsion."[4]

On Tuesday, when writing about images in churches, I pled for restraint. There is no divine command about images; only a command not to worship them. Let images be retained or removed; it is a matter of freedom. Rash destruction of altars and images only strengthen the resolve of those who want to keep them. I said, "And you rush, create an uproar, break down altars, and overthrow images! Do you really believe you can abolish the altars in this way? No, you will only set them up more firmly."[5] I concluded that sermon by saying, "This is what we must preach and teach, and let the Word alone do the work, as I said before. The Word must first capture the hearts of men and enlighten them; we will not be the ones who will do it."[6]

On Wednesday, I continued to talk about images. I said that in my opinion they should be removed because their presence in churches had deflected worship of God to the images of saints who had thereby become idols. Nevertheless, abuse itself does not make anything evil in itself. To illustrate, I said, "Again, wine and women bring many a man to misery and make a fool of him [Ecclus. 19:2; 31:30]; so we kill all the women and pour out all the wine. Again, gold and silver cause much evil, so we condemn them. Indeed, if we want to drive away our worst enemy,

---

3 LW 51:71.

4 LW 51:77.

5 LW 51:83.

6 LW 51:83.

the one who does us the most harm, we shall have to kill ourselves, for we have no greater enemy than our own heart."[7] In that sermon I made one additional point, and I think it is very important in exercising Christian freedom. If a religious requirement is laid upon you, a man-made law and not a divine law, then you must do exactly the opposite to show the freedom that God gives to Christians. On the other hand, you must be cautious not to offend the conscience of a "weak" brother or sister, or perhaps a new convert to the faith. In such cases, you must restrain your freedom out of respect for your brother or sister. Christian freedom always requires responsibility to others; responsibility to the "stubborn" to show your freedom in Christ; responsibility to the "weak" in restraint of that freedom. The distinction requires great wisdom.

The last four sermons, Thursday through Sunday, I preached mostly on the sacrament. I'll share just a few thoughts that I included in those sermons. In *The Babylonian Captivity of the Church*, I said that all Christians, not only priests, should receive the full sacrament in both bread and wine. Karlstadt had made that into a law and required that all receive both kinds. In the sermon, I said, "For if you desire to be regarded as better Christians than others just because you take the sacrament into your hands and also receive it in both kinds, you are bad Christians as far as I am concerned. In his way even a sow could be a Christian, for she has a big enough snout to receive the sacrament outwardly."[8]

The most elementary elements of our Christian faith need endless repeating. On Friday, I had to remind my congregation that simply eating the bread and drinking the wine does not have a life-saving quality; faith is required. I think it is no different in your day. I said,

> There is no external sign by which we Christians may be distinguished from others except this sacrament and baptism, but without faith outward reception is nothing. There must be faith to make the reception worthy and acceptable before God, otherwise it is nothing but sham and a mere external show, which is not Christianity at all.[9]

---

7 LW 51:85.

8 LW 51:91.

9 LW 51:92.

On Saturday, I preached about love being the fruit of the sacrament, and on *Reminiscere* Sunday, I preached on private confession. I regret that many who use my name no longer even offer private confession. Perhaps that is a reaction against the Roman Church's requirement that one must make confession to a priest at least once a year. That, my dear friends, is an overreaction, and the reason for the omission of private confession has long since been forgotten. Pastors deprive thousands the blessing of making personal confession of their sins and hearing the blessed words of forgiveness spoken directly to them personally. In the sermon, I said that I would refuse to make confession because the pope required it of me. However, I said,

> Nevertheless I will allow no man to take private confession away from me, and I would not give it up for all the treasurers in the world, since I know what comfort and strength it has given me. No one knows what it can do for him except one who has struggled often and long with the devil. Yea, the devil would have slain me long ago, if the confession had not sustained me.[10]

I concluded my final sermon with the words "I commend you to God. Amen."[11] So also, my brothers and sister in the New World, I commend you to God. Amen.

10 LW 51:98.

11 LW 51:100.

Letter 72

The reform movement had taken root in Wittenberg and surrounding communities. The fact that it had retained its strength during my ten-month absence is clear evidence that the reform of the church was not mine, but the work of God's Spirit.

The gracious Gospel that people are set free from the consequence of their sin by faith alone in the saving death and resurrection of Jesus is more than a theological doctrine to be taught and memorized; it had many practical applications. I considered it my responsibility to help people identify and understand those implications and make appropriate adjustments.

One place that continued to need reformed practices was the monasteries.

About two months after my return to Wittenberg from the Wartburg castle, I wrote *Avoiding the Doctrines of Men*.[1] That short treatise was intended primarily for monks. I began, "I, Martin Luther, have published this little book for the comfort and saving of those poor consciences who are held captive in monasteries and convents by man-made laws."[2] The specific content of that treatise related to specific prohibitions and requirements imposed upon the monks, but had no basis in the Scriptures. Two or three sentences from the treatise will give you an idea of monastic man-made laws, and the way the observance of those laws could be avoided. I referred to Matthew 15 [:11], where we hear Jesus say, "Not what goes into the mouth defiles a man, but what comes out of the mouth, this defiles a man." I followed by saying, "It liberates all consciences from all laws concerning food and drink. So it is allowable to eat milk, butter, eggs, cheese, and meat any day, be it Sunday or Friday, Lent or Advent; and no one needs to pay butter money or buy letters for that purpose."[3] Regarding "butter money" and "buy letters," a scholar from your day has noted correctly, "Indulgences could be purchased permitting the off-season use of butter, etc. Such dispensations (*Butterbriefe*)

1 LW 35:131–47.

2 LW 35:131.

3 LW 35:133.

granted upon condition of a trifling alms to a specific object, were a favorite means of raising money."[4] I continued by saying, "Second, it follows that for the pope to sell letters and grant permission to eat butter, meat, and so forth, is sheer knavery of the devil. For in this verse Christ has already permitted it and made it a matter of liberty."[5]

The issues that I addressed in this treatise are of little concern to you in your day, and for that reason I almost chose to neglect mention of it. But I have heard that there are still peddlers of man-made laws.

Some even claim that it is a sin to drink beer. Good gracious! Haven't they read Matthew 5? If drinking beer is a sin, all Germans would go to hell.

I cannot identify all the man-made laws that overzealous Christians try to impose upon others in your day. But you must be alert. Whenever the Gospel is presented in negative terms—"Christians cannot . . . must not . . . should not . . ."—be alert to requirements imposed upon the Gospel. The Gospel is always positive; it is the good news of what God has done for you.

A few months later, I preached on Matthew 7 in which Jesus says, "Beware of false prophets." In that sermon, I referred to St. Augustine and quoted him, saying, "I should not have believed the gospel, had I not been moved by the great authority of Christendom." Someone or some group, I have forgotten which, tried to defend man-made laws by quoting Luke 10, where Jesus said, "The one who hears you hears Me, and the one who rejects you rejects Me."[6] I defended my position with another very brief writing that I called *A Reply to the Texts Cited in Defense of the Doctrines of Men*. I can summarize that brief defense with one sentence. "We do not condemn the doctrines of men just because they are the doctrines of men, for we would gladly put up with them. But we condemn them because they are contrary to the gospel and the Scriptures."[7]

That's enough for now. But remember: reject all man-made laws that becloud the Holy Gospel. Take your stand on this one great principle: The Word of God Alone!

---

4 LW 35:133, n. 5.

5 LW 35:133.

6 LW 35:147.

7 LW 35:153.

LETTER 73

Another institution that needed reform was Christian marriage. The Roman Church encumbered marriage with numerous restrictions and requirements. Shortly before I was born, an Italian, Angelo Carletti di Chivasso, an authority on canon and civil law,[1] created a handbook for priests to use when hearing confession. Regarding marriage the author listed eighteen impediments to marriage, eighteen conditions under which marriage was prohibited or for which an annulment could be allowed.[2]

In the summer of 1522, I wrote *The Estate of Marriage*[3] to address this abuse. I began by saying, "How I dread preaching on the estate of marriage."[4] Nevertheless, I continued, "But timidity is no help in an emergency; I must proceed. I must try to instruct poor bewildered consciences, and take up the matter boldly."[5]

The specific impediments from five hundred years earlier are of no interest to you, but I will share two things that I said in the first part of the treatise. First, and perhaps this is even more egregious than the impediments, for the impediments could be removed for filthy money. I wrote, "Indeed, the pope himself does not adhere to them so strictly or firmly but what one can rescind any of them with gold and silver."[6] As I concluded the first part of the treatise I said, "It is a dirty rotten business that a bishop should forbid me a wife or specify the times when I may marry, or that a blind and [mute] person should not be allowed to enter into wedlock."[7]

In the second part of the treatise, I laid out three conditions that allowed for divorce: if one is or becomes a eunuch, in cases of adultery or, as I put it, "[a case] in which one of the parties deprives and avoids the other, refusing to fulfill the conjugal duty or to live with the other person."[8]

I have been told that in your culture and in your day divorce is almost

1 LW 45:22, n. 7.

2 LW 36:96, n. 166.

3 LW 45:11–49.

4 LW 45:17.

5 LW 45:17.

6 LW 45:22.

7 LW 45:30.

8 LW 45:33.

as common as marriage. That may be acceptable for pagans, but Christians are to regard marriage as a sacred, lifelong covenant. Marriage may not be a sacrament, but it certainly has a sacramental like quality. I cannot say more.

In the third part, I spoke about the blessedness of marriage. That was in contrast to the Roman Church, which taught marriage to be inferior to the state of virginity. I affirmed marriage as not only a gift of God but also a command. God said, "Be fruitful and multiply." It is within the bounds of marriage that God continues His work of creation. I said, "But the greatest good in married life, that which makes all suffering and labor worth while, is that God grants offspring and commands that they be brought up to worship and serve him."[9] Further, I said that parents are raised to the position of bishops when they raise their children in the holy faith. I used these words, "Most certainly father and mother are apostles, bishops, and priests to their children, for it is they who make them acquainted with the gospel. In short, there is no greater or nobler authority on earth than that of parents over their children, for this authority is both spiritual and temporal."[10]

In setting people free from man-made laws that restricted marriage, and in speaking of the blessedness of marriage, I had no intention of minimizing the state of virginity. I only objected to the Roman teaching that virginity was a spiritual estate superior to marriage. Indeed, I affirmed the virgin and the celibate life. Near the end of the treatise I said,

> In saying this I do not wish to disparage virginity, or entice anyone away from virginity into marriage. Let each one act as he is able, and as he feels it has been given to him by God. I simply wanted to check those scandalmongers who place marriage so far beneath virginity that they dare to say: Even if the children should become holy [1 Cor. 7:14], celibacy would still be better.[11]

I told you at the beginning that I did not want to preach on marriage. I am no more a marriage counselor than I am a historian; I am a pastor. I care only that the Gospel sets people free to marry and enjoy that blessed estate. If what I have written helps to that end, my terrible task has been worthwhile.

---

9 LW 45:46.

10 LW 45:46.

11 LW 45:46–47.

Letter 74

The Holy Mass was central to the lives of believers in my day. But that great gift of God—the body and blood of Jesus, given to poor penitent believers for forgiveness and consolation of conscience—had degenerated into a moneymaking machine for priests who would "say" a private mass for individuals; the blood of Christ was withheld from the faithful and reserved for priests only, lest the precious blood be spilled; the body and blood of Christ were presented for adoration by the faithful; and worst of all, some were claiming that the sacrament was a mere memorial of Christ's death; bread and wine was no more than bread and wine.

You will not be surprised that I felt compelled to address that confused situation. You will also recall that I wrote extensively about the sacrament of the Lord's Supper in *The Babylonian Captivity of the Church* [see Letter 47]. From 1521 to 1526, I wrote four additional treatises on that sacrament. I'll share with you some additional issues that I addressed in those treatises without repeating what I said in *The Babylonian Captivity*.

In late 1521, while still at the Wartburg, I wrote *The Misuse of the Mass*.[1] Much of what I said in that treatise I had said in *The Babylonian Captivity*, but one thing I added, although almost only in passing. I said, "No mass, if it is to conform to the institution and example of Christ, should be held unless the sacrament is broken and distributed among many by the priest."[2] This was said against the practice of priests who would "say" a mass without anyone in attendance. The faithful would pay priests to say a mass "for" or "on behalf" of someone, perhaps in purgatory. No one would be present to even witness the mass, let alone to receive the bread or wine as Jesus directed when he said "take and eat."

The second treatise was *Receiving Both Kinds in the Sacrament*.[3] I wrote this in response to the action of Karlstadt on Christmas Day 1521. Without proper education of the laity, he thrust the host into the hands of the recipients (against the practice of the priest placing the host in the mouth) and gave the cup to the faithful (against the tradition of many centuries of the priests alone receiving the cup). Karlstadt's theology

---

1 LW 36:133–230.

2 LW 36:171.

3 LW 36:231–67.

was right, but his pastoral practice was wrong. I said, "It would do just as much harm suddenly to impose on the whole church the reception of both elements, in accordance with the gospel, when the church consists of such weak, captive consciences."[4] Good pastoral care might require the use of bad theology for a while until the faithful are brought to a clear understanding of the Gospel. I put it in these words: "We must let the old misuse of the sacrament go on for a while yet, until the vessels, at least most of them, have become new and the gospel has taken root among the people."[5]

In 1523, I wrote *The Adoration of the Sacrament*.[6] The adoration of the sacrament was a consequence of the Roman teaching of transubstantiation. Once the priest transubstantiated the elements, the bread was no longer bread, but the body of Christ; the wine was no longer wine, but the blood of Christ. Consequently when the sacrament was adored, it was Christ that was adored. I thought transubstantiation to be a mere philosophical trick to explain what is inexplicable. However, I never wavered on the word of Christ that He is really present in the bread and wine. I preferred not to adore the sacrament because adoration could take one's mind from the words of Christ. The Word does everything. Consequently, I said, "Not that adoration is wrong, but simply because there is less danger in not adoring than in adoring."[7] I regret that trivial issues create such a conflict in the Body of Christ. I said, "The first group would like to compel people not to adore the sacrament, as if Christ were not there at all; and the other group would like to compel people to adore it, as if Christ's state of glory were in the sacrament as it is in heaven. With this kind of quarreling they both get off the track, so that they emphasize the sacrament and neglect the words."[8] The adoration of the sacrament is certainly one issue on which Christian freedom should be allowed.

In *The Abomination of the Secret Mass*,[9] written in 1525, I took issue with how priests celebrated the Mass. I must offer a clarification for you. What most of you call a worship service the Roman Church calls a Mass.

---

4 LW 36:251.

5 LW 36:252.

6 LW 36:269–307.

7 LW 36:297.

8 LW 36:295.

9 LW 36:309–28.

Within the worship service, you celebrate the sacrament of the Lord's Supper. That portion may be called the Eucharist, or the Communion, or simply the Lord's Supper. The Roman Mass of my day contained a longer prayer called the *canon* that referred to the Mass as a sacrifice by the priest for the sins of the people. It also called upon dead saints for their help. An editor of my treatise in your day has said, regarding the Canon of the Mass, "For the Roman Catholic it was so holy that the priest read it in a whisper."[10] He is correct. I made reference to that practice when I wrote, "Now we shall recount the words that the papists secretly read in the secret mass which they call the canon, the words which they hold to be so high and holy that they forbid the laity to know them."[11] The poor worshiping community sat in silence not knowing what was happening. There was no word to believe, only the silent action of the priest. I took it upon myself to print out the entire canon and made very critical comments about many parts of the canon. The greatest abomination, and I said this in almost every treatise that I wrote about the sacrament, was the alleged offering of the sacrifice of Christ to God, rather than receiving the gift of God in Christ for the forgiveness of sin. It is the greatest difference between giving and receiving. I used these words. "This is one part of the abomination, that they offer bread and wine to God as a pure sacrifice and yet they beseech God to be pleased with it and bless it."[12] I preferred that the entire Mass be eliminated and a new order of worship be prepared for the faithful.

Satan never stops attacking the Church of Jesus Christ. By 1524, the father of lies had diverted some leaders of the evangelical movement to deny that Christ is really present in the bread and wine of the sacrament. They were deluded by the teaching of Ulrich Zwingli in Switzerland. Even Karlstadt was teaching that Jesus words "This is My body" did not mean what they say, but that the bread must be understood as a symbol of Christ's body. Some were even claiming that Zwingli's teaching represented my view of the sacrament. By 1526, I knew that I must respond. I wrote *The Sacrament of the Body and Blood of Christ—Against the Fanatics*.[13] In the very first paragraph, I wrote, "In foreign lands a large number are already pouncing upon it and maintaining that Christ's body and blood are not present in the bread and wine, the times demand

---

10 LW 36:310.

11 LW 36:314.

12 LW 36:316.

13 LW 36:329–61.

that I say something on this subject also."[14] The main argument of the fanatics was that to believe the words of Jesus as they stand is not reasonable. I concluded my argument against them by saying, "Hence, to sum it all up, what those people keep saying—that because it is not in accord with reason it is not true—we shall simply turn about and say the opposite: God's word is true, therefore your notions must be false."[15] I had no other argument than the words of Jesus. I wrote, "In these words ["my body and blood given for you"] his body and blood are given to us. So there are two things to be believed: that it is truly present, which the papists also believe; and that it is given to us, which they do not believe, and that we should use it as a gift."[16] I also said that whenever the sacrament is offered, preaching should be included. It is the Word that accomplishes what is promised in the sacrament.

Keep the faith, even when reason is offended.

---

14 LW 36:335.

15 LW 36:343.

16 LW 36:347–48.

Letter 75

I fear that you might think of me as an academic theologian engaged with my opponents only to win a contest. I assure you that I cared nothing about winning anything; I hated the contests. I engaged in the battle for the souls of the dear people in my congregation and those throughout the German lands. My writings were not only on the theological issues that had been so badly distorted by the papacy over the previous four hundred years, but I also wrote some very practical helps for my people.

In the summer of 1522, I prepared a *Personal Prayer Book*[1] for the laity. For many centuries, the Roman Church had prepared and widely distributed prayer books. A historian in your day who prepared an introduction to my *Personal Prayer Book* wrote, "Such prayer books were regarded as essential for any layman who wished to save his soul."[2] In my day, those prayer books told the faithful when to pray, to which saint their prayers should be addressed, and what benefit they would gain by their prayers. Those prayer books removed the focus from Jesus Christ. I knew that I must prepare an evangelical prayer book.

My people did not have a benefit that you have; they had no Bible in their homes, but they knew the Lord's Prayer, the Creed, and the Ten Commandments. In my introductory comments to the *Prayer Book*, I said, "Indeed, the total content of Scripture and preaching and everything a Christian needs to know is quite fully and adequately comprehended in these three items."[3]

In that introduction, I continued, saying, "Three things a person must know in order to be saved. First, he must know what to do and what to leave undone. Second, when he realizes that he cannot measure up to what he should do or leave undone, he needs to know where to go to find the strength he requires. Third, he must know how to seek and obtain that strength."[4] The Ten Commandments tells what must be done and left undone. The Creed shows where the required help is to be found:

---

1 LW 43:3–45.

2 LW 43:6.

3 LW 43:13.

4 LW 43:13.

in the triune God Himself. The Lord's Prayer provides the way to receive that strength.

With that introduction, I began with the Ten Commandments. After providing a brief comment on each commandment, I took each of the ten and showed specific ways in which each of the ten would be violated. I'll give you one example: the Third Commandment.

> Whoever does not listen to God's Word or try to understand it.
>
> Whoever does not offer prayer to God.
>
> Whoever does not regard all that he does as God's work.
>
> Whoever, in all he does and endures, does not quietly allow God to do with him as He pleases.
>
> Whoever does not help the other person do all this and does not restrain him from doing otherwise.

I followed that with specific ways in which each of the Ten Commandments could be fulfilled.

The Creed has everything to do with faith. I began that section by noting two different parts of faith. The first is what is to be believed and the second in whom that faith must be placed. It is that second part of faith that makes one a Christian. I wrote, "So that little word *in* is well chosen and should be noted carefully; we do not say, I believe God the Father, or I believe about the Father, but rather, I believe *in* God the Father, *in* Jesus Christ, *in* the Holy Spirit."[5]

I then gave a brief comment on what is meant in each phrase of the Creed.

When I presented the Lord's Prayer, I did as I had done with the other two. I gave brief comments on what it means to call God "Father," the same with the seven petitions of the prayer, and the significance of concluding with the "Amen."

You might be surprised that I included comments of the Hail Mary. Remember, I was a pastor. My people had been taught from childhood to pray to Mary. Pastoral ministry requires gentle care of people in order to bring them slowly to an evangelical understanding of the faith. My very first words in presenting the Hail Mary were these: "Take note of this: no one should put his trust or confidence in the Mother of God or in her merits, for such trust is worthy of God alone and is the lofty service due

---

5 LW 43:25.

only to him. Rather praise and thank God through Mary and the grace given to her."[6] I followed by saying, "Let not our hearts cleave to her, but through her penetrate to Christ and to God himself. Thus what the Hail Mary says is that all glory should be given to God, using these words: 'Hail, Mary, full of grace. The Lord is with thee [Luke 1:28]; blessed art thou among women and blessed is the fruit of thy womb, Jesus Christ. Amen.'"[7]

Before concluding with eight psalms that can be used in prayer, I said, "He who has no faith is advised to refrain from saying the Hail Mary and all other prayers because to such a person the words apply: Let his prayer be sin [Ps. 109:7]."[8]

As for you, pray often, fervently, and passionately. Your Father in heaven has promised to hear and honor your payers.

---

6 LW 43:39.

7 LW 43:39.

8 LW 43:40–41.

Letter 76

I get carried away telling you about what I wrote. I must continually remind you how God protected me and allowed me to continue my work. God almost always works behind the scenes to accomplish His purpose in the flow of history. Only a person of faith sees the hidden hand of God. Today I want to tell you about several political events that God used to protect me and the task He had entrusted to me.

Pope Leo X died while I was at the Wartburg, 1 December 1521. That event took the focus off of me. The whole Western world waited and wondered who would be the next one to sit in St. Peter's chair. In early January, Pope [Adrian] VI was installed. (Hadrian was from the Netherlands and was the only non-Italian pope until Pope John Paul II took the throne in your day, in 1978.) Some have called Hadrian a reform pope. Yes, Hadrian attempted to reform the curia. When he sent a legate to the Diet of Nürnberg in 1522, he instructed the legate to blame the problems of the church on the curia. Reform was necessary, but not the reform most desperately needed: a reform in the teaching practice of the church. Hadrian had no love for me and no stomach to review the teachings and practices of the Roman Church. In fact, he remained steadfast with the late Pope Leo in opposition to the evangelical faith. It didn't matter; Hadrian died in September 1523, less than two years after he took office. That event, again, gave a respite in my case as the waiting and wondering again gripped the Western world until Clement VII was elected only a few days after Hadrian's death. The question became, how would Clement handle "the Luther case"?

Now I must tell you about three German diets that met between 1522 and 1524 and how they affected the reform movement. All three diets met in Nürnberg.

The emperor was absent from the German lands, and few of the territorial princes were anxious to act on the decrees of the Diet of Worms. A Council of Regency had been established to govern during the emperor's absence.

The first of the three diets met in March. My name was hardly mentioned. The pressing issue was the advance of the Muslim Turks in Eastern Europe.

The second diet met in the winter of 1522–23. That diet was more productive. It had received a demand from the pope that the Edict of Worms be carried out. The counselors at the diet were masters of diplomacy. They prohibited me from preaching and then said under what conditions I could preach! One of your historians found the words of the diet and then concluded, "These formulations closely approach[ed] the reformation position."[1] You will understand that the diet dealt with many more serious issues than the reform movement in Germany, but those other issues were of little interest to me.

The third diet in Nürnberg met in 1524 and concluded with this formula regarding my activities: "The gospel should be preached in accord with the interpretation of the universal Church. Each prince in his own territory should enforce the Edict of Worms in so far as he might be able."[2] Note that little phrase, "in so far as he might be able." That gave some latitude to each sovereign. It was this diet that first used the phrase *cuius regio, eius religio* (whose the realm, his the religion). That phrase was formalized at the Diet of Speyer in 1526 and became the law of the Holy Roman Empire at the Peace of Augsburg in 1555.

The papal elections and the three Diets at Nürnberg gave some breathing room for those of us committed to the evangelical faith. That faith is a precious treasure given by God. Preserve it in your day as I did in my day.

Next, I will tell about some things that I wrote in 1523.

---

1 Bornkamm, 298.

2 Bainton, 316.

Letter 77

Are Christians obligated to obey secular authorities at all times and under all circumstances? That is an issue as relevant in your time as it was in mine.

I was challenged with that issue by some folks who claimed that I used the secular authorities when it was to my advantage but ignored them at my pleasure. When I wrote *To the Christian Nobility of the German Nation Concerning the Reform of the Christian Estate* [see Letter 45], I called on the secular authorities to take a stand against the papacy that had invaded secular government. You will recall that the papacy was after my skin. But at the Diet of Worms, I would not submit to the secular authorities. Could the charge of inconsistency stand? Was I guilty of using the secular authorities only to protect myself?

Those ignorant sophomores who make charges against me know nothing about the political situation in my day. The papacy exerted great political pressure of the nobles: dukes, princes, kings, and emperors. It was against the intrusion of the church into the affairs of the secular government that I had written.

To clarify the issue I considered it necessary to help the ignorant understand the difference between the two separate kingdoms through which God rules the world. Consequently, I wrote *Temporal Authority: To What Extent It Should Be Obeyed*.[1]

I had preached six sermons on the subject in October 1522. Duke John, brother of Frederick the Wise (Frederick died in 1525, and Duke John became my sovereign) heard the sermons and asked that they be published.[2] I complied with the request but only used the ideas from the sermons to create a full treatise on the subject.

I began by affirming the divine origin of secular authority. The familiar words of Paul, writing to the Church in Rome, served as the basis of my contention that all secular law comes from God: "Let every soul [*seele*] be subject to the governing authority, for there is no authority except from God; the authority which everywhere [*allenthalben*] exists has been ordained by God."[3]

---

1 LW 45:75–129.

2 LW 45:79.

3 LW 45:85–86.

I followed by saying that the law has two functions: first, to restrain evil; second, to humble people that they might recognize their sin and flee to the grace of God in Christ Jesus.[4]

Many times in this section I mentioned that a Christian engages in secular activity for the sake of his neighbor, sometimes even at the expense of his own person. One example of what I said in this regard will be enough. "In what concerns you and yours, you govern yourself by the gospel and suffer injustice toward yourself as a true Christian; in what concerns the person or property of others, you govern yourself according to love and tolerate no injustice toward your neighbor."[5]

After affirming the divine origin of secular law, I spent more time talking about how Christians should act in civil matters rather than focusing on those who exercise the secular authority.

In the second part of the treatise, I drew the line where secular authority must end and submit to another authority: the authority of the Gospel. Temporal authority is limited to temporal issues. Temporal authority has no business telling people what they must believe or how they choose to exercise their beliefs, so long as their practice does not impinge on the rights of others. I quoted St. Augustine, "No one can or ought to be forced to believe."[6] In affirming the rights of individual consciences, both Augustine and I were well ahead of our time. What is common in your day was revolutionary in mine.

You will recall that at the Diet of Worms, secular authority convicted me for my Christian teaching. On the other hand, bishops whose responsibility is to preserve, maintain, and promote the faith were more involved in secular issues than religious ones. I think that some bishops in your day do the same. I said of our bishops,

> For my ungracious lords, the pope and the bishops, are supposed to be bishops and preach God's word. This they leave undone, and have become temporal princes who govern with laws which concern only life and property. How completely they have turned things topsy-turvy! They are supposed to be ruling souls inwardly by God's word; so they rule castles, cities, lands, and people outwardly, torturing souls with unspeakable outrages.[7]

---

4 LW 45:90.

5 LW 45:96.

6 LW 45:108.

7 LW 45:109.

Now back to the beginning. I did not use temporal authority for my own good or for my own protection. When I wrote *To the Christian Nobility of the German Nation*, I called on the nobles to keep the church out of secular matters. When I wrote *Temporal Authority: To What Extent It Should Be Obeyed*, I told the secular authority to keep out of religious issues. It was as simple as that. This seems elementary to you; in my day, it was revolutionary.

I concluded my treatise by suggesting a few ways in which princes (in your case, executives, representatives, and judges) should exercise the authority God has given to them.

Letter 78

You cannot imagine how many lies were told about me. Most were just gossip; I ignored them. But when one lie had the smell of official sanction, I knew that I must respond. Archduke Ferdinand had publicly accused me of teaching that Jesus was the natural-born child of Joseph.[1]

That was in addition to rumors spread to Elector Frederick that I taught that Mary was not a virgin when Jesus was born. Those lies originated in Nürnberg.

To affirm my orthodoxy, I wrote a short treatise titled *That Jesus Christ Was Born a Jew*.[2] My first object was to affirm that Christ was born to a Jewish mother.

To understand what I wrote about the Jews, you must understand the cultural animus against the Jews in my day. One historian in your day noted that in 1492, when I was only nine years old, Ferdinand and Isabella banished all Jews from their territories.[3] In your day, you know those territories as Spain. Another from your day wrote, "Since 1432 Jews had been forbidden to take up permanent residence in Electoral Saxony."[4] It should be clear that Jews were *persona non grata* in Europe in my day.

I was one of a very few who defended the Jews. Yes, in later years I said some very harsh words against them, but in *That Jesus Christ Was Born a Jew*, I said, "If the apostles, who also were Jews, had dealt with us Gentiles as we Gentiles deal with the Jews, there would never have been a Christian among the Gentiles. Since they dealt with us Gentiles in such brotherly fashion, we in our turn ought to treat Jews in a brotherly manner in order that we might convert some of them."[5] I continued by noting the priority of the Jews in God's mystery of salvation. I wrote, "When we are inclined to boast of our position, we should remember that we are but Gentiles, while the Jews are of the lineage of Christ. We

---

1 LW 45:197.

2 LW 45:195–229.

3 Kittelson, 273.

4 Brecht 3:336.

5 LW 45:200–201.

are aliens and in-laws; they are blood relatives, cousins, and brothers of our Lord."[6]

As for the lies circulating about me, I used several passages from the Old Testament to prove that Jesus was born of a Jewish mother; and I confirmed my belief that she was a virgin, the conception being of divine origin. I wrote, "So this mother is a virgin, and yet a true natural mother; not, however, by natural capacity or power, but solely through the Holy Spirit and divine power."[7]

That was in 1523. My tune changed in later years, and those who have used my name have been embarrassed by many of my later comments about the Jews. Nevertheless, I must live with what I said. Therefore I will share with you a few comments that I made in two other treatises that I wrote that relate to the Jews.

I received a letter from a friend who told of Christians in Bohemia and Moravia who insisted that worship must be on Saturday; they were called Sabbatarians.[8] I had no doubt that those misguided believers were influenced by the Jews who were attempting to convert them. At that time, I was lecturing on Genesis. I told my students, "In our time there arose in Moravia a foolish kind of people, the Sabbatarians, who maintain that the Sabbath must be observed after the fashion of the Jews. Perhaps they will insist on circumcision too, for a like reason."[9]

An event occurred that may have prompted a response to my friend. A very prominent Jew, Josel Bosheim, asked me to intercede with my sovereign to allow Josel to enter and pass through Saxony. About two years earlier, Elector Frederick had issued an order that prohibited any Jew from entering Saxony. (I still don't know why Prince Frederick issued that order; the prohibition order from 1432 should have been sufficient.) I refused to intercede, but told Josel, "I propose to write a pamphlet about this if God gives me space and time."[10]

I responded to my friend with a very long letter *Against the Sabbatarians: Letter to a Good Friend*.[11] I said very little about the Sabbatarians in Moravia, but wrote mostly about the Jews.

---

6 LW 45:201.

7 LW 45:204.

8 LW 47:59.

9 LW 47:60.

10 LW 47:62.

11 LW 47:57–98.

I had nothing good to say about them, as I did in 1523, but my words were quite moderate. I said that their rabbis had made them a very stubborn people,[12] and I castigated them for ignoring the prophecies of their own Bible. I said that their refusal to recognize the Messiah in Jesus was the cause of their fifteen-hundred-year exile from their homeland. I also showed convincingly that their Ten Commandments were not exclusively for them but constituted a natural law for all people, for all times.

Five years later, I was an old worn-out man and, I think, even a bitter man. That bitterness broke out in vituperative, caustic, and acrimonious language in several treatises that I wrote against the Jews. Most people would say that the worst was *On the Jews and Their Lies*.[13] Not only my words but the whole tenor of my comments and the recommendations that I made for the disposition of the Jews and their synagogues was so vitriolic that one historian from your day, who spent his entire career studying me and what I wrote, said, "One could wish that Luther had died before ever this tract was written."[14]

I have no intention of sharing any of those words with you. If you have ever been embarrassed by anything that you said or wrote, you will understand why I choose not to write them again. I take full responsibility for what I wrote. If I am embarrassed now for what I wrote, it is too late to apologize. Some apologies are inadequate; they just reopen a terrible wound. No one need remind me of my sin; I am more aware of it than any others. My Lord, God's Messiah, has redeemed me, a lost and condemned person. By His grace I now share His presence with all sinners who have been made saints by that same grace.

Some in your day have confessed my sin to the Jews of your day. I am pleased that the relation between Jews and Christians in your day is much better than it was in my day, but I am not pleased that they confess my sins; it would be much better that they confess their own sin.

I have said enough.

---

12 LW 47:65.

13 LW 47:121–30.

14 Bainton, 379.

Letter 79

The reform of the church created many practical problems. My calling was to be a professor of Bible. Nevertheless, I was frequently called upon to address some of those practical issues.

The small town of Leisnig in Electoral Saxony adopted the evangelical faith. The abbot of a local monastery was responsible for providing priests for the town parish, but the abbot refused to provide for their need. Some folks from Leisnig asked me to come to their assistance. I visited them in the fall of 1522. Subsequently, the congregation selected their own priest and preacher but apparently had some misgivings about their action. In January 1523, a delegation from Leisnig visited me in Wittenberg and asked me to prepare a written statement on the biblical basis for calling their own clergy.[1]

The request prompted me to write a short treatise, only about ten pages in length: *That a Christian Assembly or Congregation Has the Right and Power to Judge All Teaching and to Call, Appoint, and Dismiss Teachers, Established and Proven by Scripture*.[2]

On the basis of John 10, in which Jesus says, "My sheep hear My voice," I said. "He [Christ] takes both the right and the power to judge teaching from the bishops, scholars, and councils and gives them to everyone and to all Christians equally."[3] Shortly thereafter I said, "Bishops, popes, scholars and everyone else have the power to teach, but it is the sheep who are to judge whether they teach the voice [i.e., the words] of Christ or the voice of strangers."[4]

Listen to your pastors and respect them as sent from God. But remember that you, not as individuals but as a congregation, have the responsibility to judge whether you hear the voice of the Chief Shepherd or a stranger's voice. Do not fear your responsibility. I shared a truism: "Thus there cannot be a false prophet among the listeners, only among the teachers."[5]

---

1 LW 39:303.

2 LW 39:301–14.

3 LW 39:306.

4 LW 39:307.

5 LW 39:307.

When calling a pastor you must remember that I was dealing with a unique situation. The local church superior—abbot or bishop—refused to provide a priest for Leisnig.

A preacher must be made available because every congregation of believers needs to hear the Word of God. On that account, I said, "We must act according to Scripture and call and institute from among ourselves those who are found to be qualified and whom God has enlightened with reason and endowed with gifts to do so [preach and administer the sacraments]."[6] Later I wrote, "For need breaks all laws and has none. Thus it is the duty of love to help if there is no one else who could or should help."[7]

I had such a high regard for the congregation as the assembled people of God—the real Church—that I counseled even the most evangelical bishops to heed the wishes of the congregation. I wrote, "Moreover, if they were really decent bishops who wanted to have the gospel and wanted to institute decent preachers, they still could not and should not do so without the will, the election, and the call of the congregation—except in those cases where need made it necessary so that souls would not perish for lack of the divine word."[8]

I am pleased to hear that most bishops in your day who use my name are quite responsible in listening to the voice of the congregations they serve. Listen to them with respect because they are God's servants sent to serve you. But remember that you, again, not as individuals but as a congregation, must listen for the voice of the Chief Shepherd.

---

6 LW 39:309.

7 LW 39:310.

8 LW 39:311–12.

Letter 80

You will not be surprised that the reemergence of the pure Christian faith produced martyrs; it always does. Mention God in the public square, and you will be safe; mention the lordship of Jesus Christ and the free forgiveness of sins by grace alone, and you are sure to encounter opposition.

There were martyrs for Jesus Christ in my day, and that will be the topic of my comments in this letter. But before I share that story with you, I want you to recall that in the first three centuries after the time of Jesus there were several systematic persecutions of Christians for no other reason than that they would neither deny the lordship of Jesus nor give ultimate allegiance to the Roman state. After Christianity became the official religion of the Roman Empire, and even after the fall of that empire up until my day, martyrdom was quite infrequent. That terrible curse, but blessed privilege, found fertile soil in the Reformation of the church. Following the early years of the Reformation, martyrdom again became quiet until your day. I have been told that there have been more who have died for the faith in the past hundred years than in all previous history.

This letter is in memory of all the martyrs, but I want to tell you about a few of the first who died for the evangelical faith in my day.

A research historian from your day has said, "Next to Wittenberg a second strong center of Lutheran thought had developed, remarkably in the Low Countries."[1] (You know the Low Countries as the Netherlands and Belgium.) Although the Low Countries are some distance from Saxony, it probably isn't as remarkable as your historian suggests. Indeed, it was he who noted that observant Augustinian monasteries were located in that area. Because they were under German influence, those monasteries came under the vicarage of Staupitz, my mentor and confessor. You also recall that Staupitz was professor of Bible at the University of Wittenberg prior to my taking his place in 1512. During his tenure at the university, many Augustinian monks from the Low Countries came to study in Wittenberg. More than a few took the evangelical faith with them when they returned home.

---

1 Bornkamm, 100.

The Evangelicals in the Low Countries did not have the privilege of protection that I enjoyed from my sovereigns: Elector Frederick the Wise; his brother and successor, Elector John the Constant; and his son, Elector John Frederick. As your researcher noted, "The papal legate Jerome Aleander and the Hapsburg regent Margaret of Austria [1480–1530] were determined to carry out the Edict of Worms rigorously and to nip heresy in the bud."[2] In January 1522, two Augustinian friars (brothers), Henry Vos and Jan van den Eschen, were burned at the stake in Brussels, thus becoming the first martyrs of the Reformation. Two other Augustinian monks, both former students at Wittenberg and both priors of their monasteries, Jacob Probst at Antwerp and Henry von Zütphen at Dordrecht, were persecuted. Upon his return from Wittenberg, Probst was interrogated and subjected to torture. Thereupon he renounced the evangelical faith. That caused me great grief. I learned that shortly after his denial he recanted and again embraced the holy faith. It was reported that he had been killed, but miraculously, he showed up in Wittenberg. Probst escaped the ultimate witness of martyrdom.

Henry von Zütphen, on the other hand, paid the ultimate price. One researcher from your day has said that on 10 December 1524, a mob lynched him,[3] and another scholar said that they burned him at the stake.[4] The means of death is quite unimportant; Henry joined the great multitude of martyrs.

In the wake of Henry's death, I wrote *The Burning of Brother Henry* to console the congregation in Bremen on the death of their pastor. I spoke of martyrdom as precious and priceless. I said, "In our day the pattern of the true Christian life has reappeared, terrible in the world's eyes, since it means suffering and persecution, but precious and priceless in God's sight."[5] I also said, "Those who mislead the world with their doctrines of works, human righteousness, and free will, have never been able to obtain such glory."[6] I tried to bring some comfort for the bereaved by commenting on David's words in the ninth psalm. I then concluded with "The History of Brother Henry of Zütphen."[7] You can read the story of his

---

2 Bornkamm, 101.

3 LW 32:263.

4 Bornkamm, 102.

5 LW 32:265–66.

6 LW 32:266–67.

7 LW 32:272–86.

life if you choose, but I want only to tell you about his last hours so that you may know the terrible cost of faithful discipleship. I wrote, "They began beating the good martyr of Christ with all their might. One man beat him over the skull with his rapier, but John Holm of Neuenkirchen struck him with a mace. The rest stabbed him in the sides, the back, the arms, and wherever they could get at him, not just once, but as often as he attempted to speak."[8]

Then the mob attempted to burn him alive, but I noted,

> Now the fire would not burn no matter how often they tried to light it. Nonetheless they gave vent to their malice by beating him with halberds and pikes for about two hours. All that time he stood before the peasants, naked except for his nightshirt, and with eyes lifted to heaven. . . . Then the good martyr of Christ began to recite the Creed. But somebody struck him in the mouth with his fist and told him to burn first; he could recite whatever he wanted to afterwards. . . . Finally John Holm pushed forward, took his mace, and struck Henry on the chest until he died, never to move again.[9]

Thus the martyrdom of another of Christ's faithful.

You live in comfort now, but the future for you and your offspring is not as secure as you might think. Be prepared. Also, remember to pray for and offer material support for believers in other parts of the world who daily face what Jacob Probst and Henry von Zütphen faced in my day.

---

8 LW 32:286.

9 LW 32:286.

Letter 81

I want to share with you a little bit about the popes who reigned during my life. (Reign is a good verb to describe them because they assumed to themselves imperial regality, lived in opulent luxury, and distained the humility and servanthood of the apostle Peter, whom they are alleged to succeed.)

I knew nothing of Innocent VIII, who died when I was only eight years old.

Innocent was succeed by Alexander VI in 1492 and died just short of my twentieth birthday. I had already completed my bachelor of arts degree at the University of Erfurt. Alexander was the worst of the popes. One of your historians said of him,

> Doubtless, under the first [Alexander VI] and his depraved son, Cesare Borgia, the lowest depth of all papal history was reached. Alexander would go to any length to help Cesare Borgia accomplish his foul purposes. Contemporary accounts of the latter's crimes are almost beyond credibility. He is said to have been responsible for the death of over a hundred people, including his own brother, Giovanni. He caused his brother-in-law to be strangled in his presence and slew his half-brother Peroto, Alexander's favorite, in the Pope's arms, his blood spouting over the papal vestments.[1]

I need not tell you more about him; he had no effect on my life and career.

Pius III succeeded Alexander but died less than a month after his election.

Julius II reigned from 1503 to 1513. He knew nothing about me and died when I was an obscure monk teaching in Wittenberg and enduring *Anfechtung* about which I wrote in a previous letter. Julius was no more interested in the holy faith than most of the popes during my lifetime. He was known as a warrior pope. The same historian who wrote about Alexander said of Julius, "He led his armies in person through

1 Schwiebert, 29.

the streets of Rome, where the great Erasmus saw him."[2] When I was in Rome during the winter of 1510–11, Julius was absent, leading his army in war against the French. (I must share with you a brief scene from a play written by Erasmus, *Julius Excluded*. As Julius approaches the gates of heaven, Peter, allegedly the first pope, asks Julius to unlock the door of heaven with the key of faith. Julius says that he has never heard of such a key. When Julius threatens Peter with excommunication, Peter responds that he has never heard of excommunication; it was not used in his day.)

Julius's successor, Leo X, knew me very well. I was a thorn in his flesh, and he did not like the pain; it cost him indulgence money. He was another Renaissance pope, more interested in art, architecture, and other cultural embellishments than in our blessed Lord and the Holy Gospel. Leo is reported to have said, "The Lord has given us the papacy; let us enjoy it." Whether he actually said that makes no difference to me; he lived it. Money was not an issue with him. He spent what he did not have on personal pleasures, the continued construction and beautification of St. Peter's Basilica in Rome, and to prepare for war against the Turks. To pay for his extravagances, he sold papal furniture and gold and silver plates. That small stuff. He sold church offices, bishoprics, and cardinals' hats for thousands of what you call dollars. The sale of indulgences brought in vast sums from foreign countries to repay bank loans. Leo was more a businessman than a pastor of the church. At times I called Leo "Blessed Father" because of the position that he held; I had respect for the office. At other times, and more frequently, I referred to him as the Antichrist because of his obsession with this world's goods at the expense of poor souls hungering for the good news of freedom in Jesus Christ.

Pope Leo died 1 December 1521, while I was at the Wartburg. In early January, Pope Hadrian (Adrian) VI was installed. Less than two years after being installed Hadrian died, along with his attempts at reform. Waiting and wondering again gripped the Western world. Clement VII was elected only a few days after Hadrian's death, and we soon realized this new pope was a throwback to Leo X. One of your historians has said of Clement, "In place of a reform-minded churchman (Hadrian) the new incumbent was a worldly-wise politician. Foremost on his mind was the grandeur of the papal states and his own house."[3] I had little to do with Clement. By the time of his arrival, I was a condemned heretic headed

---

2 Schwiebert, 29.

3 Bornkamm, 308–9.

for hell. All hope for me was lost, or so he thought. His thought meant nothing to me; I cared only for the thought of my Savior, Jesus Christ. He had released me from my *Anfechtung* and given me a new life of freedom in the Holy Gospel.

Clement died in 1534 and was succeeded by Paul III. Paul convened the Council of Trent in 1545. It was intended to be a reform council, a council for which I had called twenty-five or thirty years earlier. The council came much too late; the reform of the church had already taken hold. Although intended to be a reform council, I think Trent caused more problems for the unity in the church than it solved.

That's enough about those gilded gentlemen. Next, I'll share with you some other things that I wrote.

Letter 82

The Christian faith is not exclusively religious; it has serious implications for daily living. In 1524, I wrote several treatises on issues for Christian life in society. I will share with you two or three of those articles.

One of the greatest temptations for all people, Christians included, is greed, the temptation to get as much of this world's goods as one possibly can. Because of that temptation, I wrote the treatise *Trade and Usury*.[1] What authority do I have as a theologian to write about economic issues? One from your day who read my treatise has said, "Of the far-reaching economic revolution which was gradually transforming Germany from a nation of peasant agriculturalists into a society with at least the beginnings of a capitalist economy, he had no conception whatsoever."[2] That person is quite accurate. But, in every economic system, greed and avarice threaten every believer. (I never wrote for unbelievers; they care nothing for the new life offered by Jesus.)

I was always suspicious of charging interest; it smacked to me of getting money without work. Greed in business dealing was as repugnant to me as blasphemy against God.

Near the beginning of the treatise, I said, "It is our purpose here to speak about the abuses and sins of trade, insofar as they concern the conscience."[3] To make it clear that my interest was only religious, and not economic, I added, "The matter of their detrimental effect on the purse we leave to the princes and lords, that they may do their duty in this regard."[4]

I was never opposed to trade. I said, "Now it is fair and right that a merchant take as much profit on his wares as will reimburse him for their cost and compensate him for his trouble, his labor, and his risk."[5] What is fair compensation for trouble, labor, and risk? In my day, I thought that 5 or 6 percent might be fair. I cannot speak for life in your day, and

1 LW 45:231–310.

2 LW 45:233.

3 LW 45:247.

4 LW 45:247.

5 LW 45:249.

I will not revert to legal restrictions and requirements. Every Christian has a conscience molded by the Spirit of God. Pay attention! Only remember that in your business you are dealing with "your neighbor," the one of whom Jesus spoke when He said that believers are to love their neighbors as they love themselves.

Remember, your closest neighbors are those in your household. I wrote, "Your first and greatest obligation is to provide for the needs of your wife and children and servants; you must not divert from them what you owe them."[6] Note "the needs." I am embarrassed to see the opulence of Christians in your day who have larger homes than they need, sometimes even more than one home, all furnished with the finest that can be purchased. That is to confuse need with greed. Forgive me, I am now off the subject of trade and usury, but my embarrassment remains.

I thought that it is not right for a Christian to loan money and expect to get it back with added interest. If your neighbor has a need, give what you have. If he is able to repay you, well and good; if not, you have done only what is required of you. Money should be earned by work. I did, however, allow the elderly who are not able to work to charge interest on their loans.

I suggested that if credit was needed, both the creditor and debtor should share the risk. Your bankers will laugh at me. I thought the debtor rather than the creditor should set the interest rate. With that, I know that I have lost the business people, especially the bankers of your day.

My words will mean nothing to unbelievers; they will continue their legalized robbery with a clear conscience. I spoke of kings and princes (in your day, that might include politicians and wealthy entrepreneurs) and said, "They hang thieves who have stolen a gulden or half a gulden, but do business with those who rob the whole world and steal more than all the rest, so that the proverb remains true, 'Big thieves hang little thieves.' As the Roman senator Cato said, 'Simple thieves lie in dungeons and stocks; public thieves walk abroad in gold and silk.'"[7]

I think that I have said both less and more than I said in the treatise, but you live in quite a different time than I. Consequently, I am sure that what I have written today is a fair representation of the sentiment contained in the treatise *Trade and Usury*.

Live the faith!

---

6 LW 45:259.

7 LW 45:272.

Letter 83

A financial crisis developed in communities that adopted the Reformation. Until I upset the social order—the ecclesiastical structure and the social order were quite intertwined—finances for the clergy and all church needs came, as one from your day has noted, from "income-producing foundations or properties, endowments of altars at which special masses were celebrated, compulsory tithes, and fees for ministerial acts, especially those performed for souls of the departed."[1] Church buildings continued to need repair, people who served the ministry of the church needed a livelihood, and the poor needed help. (A student of history has estimated that between 15 and 30 percent of the population "may have been paupers and vagrants in towns of that period."[2]) From where would the financial resources come?

Several communities established a community chest to provide for the needs of the citizens. One such community was Leisnig in Electoral Saxony. One who knows something about my interaction with Leisnig has noted that I visited the town in 1522 for that and another purpose, as he said, "Presumably two items were discussed: first, the right of the parish to select its priest and preacher; second, the establishment of a common chest for the parish."[3] The Leisnig parish did a masterful job of preparing a *Fraternal Agreement on the Common Chest of the Entire Assembly at Leisnig*.[4] (I was pleased to see that one from your day who is familiar with the Leisnig ordinance said, "It was one of the most thoroughgoing of these ordinances, almost a rudimentary congregational constitution."[5]) Subsequently, I wrote a preface to their effort with the simple title *Ordinance of a Common Chest*.[6] I then appended my preface to their ordinance and had it published.

The Leisnig ordinance was far superior to my introduction. I made only five suggestions of what should be done with the monasteries that

1 LW 45:161.

2 LW 45:161.

3 LW 45:163.

4 LW 45:176.

5 LW 45:162.

6 LW 45:159–76.

closed and with their possessions. First, I suggested that monasteries should be allowed to simply die out, but with the assurance that aged monks and all who desired to remain in the monasteries receive adequate care. Second, that properties taken by the governing authorities should be used to support the monks that remain and help those who leave start a new life, and the remainder should be used to provide a common chest to support those in need. Third, I said the same procedures should be used for other very wealthy ecclesiastical entities that had grown within the church, but which were more of a hindrance than a help to the proclamation of the Gospel. The fourth suggestion relates to a complicated formula in my day, called "repurchase," for charging interest. It is quite irrelevant in your day. Finally, and this was perhaps my best suggestion: "Mendicant houses located in cities might be converted into good schools for boys and girls, as they were before."[7] Few in my day ever thought about schools for girls.

I had no expectation that my suggestions would be followed. Once (some but not all) politicians get their hands on money or property, they find ways to use those resources for their own interests or the interests of their supporters rather than for the common good of the community, particularly care for the poor. I wrote, "I fear that very few will be guided by my advice, for Greed is a disobedient and unbelieving scoundrel."[8]

Next, I will tell you about the rights of a congregation.

---

7 LW 45:175.

8 LW 45:170.

Letter 84

The congregation in Leisnig got into a little contest with the abbot of Buch, who, by the authority of the bishop of Meissen, had been granted the right to name the Leisnig parish priest. The abbot, Antonius, got caught, as you say, between a rock and a hard place. (What a strange, but quite appropriate, metaphor.) He had appointed Heinrich Kind, one of his monks, to be the parish priest. Father Kind converted to the evangelical faith, whereupon the abbot recalled him from his parish responsibilities. The recall by the bishop notwithstanding, the congregation elected Father Kind to be their priest and selected another to be the preacher. The abbot felt snubbed by the action of the congregation and appointed a different priest to take the place of Father Kind. The congregation made it quite clear to the new appointee that he had not been called by the congregation, and they did not want and would not accept him as their priest. The new appointee departed peacefully. One of your own, who told this story, said that there was an attempt for the two parties to compromise but concluded, "An agreement never was worked out between the parish and the monastery."[1]

To stand against a bishop in my day was an unheard of scandal. Therefore, the congregation contacted me and asked for a written statement confirming their action. They also asked me to provide them with an appropriate evangelical order of worship. It was that request that prompted me to write *The Right and Power of a Christian Congregation or Community to Judge All Teaching and to Call, Appoint, and Dismiss Teachers, Established and Provided from Scripture.*[2] Lest there be any misunderstanding, I made it clear that when I referred to teachers, I also included pastors. I wrote, "No bishop ought to appoint anyone without the consent, choice and call of the congregation; it is his duty rather to confirm the man whom the congregation has elected and called."[3]

Among nonbelievers every Christian has a right and obligation to preach and teach the faith, without a call. The need itself is the call. It was in that context that I said, "For necessity breaks every law and knows no

1 LW 45:164.

2 PE 4:73ff.

3 PE 4:82.

law."[4] When other believers are present no one should assume the office of preacher or teacher; let the community appoint the one who is to be their servant in preaching and teaching. I concluded my letter to Leisnig by saying, "Therefore the man to whom has been committed the office of preaching has committed to him the highest office in the Christian Church."[5] So high did I consider the office of preaching that I followed by saying, "Or if he prefer, he may confine himself to preaching, and leave baptizing and such minor offices to others."[6]

In that same letter, I said that because all Christians are priests, all have the right to judge what is being preached and taught. But, be careful. It is the community of believers, not one individual or a faction within the community, that is to judge. I noted the words of Jesus quoted by John, "My sheep hear My voice"; and, "My sheep do not follow a stranger, but flee from him; for they know not the voice of strangers."[7] Because of that blessed assurance, I wrote, "Indeed there can be no false prophets among the hearers, but among the teachers alone. All teachers should and must, therefore, be subject with their teaching to the judgment of the hearers."[8]

When I responded to the Leisnig congregation's request for an evangelical order of service, my suggestion for worship is so foreign to anything that you would even consider that I am tempted to refrain. Nevertheless, because you are so negligent in worship, usually only once a week, I will give you my thoughts in the hope that a few might learn the necessity of more frequent worship. *Concerning the Ordering of Divine Worship in the Congregation*[9] is one of my shortest writings.

I began by stating three ways in which the Roman worship liturgy of my time had been misused: (1) Preaching had been mostly eliminated. (2) What should have been preaching of the Word of God had become only fables, lies, and legends. (3) The worship service was considered to be a good work to merit God's salvation.[10] On the positive side, I wrote, "The Christian congregation never should assemble unless God's Word

4 PE 4:80.

5 PE 4:84.

6 PE 4:84.

7 PE 4:77.

8 PE 4:78.

9 PE 6:60ff.

10 PE 6:60.

is preached and prayer is made, no matter for how brief a time this may be."[11] Worship should be a daily experience, morning and evening. I said, "We should assemble daily in the early morning, say at four or five o'clock, and have God's Word read. . . . Thereupon the preacher . . . shall come forward and expound a part of the same lesson."[12] The reading and preaching should not last more than half an hour. Then, I wrote, "The congregation shall immediately unite in giving thanks to God, in praising Him, and in praying for the fruits of the Word."[13] The same should be done in the evening at about five or six o'clock. Each service should last for not more than an hour because, as I said, "One must not overload the souls so that they become weary and bored."[14] I need not tell you that believers should all congregate on Sundays for worship in the morning and evening. I had some instructions for that worship also, but you have your own ways of worship in your day so that I need not tell you how to worship. I need only to tell you that you worship all too infrequently. Perhaps that last sentence is the most important of all that I have written today.

Keep worshiping.

---

11 PE 6:60.

12 PE 6:61.

13 PE 6:61–62.

14 PE 6:62.

Letter 85

Education of the youth in my day was a disaster. Few children went to school, and those who did got their learning in either monasteries or cathedral schools. At one time I said, "I would wager that in half of Germany today there are not four thousand pupils in the schools."[1] You can imagine the education they received was almost entirely religious. The common people (what a shameful term; are not all people common?), nearly all of whom were uneducated, thought the need for education belonged only to those who entered one of the three professions: theology, medicine, and law. There was a pejorative phrase used in my day that characterized the popular sentiment of the common people: *die Gelehrte sind verkehrte* ("the learned are daft").

As early as 1520, when I wrote *To the Christian Nobility of the German Nation*, I was thinking only about the need for the youth to read the Scriptures. Schools were needed to teach them to read. I wrote, "Above all, the foremost reading for everybody, both in the universities and in the schools, should be Holy Scripture—and for the younger boys, the Gospels. And would to God that every town had a girls' school as well."[2]

Only four years later, I wrote an entire treatise asking all towns to establish schools: *To the Councilmen of All Cities in Germany That They Establish and Maintain Christian Schools*.[3] I put the issue quite clearly. "My dear sirs," I wrote, "if we have to spend such large sums every year on guns, roads, bridges, dams, and countless similar items to insure the temporal peace and prosperity of a city, why should not much more be devoted to the poor neglected youth—at least enough to engage one or two competent men to teach school?"[4] To further my appeal, I said, "A city's best and greatest welfare, safety, and strength consist rather in its having many able, learned, wise, honorable, and well-educated citizens."[5]

I was not a specialist in formal education; I only knew education of

1 LW 46:234.

2 LW 44:205–6.

3 LW 45:339–78.

4 LW 45:350.

5 LW 45:356.

the young to be a crying need. I left the details of forming schools to my younger colleague Philip Melanchthon. He was such a good teacher that he became known as *praeceptor Germaniae* (teacher of the Germans). One from your day quoted Philip: "'I call that man a philosopher,' Melanchthon writes, 'who, having learned many things that are good and useful to the human race, takes his learning [*doctrinam*] out of the shadow of the school and applies it for the public welfare, teaching people what he knows, whether it be about nature, religion, or civil government.'"[6] I was always proud of that brilliant teacher.

I was not finished publishing about education. I have been told recently that somebody from your time has said that people have to hear something seven times before they take it seriously or act on it. I don't know if that is true, but I knew that education needed further encouragement. In 1530, I wrote *A Sermon on Keeping Children in School*.[7] The sermon actually became a fifty-page book. Education was so bad that even priests were deficient in learning. I said, "In a word, a priest was a man who could say mass, even though he could not preach a word and was an unlearned ass."[8] I spent the first half of the "sermon" on pleading for an educated clergy; in the second part, I promoted education in temporal matters for the civic good. I began that section by saying, "Therefore as it is the function and honor of the office of preaching to make sinners saints, dead men live, damned men saved, and the devil's children God's children, so it is the function and honor of worldly government to make men out of wild beasts and to prevent men from becoming wild beasts."[9] Further, I said, "And just as in the kingdom of Christ, a pious theologian and sincere preacher is called an angel of God, a savior, prophet, priest, servant, and teacher . . . so a pious jurist and true scholar can be called, in the worldly kingdom of the emperor, a prophet, priest, angel, and savior."[10] To keep children from years of schooling so that they can rush out and earn money is a disgrace. I wrote,

> We shamefully despise God when we begrudge our children this glorious and divine work and stick them instead in exclusive service of the belly and of avarice, having them learn nothing but how to make a living, like hogs wallowing

---

6 Ozment, 313.

7 LW 46:207–58.

8 LW 46:221.

9 LW 46:237.

10 LW 46:239–40.

> forever with their noses in the dunghill, and never training them for so worthy an estate and office [as government service].[11]

I reached the climax of this section with the following words,

> Indeed, there is need in this office [public service] for abler people than are needed in the office of preaching, so it is necessary to get the best boys for this work; for in the preaching office Christ does the whole thing, by his Spirit, but in the worldly kingdom men must act on the basis of reason—wherein the laws also have their origin—for God has subjected temporal rule and all of physical life to reason (Genesis 2 [:15]). He has not sent the Holy Spirit from heaven for this purpose.[12]

Your day is not like mine. Give thanks to God every day that your governing authorities require you to keep your children in school. Get the best teachers available and pay them well for the great God-given work they do.

---

11 LW 46:241.

12 LW 46:242.

Letter 86

The reform of the church is a necessary but hazardous task. It is no different in your day than in mine. If the reform is not grounded in the Word of God, with a clear distinction between Law and Gospel, the reform degenerates into a religious movement that flirts with heresy. In addition, if the reform falls into the hands of fanatics, it turns sour and dives into schism and, sometimes, heresy.

Two in my day were captured by the call to reform, embraced the Gospel of forgiveness of sin by grace through faith, and affirmed the changes necessary, but carried the changes to a radical and heretical dimension. The two were Andreas Karlstadt and Thomas Münzer. One from your day accurately noted, "Both were sensitive and gifted, neither was balanced and stable."[1]

Karlstadt (we seldom used first names) was a senior colleague at the University of Wittenberg. He was the dean of the faculty when I arrived, and it was he who presented me with the doctor of theology degree when I had completed the academic requirements.

Karlstadt was a devoted Thomist (dedicated to the theology of Thomas Aquinas), but after buying and reading a complete set of St. Augustine's writings, he became a staunch supporter of the reform theology. After being "converted," he became an enthusiastic supporter of the reform. He even preceded me to the door of the Castle Church with his posting. Six months before I posted my Ninety-five Theses, your historian noted, "Carlstadt now became an ardent exponent of the new approach, and in April, 1517, he posted 151 theses on the door of the Castle Church to expound the cause of the gospel further with the rest of the faculty."[2]

I was pleased with Karlstadt's enthusiasm for the Gospel; I wish that all who use my name would show greater enthusiasm than I have seen over the years. I got exasperated with the dear doctor on several occasions, but all went quite well between us until I was confined to the Wartburg castle and no longer present to give direction to the reform movement.

---

1 Bainton, 258.

2 Schwiebert, 295.

In December 1521, his excessive enthusiasm took a drastic turn. At the Christmas worship service, he faced the congregation of about two thousand without wearing the traditional clerical vestments, and he offered the sacrament to the laity in both kinds (bread and wine). "He officiated without vestments, omitted the Eucharistic prayer, and spoke the words of institution in German," as one of your historians has noted.[3] You might think those issues to be trivial and inconsequential. That is precisely the point. Karlstadt made the trivial into a major issue. Trivial issues could have been addressed later, after the laity had been properly educated. Reform does not come by unnecessarily confusing the people. Let the Word of God lead them slowly into the freedom of worship.

One who studies what I wrote found this quote: "Give men time. I took three years of constant study, reflection, and decision to arrive where I now am, and can the common man, untutored in such matters, be expected to move the same distance in three months?"[4]

Confusion in Wittenberg got worse only two days later when, on 27 December, three fanatics arrived from Zwickau claiming direct communication from the Holy Spirit. They were real iconoclasts.

I'm quite certain that the unstable Karlstadt was influenced by those Zwickau fanatics. Subsequently, he renounced infant Baptism, denied the real presence of Jesus Christ in the sacrament, removed all pictures and images from churches, and as one of your own has noted, said the church should "relegate organs, trumpets, and flutes to the theater."[5]

Only a month after the Christmas confusion, Karlstadt persuaded the City Council to make some radical changes. The elector had had enough. He forbade Karlstadt to do any further preaching.

In the same month, January, the poor professor again confused the laity by marrying, which was an unheard of scandal at that time, and saying that all clergy should be required to be married. That requirement would have been a clear violation of Christian freedom to marry or remain celibate.

Brother Andreas (he no longer wanted to be called "Herr Doctor") left his teaching position and installed himself as pastor in the nearby community of Orlamünde. There his fanaticism increased. He preached against theological education and thoroughly confused the congregation.

---

3 Loewenich, 218.

4 Bainton, 214.

5 Bainton, 208.

He began a campaign of writing violent, scurrilous tracts against me, especially against my defense of the real body and blood of Jesus in the Lord's Supper, which is a denial of what Jesus said to His disciples the night before His crucifixion. The now "Brother Andreas" taught that the sacrament was no more than bread and wine, a mere memorial of Jesus' suffering and death.

Duke John, brother and successor to Frederick the Wise, finally, in 1524, dismissed Karlstadt from the Saxon territory. Karlstadt then went to Strassburg, where he confused even the clergy. Under the pastoral leadership of Martin Bucer, the clergy wrote to me asking for clarification on infant Baptism, the real presence of Jesus in the Lord's Supper, and the use of images in worship. I provided a short response: *Letter to the Christians at Strassburg in Opposition to the Fanatic Spirit*.[6] I did not give specific answers to their questions but promised to write a longer statement later. My immediate response was quite brief: "Now my very dear friends, I am not your pastor. . . . My sincere counsel and warning is that you be circumspect and hold to the single question, what makes a person a Christian? Do not on any account allow any other question or other art to enjoy equal importance."[7] In regard to the real presence of Jesus in the sacrament, I wrote,

> I confess that if Dr. Karlstadt, or anyone else, could have convinced me five years ago that only bread and wine were in the sacrament he would have done me a great service. At that time I suffered such severe conflicts and inner strife and torment that I would gladly have been delivered from them. . . . But I am a captive and cannot free myself. The text is too powerfully present, and will not allow itself to be torn from its meaning by mere verbiage.[8]

I had already begun to write *Against the Heavenly Prophets in the Matter of Images and Sacraments*.[9] That treatise was directed against my former colleague Karlstadt. Issues such as infant Baptism, the real presence of Jesus Christ in the Lord's Supper, and the use of pictures and images in the church are no longer issues with you. I did, however, reference Karlstad's inclination to make minor issue into major issues, and I do

6 LW 40:61–71.

7 LW 40:67.

8 LW 40:68.

9 LW 40:72–223.

think that is also a significant issue in your day. My comment regarding Karlstadt is equally valid for you: "Bear in mind that the devil is eager to spruce up such minor matters, thereby drawing the attention of the people so that the truly important matters are neglected, as long as they gape in his direction."[10]

Karlstadt was swiftly rejected in Strassburg; he moved to Rothenberg. The Peasants' War forced him to flee that city after enduring physical wounds.

The poor soul had no place to go. He wrote to me asking my pardon for what he had written against me and asked me to intercede with the elector so that he and his family could return to Saxony. I did, and the elector relented. Upon his return with no place to stay and no income to provide food, Katie and I took the family into our home, where they resided for a few weeks.

The wandering spirit left Wittenberg and found his way to Basel, where his life ended.

Such was the tragic life of an enthusiastic Christian whose enthusiasm conquered wisdom. His enthusiasm did more to harm the Reformation than to promote it.

In my next letter, I will tell you about Thomas Münzer and the three Zwickau fanatics.

---

10 LW 40:84.

LETTER 87

Andreas Karlstadt was a want-to-be reformer with a warm heart, a good mind, but completely lacking in wisdom. His enthusiasm for the Gospel lead him into strange and heretical teachings. Thomas Münzer, a compatriot with Karlstadt in late 1521, was of a different spirit; he was a radical revolutionary who willed not merely the reform of the church but, more important, a fundamental change in society. One of your own has correctly noted, "Münzer . . . resorted to force when [he] found that political power could not be gained and maintained peacefully."[1] He, more than any other one individual, was responsible for the tragic Peasants' War from 1524 to 1526. But of that ill-conceived event, I will write to you in my next letter.

Thomas had been a student in our university 1517–18. I do not remember him from that time, but perhaps we had some influence on him. It is well known that he attended the Leipzig Debate in 1519. I cannot imagine that he supported the Roman position in that debate, but I cannot be absolutely certain. I do know that Thomas had a close relationship with Karlstadt. It was they, along with Gabriel Zwilling, who created confusion and restlessness in Wittenberg around Christmas 1521 when I was absent, staying at the Wartburg.

In May 1520, Thomas was invited to serve as an interim pastor in Zwickau. To my regret, it was I who recommended him for that position. Within a year, he was in trouble with the town council for participating in social protests. He wrote to me and asked for my support, saying that he wanted me to be his advocate before our Lord. Then he begged me not to listen to those who brought charges against him. He also said that I had brought him to birth through the Gospel. Those were probably the last two kind words that he said about me. A scholar from your day, who knows more about me than I know about myself because he has spent his entire life studying me and other persons and events around my time, has said, "The likes of Münzer's hatred of Luther, in style and substance, recurred only once again, in Friedrich Nietzsche."[2]

In April 1521, Münzer was dismissed from Zwickau by the civil

1 Ozment, 349.

2 Bornkamm, 161.

authorities. A large armed crowd came to his defense. (Note that they were armed. That was Thomas's mode of operation when he couldn't have his way.) About fifty of his supporters were arrested, and his support dissipated. Thomas then fled during the night. (Be very suspicious of pastors who surround themselves with loyal followers. Loyalty in the church belongs exclusively to the Lord Jesus.)

Thomas moved to Prague, where after a short time he was arrested and expelled from that city.

His next stop was Allstedt, where, in the spring of 1523, without the consent of Elector Frederick, he installed himself as pastor. It took only about a year to establish his "League of the Elect." These were, according to the warped theology of Thomas, the real Christians. I never knew the size of the "special forces" that Thomas created, but another scholar from your day said that it numbered five hundred.[3] A different scholar said that three hundred were outsiders.[4] I certainly hope that you do not have outside rabble-rousers in your day who travel from one protest to another. There can be no doubt that Thomas was a gifted speaker who could attract the masses. But his preaching was not Gospel preaching; it was revolutionary preaching. The count of Mansfeld noted the results of his preaching. A scholar wrote, "The new way of worship and Münzer's thunderous preaching attracted crowds even from afar, so much so that Count Ernest of Mansfeld, citing a mandate of the Nuremberg Diet, forbade his subjects to leave their local church and attend in Allstedt."[5] How did Thomas respond? I'll let your scholar tell you; he knows better than I. "Münzer had sent the count a threatening letter: 'Don't move, or the old coat will tear. You just dare to stop me, and I'll treat you a hundred thousand times worse than Luther treated the pope.'"[6] Decorum may be dead in your day, but in my day that is not how we spoke to the nobility. Incendiary words were not enough for Thomas. Your historian noted, "The only overt act, however, was the burning of a chapel dedicated to the Virgin Mary."[7] *Only*, he says! Is that not more than enough? I am surprised that the authorities did not act sooner. Finally, in August 1524, Münzer was summoned to Weimar for an interrogation by the civil authorities. "An eye witness reported that he came out of that hearing as

3 Loewenich, 254.

4 Bornkamm, 155.

5 Bornkamm, 153.

6 Bornkamm, 153.

7 Bainton, 262.

white as a sheet."[8] At some point Münzer fled Allstedt, as another of your historians has said, "By night [he] escaped over the walls of Allstedt and fled from Saxony."[9] As usual, he left his followers leaderless and in disarray. A year earlier, in a letter to Spalatin, I said, "I advised the collector of Allstedt, when he was here, that he should have nothing to do with the spirit of the prophet Thomas."[10] Finally, in the summer of 1524, I felt compelled to warn the elector about the danger Thomas posed to the whole society. I wrote *Letter to the Princes of Saxony Concerning the Rebellious Spirit*.[11] I had nothing profound to say, but I reminded them of their responsibility to maintain peace and order in society. Thomas was a threat to that peace.

After Thomas fled Allsedt, he surfaced in Mühlhausen. You will hear more about him when I tell you about the peasants' uprising.

Thomas was a poor soul. Having heard the Gospel, he traded that spiritual liberation for a political and social revolution. He relied not on the Bible but on inner inspiration of the Holy Spirit. Of the Bible, he said in disdain, "Bible, Babel, bubble."[12] Of course, if God speaks directly to an individual, there is no need for the mediation of the written Word of God. I, too, relied on the Holy Spirit, but not on His direct inspiration within me. When I wrote the Small Catechism in 1529, I said, "I believe that I cannot by my own reason or understanding believe in Jesus Christ my Lord or come to him, but the Holy Spirit has called me through the gospel." Two ways to be engaged by the Holy Spirit of God: directly within or mediated by the written Word of God. The belief that one can hear the Holy Spirit directly and clearly has led to great disasters within the church. For me, it has always been the Word alone.

Beware of charismatic preachers who gain a great following by claiming that God has spoken to them directly.

---

8 Bornkamm, 163.

9 Bainton, 264.

10 Smith 2:193.

11 LW 40:45–59.

12 Bainton, 260.

Letter 88

This is not an easy letter to write; it's about the social uprising of the common man: peasants, townsmen, miners, and even a few lords, against the elite of society: nobles, bishops, and priests. The uprising led to war.

I wrote a few things against both sides engaged in the war and have been viciously maligned for what I wrote. I never had the gift of soft speech; I always spoke candidly and with passion. I stand by the substance of what I wrote but am quite aware that the form and phrasing caused needless harm to the reform of the church. That I regret.

You must know the plight of the peasants (distinct from the townsmen) of my day. A historian of your day said it well,

> Most of them lived in small huts, with thatched roofs of straw, wooden chimneys covered with clay, dirt floors, and rude tables, benches, stools, and beds. Cattle, poultry, and peasants often occupied the same buildings. . . . Usually isolated from the outside, their world was a dreary one, brightened only by church festivals, local market days, and occasionally traveling entertainers.[1]

Another historian said that the cause of the uprising included overpopulation and crowding aggravated by the authorities expropriating the common lands, added imperial taxes dating from 1495, and severe crop failures in 1523 and 1524.[2]

In 1525, the peasants presented their grievances in *Twelve Articles*. One of the two authors of those articles was an evangelical (you would say Lutheran) pastor.

I will share the *Twelve Articles* with you so that you can see the moderate nature of their requests.

1. The right of each community to choose and dispose its own pastor.
2. An end to the small tithes of cattle for lay and ecclesiastical lords.

---

1 Grimm, 16.

2 Ozment, 273.

3. Release from serfdom.
4. Free access to fish and game.
5. Free access to firewood as needed.
6. An investigation of excessive tenural services.
7. Strict observance by the lords of the agreements made with their servants.
8. New rent assessments, based on equity and justice.
9. The basing of legal judgments, that is, punishments, on customary law rather than on constantly appearing arbitrary new laws.
10. The return of expropriated common fields.
11. Abolition of the death tax.
12. A willingness of the peasants to withdraw any articles contrary to the Word of God.

No one need tell you that the peasants' requests were quite moderate and that they had been influenced by the evangelical movement.

Shortly after I became aware of the *Twelve Articles*, I wrote *Admonition to Peace, a Reply to The Twelve Articles of the Peasants in Swabia*.[3] There were two parts to what I wrote. To the princes and lords, I warned of the seriousness of the situation and urged them to be moderate in their demands, telling them bluntly that they were to blame for the current uprising. To the peasants, while admitting that their demands were just, I said they must not use force to secure their demands. I was particularly pleased with their twelfth statement: bound by the Word of God!

I began by saying, "We have no one on earth to thank for this disastrous rebellion, except you princes and lords, and especially you blind bishops and mad priests and monks."[4] Further I said, "These protests are also right and just, for rulers are not appointed to exploit their subjects for their own profit and advantage, but to be concerned about the welfare of their subjects."[5]

I warned the peasants against insurrection. I said, "For here is God's word, spoken through the mouth of Christ, 'All who take the sword will perish by the sword' [Matt. 26:52]. That means nothing else than that

---

3 LW 46:3–43.

4 LW 46:19.

5 LW 46:22–23.

no one, by his own violence, shall arrogate authority to himself, but as Paul says, 'Let every person be subject to the governing authorities with fear and reverence' [Rom. 13:1]."[6] I had other words of warning for the peasants, but to no avail.

Under the guidance of the evil-spirited Thomas Münzer, war erupted. One of your historians said, "In Saxony there would have been no Peasants' War without Thomas Münzer."[7] "Now is the time," he cried, "if you be only three wholly committed unto God, you need not fear one hundred thousand. On! On! On! Spare not! Pity not the godless when they cry. . . . The whole countryside is in commotion. Strike! Clang! Clang! On! On!"[8]

The peasants were well organized. I never knew how well they were organized, but someone told me that they were organized into companies with numbers between two thousand and fifteen thousand. I never heard how many companies constituted the peasant forces, but the full sum of fighters was very large. I didn't track all the events as your historians have. I lived through the event; they have the advantage of historical retrospect. The revolution was strongest in central and southern Germany between February and May 1525. Münzer was a little late joining the fray. It's always easier to send others into battle. In mid-May, Münzer aligned his civilian troops with about seven thousand peasant troops. Münzer was captured and taken back to Mühlhausen on 25 May. There he was executed and his head impaled for public warning.

The capture of Münzer near Frankenhausen marked the end of the Peasants' War. People in your day have estimated that one hundred thousand peasants were killed in that war.

When I discovered that the uprising had developed into outright war, I wrote *Against the Robbing and Murdering Hordes of Peasants*.[9] I charged the peasants with three sins against God. First, they have sworn to be true and faithful, submissive and obedient to their rulers. Second, they were starting a rebellion. Third, "They cloak this terrible and horrible sin with the gospel, call themselves 'Christian brethren.'"[10] I have no regret for those words. My words to the princes and lords have earned for

---

6 LW 46:24–25.

7 Bainton, 277.

8 Bainton, 278.

9 LW 46:45–47.

10 LW 46:50.

me eternal damnation from all revolutionaries. My words were much harsher when I spoke to the rulers. I said, "If he is able to punish and does not do it—even though he would have had to kill someone or shed blood—he becomes guilty of all the murder and evil that these people commit. . . . This is not a time to sleep. And there is no place for patience or mercy. This is the time of the sword, not the day of grace."[11] I concluded by saying, "If anyone thinks this too harsh, let him remember that rebellion is intolerable."[12]

If those words were from my natural evil spirit, God has forgiven me even though all revolutionaries never will. Perhaps God has forgiven Münzer also. We all live before God on the basis of forgiveness, never on the basis of our own natural self-deluded righteousness.

I received very harsh criticism in my own day for this writing, one of the shortest in my career. Friends urged me to write an explanation. Reluctantly, I agreed. I wrote *An Open Letter on the Harsh Book against the Peasants*.[13] I addressed it to my friend Caspar Müller, chancellor of Mansfeld. I think that it came out more as a defense of what I wrote than an explanation. If you think it useful, you can read it at your leisure. I think that you will not gain much from it.

---

11 LW 46: 53.

12 LW 46:55.

13 LW 46:57–85.

Letter 89

In 1519, I wrote *Treatise on the Holy Sacrament of Baptism*.[1] I had no significant argument with the Roman Church regarding this sacrament, and the Anabaptists had not yet surfaced.

There are three parts to this sacrament. I said, "Therefore in this sacrament we must have regard to three things—the sign, the significance thereof, and the faith."[2]

The sign, of course, is the water. You might be surprised to hear me say that immersion is the proper mode of Baptism. That was not the mode used in my day, nor is it in your day, in the Roman and evangelical churches. The first words in the treatise emphasized the proper mode. "Baptism," I wrote, ". . . is called in the Greek language *baptismos*, in Latin *mersio*, which means to plunge something entirely into the water, so that the water closes over it."[3] Shortly thereafter I wrote, "This usage is also demanded by the significance of baptism, for baptism signifies that the old man [old nature] and the sinful birth of flesh and blood are to be wholly drowned by the grace of God."[4] (I have often wondered whether the Anabaptists who emerged during the next decade had read only the first page of my treatise.)

Now you have the sign, immersed into water, and the significance of the sign, the old sinful nature drowned. What then of faith? As always, faith clings to the promise that in Baptism we have died to sin and have been raised from death to a new life with God. I put it this way, "This faith is of all things most necessary, for it is the ground of all comfort."[5] From early in my career, I insisted that those who are saved from the consequence of sin are saved by faith alone. Please do not understand me to say that grace is thereby excluded. Faith is of no value if it is not preceded by God's grace through which God offers salvation.

Some might expect that those who have died to sin in Baptism would

1 PE 1:51ff.

2 PE 1:56.

3 PE 1:56.

4 PE 1:56.

5 PE 1:63.

demonstrate no evidence of sin and be as pure as the angels of God. No! Sin clings to the baptized until they take their last breath. Only then is the fullness of Baptism realized. The inclination of the old self-centered nature, the attractive dead ends of the decaying cultures in which we all live, and the empty promises of Satan entice every believer. Time and again we fall. But the believer turns in daily repentance; he lives in the forgiveness of sins just as a fish lives in water. I quoted St. Augustine, "Sin is altogether forgiven in Baptism; not in such wise that it is no longer present, but in such wise that it is not taken into account."[6]

Flee from sin because you have died to it, but do not despair when you fail or fall. Return daily, hourly, to your Savior. Embrace the cross; Satan cannot endure the sight of Jesus' crucifixion because therein he received his eternal death sentence.

Take comfort in your Baptism. There God made a promise to you. Take more comfort in God's promise than in your despair.

I added a short warning at the conclusion of the treatise. I said, "At the same time, however, we must have a care that no false security creeps in and says to itself: 'Everything is right by virtue of baptism; meanwhile, therefore, I will live and do my own will, and afterwards, or when about to die, will remember my baptism and remind God of His covenant.'"[7]

You were baptized into a life of perpetual struggle. The struggle is between your old self-centered nature and the new nature given to you when you were baptized. Do not fear the struggle. As long as faith in God's promise is alive, you have won the battle. God has given you the victory. Your sin is canceled and you are an heir of eternal life.

---

6 PE 1:62.

7 PE 1:71.

Letter 90

When I wrote *A Discussion of Confession*[1] in 1520, I was thinking primarily about private confession that a person made to a priest. Primarily does not mean exclusively; I also referred to confession made directly to God. I wrote, "Before a man confesses to a priest, who is the vicar, he ought first confess to God who is the Principle."[2]

I grieve that most people who use my name in your day no longer have the privilege of private confession. What are your pastors doing if not hearing confession and offering absolution? What are your seminary professors teaching if they exclude training pastors in hearing confessions? I have noticed that many pastors, or others who teach my catechism, simply ignore the part on private confession. Why eliminate one major part of Christian living?

I urge your pastors to think again about their failure to offer believers the opportunity to make private confession and hear God's word of forgiveness. I urge the laity to call their pastors to faithful service by encouraging them to offer the privilege of private confession.

In my day, private confession was a requirement. Three hundred years before I did any writing, the Fourth Lateran Council of the Roman Church decreed, "All the faithful of either sex, after they have reached the age of discernment, should individually confess all their sins in a faithful manner to their own priest at least once a year."[3] When the Roman Church says "should" it means "must." (The 1983 Code of Canon Law uses the word "obliged.") What a tragedy! A privilege became an obligation; the Gospel became a law.

For my dear German people, I wrote about confession. The "Discussion" is also of value for you who make confession only to God.

Be careful that you do not take comfort in your confession, but only in God's promise of forgiveness. I put it in these words, "Therefore, for him who is about to go to confession, it is before all things necessary that he should not place his trust in his confession . . . but that, with com-

---

1 PE 1:75ff.

2 PE 1:83.

3 Decrees 1:245.

plete fullness of faith, he put his trust only in the most gracious promise of God."[4] I even suggested that occasionally, not often, but occasionally, one should go to the Communion without making confession. "Would you know why such advice is given?" I asked. "Listen!" I continued, "It is in order that a man may learn to trust more in the mercy of God than in his own confession or his own diligence."[5]

What sins should you confess? All of which you are aware. In my day, the Roman Church insisted that each individual sin must be confessed to a priest. The penalty imposed by the priest for each sin was determined by the severity of the sin. I thought confession of all sins to be impossible. No one can name all his sins; we are mostly blind to our own sins, but we see very clearly the sins of others. "Against these teachers," I wrote, "it should be known that a man ought to give up in despair the idea that he can ever confess all his mortal sins."[6] If you are aware of no sin, consider the words of Jesus to the effect that one must love the Lord his God with all that is in him, and must love his neighbor as he loves himself. If that reflection doesn't call you to attention, neither I nor any pastor can be of any help. Your only hope is to pray that God will show you your sin.

Confession of sin is predicated upon the intent to be free from sin and live a godly life. If that intent is not present, it would be better that you not make confession. I said, "For if there is anyone who does not find himself seriously inclined toward a good life (and by "good life" I meant something quite different than those words mean in your day), I know not whether it is safe for him to make confession. This I do know, that it were better for him to stay away from confession."[7]

---

4 PE 1:81.

5 PE 1:95.

6 PE 1:88.

7 PE 1:84.

LETTER 91

The year 1525 may have been the most important year in my career. I married Katharina von Bora, a woman about fifteen years younger than I, and engaged the most brilliant mind in Europe on the most important issue facing the church. The man was Desiderius Erasmus, a man about seventeen years older than I.

In this letter, I will you about the contest for Erasmus; in the next, a little about my marriage, wife, and family.

Erasmus had chided the church on the need for reform long before I saw the need, but he was a cautious man, fearful of taking a firm stand on any issue that might raise a controversy. Early in my career, probably up until 1519 or 1520, Erasmus seemed to support my call for reform. I wrote to him and asked for his support, but he was reluctant to commit. The Romans also solicited his support. They got the same treatment as I. The brilliant scholar tried to remain neutral. What a tragedy!

With his early support of my reform efforts and his desire to remain faithful to the Roman Church, Erasmus was caught in a dilemma. Whichever way he turned, he would be charged with duplicity and would offend somebody.

Finally, he found a way to remove himself from my camp without totally committing to the other. He wrote *On the Freedom of the Will*. Even in that book he did not take a firm stand but presented some options, as one who has read Erasmus's book has said, "He proposes a mediating solution and leaves the reader to judge."[1]

I did not particularly want to respond but felt I must because Erasmus had captured the essence of the issue in contention between me and Roman theology. I responded with perhaps the longest treatise of my life, nearly three hundred pages: *The Bondage of the Will*.[2]

Near the beginning of the book, I affirmed that Erasmus had found the kernel from which our theological controversy had grown. I wrote, "Indeed, as you should know, this is the cardinal issue between us, the

1 LW 33:9.

2 LW 33:3–295.

point on which everything in this controversy turns."[3] Again, at the conclusion of the book, I wrote,

> Moreover, I praise and commend you highly for this also, that unlike all the rest you alone have attacked the real issue, the essence of the matter in dispute, and have not wearied me with irrelevancies about the papacy, purgatory, indulgences, and such like trifles (for trifles they are rather than basic issues), with which almost everyone hitherto has gone hunting for me without success. You and you alone have seen the question on which everything hinges, and have aimed at the vital spot; for which I sincerely thank you.[4]

I hope that you understand that I cannot provide an adequate summary of three hundred pages in a short letter, but I must clarify one item and then give you a brief sample of my firm conviction that the human will is in bondage.

First, the clarification. When I wrote that the human will is in bondage, I was not being a determinist or fatalist. Indeed, you have vast freedom of choice. You can choose your occupation, whom to marry, if you choose to marry, the furnishings for your dwelling, how much to hoard for yourself and how much to give so that others may have food and warmth. There are more issues over which you have freedom than places where your will is bound. I affirmed the freedom of the will under certain conditions with these words, "Let us at least teach men to use it honestly, so that free choice is allowed to man only with respect to what is beneath him and not what is above him."[5]

Only in relation to God is your will bound. You are not fee to choose to believe in God, the Father, Son, and Holy Spirit, and all that pertains to the blessed Trinity. You must wait for God's Spirit to call you to faith. I said the same when I wrote the Small Catechism in 1529. In writing about the third part of the Apostles' Creed I wrote, "I believe that I cannot by my own reason or strength believe in Jesus Christ, my Lord, or come to Him; but the Holy Spirit has called me by the Gospel." Even after having been called, you are free to reject the call and submit to the lies of Satan and the lures of this world, but you are not free to initiate the

---

3 LW 33:35.

4 LW 33:294.

5 LW 33:70.

call from God. These were my words, "On the other hand in relation to God, or in matters pertaining to salvation or damnation, a man has no free choice, but is a captive, subject and slave either of the will of God or the will of Satan."[6]

Consider the implication of affirming free will in relation to God. If you have a free will, then God is in your hands; He awaits a decision from you. Don't you see the blasphemy? God is at your disposal; you can accept Him and His promises or reject the same. In either case, you are in control of God.

In writing to Erasmus, I said, "It follows now that free choice is plainly a divine term, and can be properly applied to none but the Divine Majesty alone; for he alone can do and does (as the psalmist says [Ps. 115:3]) whatever he pleases in heaven and on earth."[7]

I realize that these words are quite inadequate to give you the entire argument in *The Bondage of the Will*, but I hope that you catch the importance of the issue. I will close with one further comment, near the end of the book. "For we cannot have it both ways; the grace of God cannot be both so cheap as to be obtainable anywhere and everywhere by any man's puny endeavor, and at the same time so dear as to be given us only in and through the grace of one Man and so great a Man."[8]

---

6 LW 33:70.

7 LW 33:68.

8 LW 33:279.

LETTER 92

I had no intention of ever being married. I recognized the married estate as a divine institution, but it was not meant for everyone. For many years, I considered myself to be among the latter group.

In 1519, I wrote *A Sermon on the Estate of Marriage.*[1] From mere observation I could see the vastly different consequences of marriage. Near the end of the sermon I said, "O what a truly noble, important, and blessed condition the state of marriage is if it is properly regarded! O what a truly pitiable, horrible, and dangerous condition it is if it is not properly regarded!"[2]

In spite of the positive potential in marriage, I had made a vow when I entered the monastery in 1505. I had promised to lead a chaste life, and that implied a celibate life. By the time Father Staupitz released me from that vow in 1518, I was already thirty-five years old, up to my neck in writing, working to protect the precious Gospel that I had discovered, and simply exhausted at the end of the day. I had neither energy nor desire to consider marriage. In early 1521, I had been branded a heretic by the Roman Church. In my day, heretics were executed. Later in the same year, I was declared a criminal, an outlaw, by the emperor of the Holy Roman Empire. Life expectancy for me was very short. Even if I had considered taking a wife under those conditions, I thought I would have brought a bride into immediate widowhood. That would have been cruel.

A few items that I wrote got into the hands of some nuns in Ducal Saxony, not far from the border with Electoral Saxony. I think that my friend Leonard Koppe from Torgau, who delivered herring to the convent, may have been the smuggler. Having discovered freedom in Christ through the Gospel, several of the nuns yearned for release. Do not think that they could just announce their resignation and walk away; it was not so simple. For all practical purposes, they were imprisoned. In your day, those who held them would be charged with kidnapping.

My friend Leonard consented to devise a plan to rescue the ladies. To even attempt such an endeavor was a capital crime.

---

1 LW 44:3–14.

2 LW 44:13–14.

I was not privy to how Leonard arranged the rescue with the nuns, but apparently the nuns selected Easter Eve as the night of their escape. On that night there was a vigil, and the nuns were allowed to stay up much later than usual. When most of the sisters grew tired and returned to their beds, twelve nuns gathered and waited anxiously for their rescue. It was after midnight, says one from your day who knows more than I, that Leonard arrived with his covered wagon and swiftly moved the ladies into Electoral Saxony. In that territory, they had some measure of relief.[3]

It took a day or two before the twelve arrived in Wittenberg. Three went immediately to their homes of origin. That left nine nuns, who had nothing except the clothes they were wearing.

I felt responsible for those nine, but what could I do? I had a very meager income from teaching. But even that had been suspended, as a researcher from your day has noted, "In 1523 the university inspectors had cancelled the nine gulden he [Luther] had received as income, and he was teaching at the university practically without pay."[4]

Fortunately, a few local families took pity on the poor ladies and gave them temporary shelter and board. That was no permanent solution. On 10 April, I wrote to Spalatin and said, "I pray you also to do the work of charity and beg some money for me from your rich courtiers, by which I can support the girls a week or two until their kinsmen or others provide for them."[5] A day later, Ambrose also pleaded with Spalatin, "If you want to give anything to the poor," he wrote, "give it to them, for they are poor, wretched and deserted by their kinsfolk. I pity the poor things; they have neither shoes nor clothes. I beg of you, my dear brother, to see if you cannot get something for them from the people of the court, so that they may be provided with food and clothing."[6]

The permanent solution would be marriage. It was not long before eight of the nine nuns had either married or been taken in by relatives. One was left: Katharina von Bora. Katie worked as a domestic maid for a local family.

Jerome Baumgartner, a former student of the university, returned for a visit. Through some mutual interest, occasioned by Melanchthon,

---

3 Markwald, 46.

4 Markwald, 70–71.

5 Smith 2:180.

6 Smith 2:181.

he met Katie; they fell in love and planned to wed. Jerome returned to his home in Nürnberg with the promise to return shortly, but he never did. Katie was heartbroken.

On my own initiative, I wrote to Jerome urging him to return and fulfill his promise, but got no reply.

After a time of grieving on Katie's part, I made a suggestion to her. Dr. Kaspar Glatz, pastor in Orlamünde, would make a good husband. Katie showed her independent spirit; she would have nothing to do with Dr. Glatz.

What more could I do? In my next letter, I will tell you about Katie's fate.

Letter 93

Two years after her escape from the convent, Katie was still working as a domestic servant, and I still had no intent of a married life. As late as 16 April 1525, I wrote to Spalatin and said, "You write about me marrying. . . . But look out, or I, who have no thought at all of marriage, may sometime get ahead of you prospective bridegrooms."[1]

When I had suggested that Katie marry Dr. Glatz, she, with her independent, indomitable spirit, asked Amsdorf to tell me that she would not have Glatz, but as your historian has noted, "She would take Amsdorf himself or Luther."[2] Amsdorf later told me of that conversation.

I created quite a stir around Wittenberg when on 13 June, Katie and I were betrothed in the presence of Johannes Bugenhagen, pastor of the city church, and four others: Justus Jonas, Johann Apel, Lucas Cranach, and his wife, Barbara. In my day a betrothal amounted to a marriage.

The following day, Jonas wrote to Spalatin and said, "Our Luther has married Catharine von Bora."[3]

Lest there be any question of our marriage, one of your researchers has correctly noted, "After the blessing, on the same night, Katie and Martin's betrothal was consummated according to an ancient German custom: in the required presence of a witness. Martin and Katie's good friend Jonas was asked to be the witness."[4]

You may wonder why, at age forty three, I chose to be married. It was not love nor because I felt sorry for the poor domestic. One of your own got it right. He said that I married "to please his father, to spite the pope and the Devil, and to seal his witness before martyrdom."[5]

If I did not love Katie when we married, love has a way of growing. Later in life, I said, "I would not exchange Katie for France or Venice, because God has given her to me."[6]

---

1 Smith 2:305–6.

2 Bainton, 288.

3 Smith 2:322.

4 Markwald, 71.

5 Bainton, 288.

6 Bainton, 288.

I sometimes playfully referred to Katie as "my rib" [Genesis 2:21–22]. Once, when writing to Spalatin, I concluded by saying, "My rib and I send greetings to you and your rib."[7]

What did I have to offer Katie for a home? A monastery. The Black Cloister was practically empty of monks; almost all had left. Only one other monk and I remained. Upon my marriage, the other monk moved out. Katie was energetic and creative; she turned that monastery into a lovely home.

I regret that I did not write a long book about Katie; she was an extraordinary woman. I'll let one of your researchers tell about her. "Out of bed at 4 o'clock, she was known as 'Käthe von Bora, Morning Star of Wittenberg.' Katie was in good physical condition and often worked until 9 o'clock at night."[8] What did she do? The same researcher said, "Katie became gardener, fisher, brewer, fruit grower, cattle and horse breeder, cook, bee-keeper, provisioner, nurse, and vintner. . . . Kate carefully tended chickens, geese, pigs, cows, and work and riding horses."[9] If your researcher only knew! She did so much more than he could even imagine.

I would like to tell you much more about my devoted wife, but I must rush on to tell you about the six wonderful children she gave to me. Children can be God's greatest blessing or a source of profound grief; I experienced both.

Fifty-one weeks after we were married, God gave us a baby boy. We named him Johannes, after his godfather, my friend Johannes Bugenhagen. We always called the little one Hans. In adulthood, Hans became a lawyer.

In December 1527, Katie gave me a baby girl. We named her Elisabeth after the mother of John the Baptist. Only eight months later, Katie and I were devastated when death robbed the cradle.

When our third child was born in 1529, we named her Magdalene after Katie's aunt. We called her Lenchen. But our lives were shattered for a second time when, at the tender age of thirteen, Lenchen died while I held her in my arms. Lenchen was laid to rest beside the baby sister that she never knew. Someone has found the headstone on which I had

---

7 Smith 2:356.

8 Markwald, 81.

9 Markwald, 82.

written in Latin, "I Lenchen, Luther's daughter, rest here in my little bed, surrounded by all the saints."[10]

No child is ever replaced, but I had the joy of another son, born on 9 November 1531, one day before my forty-eighth birthday. We named him Martin. In adulthood, he followed in his father's footsteps and studied theology. He died at the age of thirty-four, never having served as a pastor.

Paul was born in 1533. We gave him the name, as someone discovered, "out of thankfulness to St. Paul, who has given us so many great teachings and writings, that we should have named two sons after the apostle."[11] Paul became a distinguished physician.

Our sixth child, the only daughter to live to maturity, was Margareta, born in 1534 and named after my mother. She married a Wittenberg student but died at the early age of thirty-six, leaving several children to her husband. Some of Margareta's progeny still live in your day.

Joy fills my heart as I think of my dear Katie and the six wonderful children she gave to me.

---

10 Markwald, 97.

11 Markwald, 99.

Letter 94

After about 1525, I wrote very little worth sharing with you. One of your own historians didn't put the issue quite in those terms, but he wrote, "As the decade advanced, issues involving government and law also demanded Luther's attention."[1] He failed to mention that I was also busy visiting congregations, assisting them in securing evangelical pastors, and addressing specific local problems that are of no interest to you.

There are, however, a few things that I still want to share with you.

I had a friend, Assa von Kram, who had made a career in military service. His conscience was pricked by the massacre of thousands of peasants in the recent peasants' uprising. He wondered and worried whether military service is compatible with being a Christian. In July 1525, he asked me to reflect on that issue and write something about it. It took a while, but by January 1527, I had written *Whether Soldiers, Too, Can Be Saved*.[2]

Someone who provided an introduction to that treatise, after translating it into your language, wrote, "In *Whether Soldiers, Too, Can Be Saved* Luther affirms the legitimacy of the military profession."[3] Of course, that statement does not answer the question whether Christians can legitimately participate in military service and be saved. The answer to that question is more difficult and requires some clear distinctions.

The first issue regards the legitimacy of war. War is a tragedy, a scourge, and the joy of Satan. Until the new age arrives in its fullness, believers and nonbelievers live together under the curse of human sin, one fighting for superiority over the other. In my treatise, I wrote, "What men write about war, saying that it is a great plague, is all true. But they should also consider how great the plague is that war prevents."[4] I also put it a different way, "For if the sword were not on guard to preserve peace, everything in the world would be ruined because of lack of peace."[5]

1 Bornkamm, 581.

2 LW 46:87–137.

3 LW 46:90.

4 LW 46:96.

5 LW 46:96.

I distinguished between three kinds of wars.

The first kind of war is insurrection—people rising up against duly constituted government. Such wars are simply intolerable. I can think of no circumstance in which insurrection is justified. I said, "I feel that there can be no stable government unless a nation respects and honors its rulers."[6] Further, I wrote, "There is as great a difference between changing a government and improving it as the distance from heaven to earth."[7]

The second kind of war is between equals. I am quite aware that absolute equality is a fiction. My intent was in reference to two separate governments, both of which have been instituted by God. In that setting, I wrote, "I want to say that whoever starts a war is in the wrong. And it is only right and proper that he who first draws his sword is defeated, or even punished, in the end."[8]

The opposite of starting a war is self-defense. I used the example of my sovereign, Duke John. "When he was asked why he let them [wicked plots on the part of his neighbors] threaten him so, he replied, 'I shall not start anything; but if I have to fight, you will see that I shall be the one who decides when it is time to stop.'"[9]

The third kind of war is when lords rise up against their own subjects. Such action should never happen. It is the responsibility of the government to create and maintain peace among its subjects. I also said, "However, if the subjects rise up and rebel, as the peasants did recently, then it is right and proper to fight against them."[10]

So much for wars. But can a Christian, in good conscience, participate in any war? Can a Christian soldier be saved? Here a clear and careful distinction must be made. A Christian does not go to war as a Christian, but as a citizen, called to service by his sovereign. I wrote, "Christians do not fight and have no worldly rulers among them. Their government is a spiritual government, and, according to the Spirit, they are subjects of no one but Christ."[11] But, as I said earlier, sometimes wars are inevitable; they can prevent a worse plague and preserve the peace. I said, "No king

6 LW 46:107.

7 LW 46:111–12.

8 LW 46:118.

9 LW 46:119–20.

10 LW 46:125.

11 LW 46:99.

can go to war alone."[12] Should a Christian sit by in comfort and let others protect him and his family? Christians also are responsible for life, peace, and security in this world. As subjects of an earthly ruler, Christians can legitimately participate in war, with the caution that they must not participate to gain wealth or honor. I finally answered the question whether soldiers, too, can be saved. I wrote, "Leave out greed and other evil thoughts, and it is not sin to fight in a war."[13]

One of your historians has said, "The problem of conscience pervades this entire work."[14] That is an overstatement, but a Christian conscience must be consulted. I did say, almost as a concluding statement, "If you know for sure that he [your ruler] is wrong, then you should fear God rather than men, Acts 4 [5:29], and you should neither fight nor serve."[15]

What if you reap the ire of your government for refusing to go to war when your conscience forbids and you are penalized for your refusal? My only response was "You must take that risk and, with God's help, let whatever happens, happen."[16]

Can soldiers, too, be saved? Without a doubt. Do you think that Jesus Christ died exclusively for farmers, priests, and nobles? No! For soldiers also.

---

12 LW 46:127.

13 LW 46:130.

14 Bornkamm, 581.

15 LW 46:130.

16 LW 46:130.

Letter 95

Someone who thinks he knows more about me than I know about me said, "The year 1527 was one of the most difficult in Luther's life."[1] That man knows nothing about *Anfechtung* and the terrifying trials that accompany it. I would take a thousand 1527s in exchange for one year of *Anfechtung* [see Letter 11].

I did not think about the difficulties of 1527 while I was living that year. Only after noting what your correspondent said did I reflect on that year; it was indeed trying. Satan came again with spiritual torments; I had an illness that I thought would end my life; the plague struck Wittenberg in August, and the University was required to relocate for a short time. The plague added additional pastoral duties; Katie endured suffering as she awaited the birth of Elisabeth. Her pain was my pain. My oldest son, Hans, became ill, and the elector expected me to visit the congregations in Saxony. In addition, I was translating the prophets from Hebrew into German, and I had to settle a feud between John Agricola and Melanchthon.[2]

Those were nothing more than life issues that many have had to endure. They are not worth comparing with the spiritual strife of *Anfechtung*.

The dreaded Black Death (you know it as the bubonic plague) that swept over Europe about two hundred years earlier, destroying about 25 percent of the population, reappeared in Wittenberg in August.

The university was transferred to Jena for a short time in order to protect the students and faculty from the deadly plague. I was ordered to depart Wittenberg along with the rest of the faculty, but I could not and I did not. There were the sick and dying who needed the comfort and consolation of the Gospel.

The onset of the Black Death and the transfer of the university prompted me to write *Whether One May Flee from a Deadly Plague*.[3]

You will almost certainly never encounter the plague. Familiarity

1 LW 37:155.

2 LW 37:155.

3 LW 43:113–38.

with the disease, public health awareness, and better medicines have crippled the Black Death in your part of the world. But what I said about fleeing the Black Death is pertinent to any public threat to your health. Ought you, as a Christian, flee when your life is in peril? I did not think it prudent to give an absolute answer that would be appropriate for every Christian. I said, "Since it is generally true of Christians that few are strong and many are weak, one simply cannot place the same burden upon everyone."[4]

What is true of the majority is not true of those who bear the public trust. Regarding priests and pastors, I said, "Those who are engaged in a spiritual ministry such as preachers and pastors must likewise remain steadfast before the peril of death."[5] Public officers also have a responsibility to remain. A few others have the responsibility to remain and serve their neighbors. That is not to say that all pastors, public servants, and others with personal obligations must remain in the face of death. Some may depart, and no one should judge who those may be, so long as there are others willing to remain and fill the required spiritual, governmental, and civic responsibilities.

To leave the option open, I wrote, "If someone is sufficiently bold and strong in his faith, let him stay in God's name; that is certainly no sin. If someone is weak and fearful, let him flee in God's name as long as he does not neglect his duty toward his neighbor but has made adequate provision for others to provide nursing care."[6]

That was about all that I had to say about fleeing the Black Death. But remember, the issue is much bigger than the plague; it relates to serving your neighbor before considering your own safety and welfare in the face of physical harm.

Every Christian wants to serve God. Those who seek to serve only their own interests, the interest of their family, their nation, their ethnic community, or their congregation are fake Christians. In my comments, I wrote, "Godliness is nothing else but service to God. Service to God is indeed service to our neighbor."[7] I mentioned the words of Jesus in Matthew's Gospel [Matt. 25:40], "As you did it to one of the least . . . you did it to Me."

---

4 LW 43:120.

5 LW 43:121.

6 LW 43:123.

7 LW 43:128–29.

I made some comments about using physicians and medicine as gifts from God, but you know more about that than I.

In my day, there were concerns about the location of a cemetery. I wrote a few lines about that, but it is not an issue for you.

Death is at our door every day. I thought it wise and prudent to write a few words about how one should care and provide for the soul as death approaches.

First, "Attend church and listen to the sermon so that they learn through God's word how to live and how to die."[8]

What I said about those who ignore God's Word may sound harsh, but I haven't changed my mind in five hundred years. I said, "A person who wants to live like a heathen . . . and does not publicly repent should not expect us to administer the sacrament to him or have us count him a Christian. Let him die as he has lived."[9]

Second, in preparation for death, I said, "Everyone should prepare in time and get ready for death by going to confession and taking the sacrament once every week or fortnight."[10]

Again, I was quite blunt. "Those who have been careless and negligent in these matters must account for themselves. That is their own fault. After all, we cannot set up a private pulpit and altar daily at their bedside simply because they have despised the public pulpit and altar to which God has summoned and called them."[11]

The third thing in preparation for death is to call for a chaplain or pastor as early as possible. Any faithful pastor will gladly respond to such a call.

My dear friends, be prepared for death because it will surely reach out and grab you, perhaps when you are not expecting it. But you, dear brothers and sisters, face death fearlessly because our Lord has won your victory. Death has no power or authority over you. You are home free.

---

8 LW 43:134.

9 LW 43:134.

10 LW 43:134.

11 LW 43:134–35.

Letter 96

During the entire decade of the 1520s, I was compelled to return time and again to defend the words of my Lord, "This is My body; this is My blood." I continued the defense because of the many attacks against what I wrote. Someone counted and said, "More than two dozen published writings had directly or indirectly attacked Luther's view of the Lord's Supper between late 1524 and early 1527."[1] I didn't count, but he didn't count the many attacks by the Romans following my publication of *The Babylonian Captivity of the Church* in 1520. In the early part of the decade, I challenged the Roman Church's teaching of transubstantiation, a teaching that materialized the Lord's Supper. In the middle of the decade, I had to contend with some of my early supporters whose reason was offended by the words. Rather than believing the words of Jesus, they transformed the sacrament into a mere memorial of Christ's death. Finally, toward the close of the decade, I defended the words of my Lord against the Swiss reformer Ulrich Zwingli and his colleague Johannes Oecolampadius. They used several arguments to deny that Jesus was really physically present in the sacrament. My erstwhile friends and the Swiss spiritualized the sacrament. I called them both fanatics.

In 1527, I wrote *That These Words of Christ, "This Is My Body," etc., Still Stand Firm against the Fanatics*.[2] A year later, I wrote *Confession Concerning Christ's Supper*.[3] One who has read these treatises has said, "The two treatises in this volume [LW 37] are Luther's most comprehensive and profound discussions of the Lord's Supper doctrine."[4]

I intended those to be my last words on the blessed sacrament. However, about sixteen years later, I felt a need to challenge Caspar Schwenkfeld's view of the Lord's Supper. Casper joined the reform movement under the influence of Karlstadt and Münzer. You will not be surprised that his view of the Lord's Supper rejected the real body and blood of Jesus in the sacrament. He spoke of receiving a "heavenly body." I

---

1 LW 37:5.

2 LW 37:3–150.

3 LW 37:151–372.

4 LW 37:xv.

have no idea what that might be. To challenge Schwenkfeld, I wrote *A Brief Confession on the Holy Sacrament*.

In previous letters [46 and 74], I have shared with you my firm belief in the real presence of Jesus in the Lord's Supper. Real has always meant the whole Jesus, not just a spiritual Jesus.

I need not say much about these last two writings on the sacrament. A few comments on the 1527 treatise will be enough. I chose this treatise because I have not previously mentioned Zwingli or Oecolampadius. You will meet Zwingli again when I tell you about our meeting in Marburg in 1529.

I wrote the treatise—true of all my treatises—not to convert anybody. I said, "For I have no hope that the teachers of a heresy or fanaticism will be converted. . . . It has never been reported that an author of false doctrine was converted."[5] I wrote only for the laity. Again I said, "So I shall once more set myself against the devil and his fanatics, not for their sake, but for the sake of the weak and simple."[6]

I spoke sharply, as was my custom, and said, "There is no middle ground."[7] Either the whole Jesus Christ is present in the sacrament or He is not. On that issue, Zwingli and I could not agree.

I did not conceive clever arguments against the Swiss. I simply clung to the clear words of Jesus, "This is My body; this is My blood." If you ask how Jesus can be present in the bread and wine, I must confess my ignorance. I wrote, "But how this takes place or how he is in the bread, we do not know and are not meant to know."[8]

This issue presents a fine example of how to interpret the Scriptures. I wrote, "For anyone who ventures to interpret words in the Scriptures any other way than what they say, is under obligation to prove this contention out of the text of the very same passage or by an article of faith."[9]

I had remained consistent throughout the decade. Your historian has said,

---

5 LW 37:19–20.

6 LW 37:19.

7 LW 37:26.

8 LW 37:29.

9 LW 37:32.

> Luther himself held fast to the same basis from which he had contested the Roman sacraments down to the biblical foundation of the Supper and of baptism. In his *Babylonian Captivity* he had laid down the rule against doing violence to the Word of God: the sacraments (unless clear circumstances prove otherwise) are to be understood "in no other than their grammatical and proper sense."[10]

I had no trouble admitting that Jesus is spiritually present as well as physically present in the sacrament. But, I insisted, "Not a single article of faith would remain if I followed the rancor of reason."[11]

When the Swiss confronted me with the words of Jesus recorded by St. John in chapter 6 [:63], "The flesh is of no avail," I had to remind them that if the flesh is of no avail in the sacrament then neither is it of avail in the womb of Mary. In that case, Mary gave birth to a spiritual being. The incarnation is lost; no flesh and blood suffered under Pontius Pilate; only a spiritual phantom died on the cross. The case for Christ and the holy faith is lost. I wrote, almost five-hundred years ago:

> Now I ask: When the Virgin Mary was bodily pregnant with the Son of God and carried Jesus Christ our Lord nine months in her womb, and then as a mother brought him bodily into the world, as our Creed and the Gospels say, did she also carry and bear Christ's flesh bodily in and through her flesh? As a fanatic I simply do not believe it. Why? Because Christ's flesh, bodily conceived, borne, and handled, is of no avail. If it is of no avail, then nothing took place, as our (Fanatic) argument declares, "Christ's flesh is of no avail." Therefore nothing is there. For if his flesh is not present in the sacrament for the reason that flesh is of no avail, neither is it in his mother's womb, precisely for the same reason that it is of no avail.[12]

In John 6, flesh does not refer to the flesh of Christ, but to human nature that is set against the Spirit of God. I'm surprised that I had to teach theologians that simple fact. I said to Zwingli and Oecolampadius,

> Since it is true and incontrovertible, then, that where flesh is placed in opposition to spirit, it does not mean Christ's

---

10 Bornkamm, 531–32.

11 LW 37:53.

12 LW 37:82.

> body but the old Adam [human nature] born of the flesh, it is certain this verse also, John 6 [:63], "Flesh is of no avail," cannot be understood of Christ's body, because Christ in this passage contrasts flesh with spirit.[13]

When I affirmed the physical of Jesus in the sacrament, I did not mean a localized presence. I said, "We poor sinners, indeed, are not so foolish as to believe that Christ's body is in the bread in a crude visible manner, like bread in a basket or wine in a cup."[14] Some in your day, trying to clarify my understanding of Christ's real presence in the sacrament, have called the union of Christ's body with the bread a "sacramental union."[15] I do not recall ever using that phrase, and while not wrong, I do not find it particularly helpful. Let the mystery of how Christ's body and blood are really present in the sacrament remain.

I also wanted to affirm the spiritual dimension of the sacrament. I said, "He [Jesus] joined both together, the Word and his body, to be eaten spiritually with the heart and physically with the mouth."[16]

The Swiss also argued that because Christ is localized in heaven at the right hand of the Father, he cannot be in the sacrament. But again they are shortsighted. If Christ is localized in heaven, then he cannot be in his Word that I read, nor in the heart of believers, nor with believers as they assemble to worship. Where does that leave us believers? A Christianity with an absent Christ.

I've said enough. That's my last word on the Holy Supper. As for you, keep the faith.

---

13 LW 37:96.

14 LW 37:65.

15 LW 37:xix.

16 LW 37:88.

Letter 97

Sometimes I regret having posted the Ninety-five Theses in 1517. Those theses lit a fire that later felt like a volcanic eruption of diverse theological opinions that further fractured the Body of Christ.

In 1527, two pastors from a Roman Catholic territory asked me for an opinion about people who were rebaptizing adults. I knew very little about those rebaptizers. They originated, according to one of your historians, in Switzerland, far from Saxony. They called themselves Anabaptists, which simply means rebaptizers.

Your historians know a lot more about Anabaptists than I did. One historian said, "Anabaptism began in Zurich in January 1525 with the administration of believer's baptism."[1] He said, "Men everywhere had to be called to follow Christ and to signify their commitment with the reception of adult baptism."[2] That attitude certainly caught my attention. Anabaptists robbed God of His activity and made it their own. Baptism was merely a sign of their commitment. How tragically people want to seize the initiative from God and make it their own work!

I'll share just two more comments from the same historian to give you a little idea of who those Anabaptists were. "Anabaptism was a network of loosely knit congregations. There was no formal training for the leaders."[3] And, "When talking about Anabaptism we must keep in mind that it was an underground movement. . . . It had no organizational structure. . . . It had no generally binding confessional statements."[4]

Please understand that I knew none of what I just quoted when I was asked to comment about rebaptism of adults. I had so little information that I hesitated to write anything. I told the two pastors, "Since there has not been much occasion here for it, I have not, for my part, given much thought to these baptizers."[5] Nevertheless, I thought it wise to provide some clarification on the subject.

---

1 Hillerbrand, 72.

2 Hillerbrand, 73.

3 Hillerbrand, 76.

4 Hillerbrand, 76.

5 LW 40:230.

One who read my letter *Concerning Rebaptism*[6] said that I was working on it in December 1527 and January 1528. But, if I recall correctly, I must have continued on the letter into at least early spring. The same reviewer says, "In March 1528 one of their [Anabaptist] noblest leaders, Dr. Balthasar Hubmaier, was burned in Vienna, and his wife drowned."[7] I deeply regretted that action. I wrote, "Still it is not right, and I truly grieve, that these miserable folk should be so lamentably murdered, burned, and tormented to death. We should allow everyone to believe what he wills."[8]

I wish that had been my final and conclusive statement on freedom of belief. But telling the truth and confessing one's sin belongs to every Christian. A different researcher noted correctly, "Because of the changed situation, though with heavy heart, Luther in 1531 signed the opinion drafted by Melanchthon for the Wittenberg theological faculty approving the application of the death penalty against Anabaptists."[9] Remember, I was a sinner just like you, and like you I have a great need for a Savior. Thank God for Jesus Christ, my Lord.

Now I must share with you a little of that letter that I wrote *Concerning Rebaptism*.

At the outset, I shared my frustration with all the diverse teachings that had arisen. I wrote, "I have long ago found that if I stop one mouth of the devil, he opens ten others, and the lie grows constantly greater."[10]

Perhaps it was my frustration with all the heresies that had come to my attention during the past decade, or perhaps it was nostalgia, that prompted me to write positively about the Roman Church. I said, "We on our part confess that there is much that is Christian and good under the papacy; indeed everything that is Christian and good is to be found there and has come to us from this source."[11]

Again I said, "We do not rave as do the rebellious spirits, so as to reject everything that is found in the papal church."[12]

---

6 LW 40:225–62.

7 LW 40:227.

8 LW 40:230.

9 Bornkamm, 605.

10 LW 40:229.

11 LW 40:231.

12 LW 40:232.

When I gave myself to the subject of Baptism, I began in the first few sentences, "Not only is my conscience at rest in this, but my reputation is sufficiently safeguarded by the number of my sermons and especially by the latest Postil . . . wherein I have made known abundantly my faith concerning infant baptism."[13]

The Anabaptists rejected infant Baptism because, they claimed, an infant knows nothing about his Baptism. In adulthood, the person may even question whether he has been baptized. To that argument I said, "My friend, how do you know that this man is your father, this woman your mother? You cannot trust people, you must be sure of your own birth."[14]

A more serious argument insisted that faith must precede Baptism, with the corresponding certainly that infants cannot have faith. To the little certainty I responded, "When they say, 'Children cannot believe,' how can they be sure of that? Where in the Scripture by which they would prove it and on which they would build? They imagine this, I suppose, because children do not speak or have understanding. But such a fancy is deceptive, yea, altogether false, and we cannot build on what we imagine."[15]

The rebaptizers apparently understood faith to be an intellectual activity. Consequently, they create another human work, thereby robbing God of the gift of faith that He desires to give.

As for the necessity of faith preceding Baptism, I said that no one can know the faith of another. "Have they now become gods," I wrote, "so that they can discern the hearts of men and know whether or not they believe?"[16] I followed by saying, "So whoever bases baptism on the faith of the one to be baptized can never baptize anyone."[17]

Indeed, faith is necessary for salvation, but whether faith precedes or follows Baptism makes no difference. I wrote, "When faith comes, baptism is complete. A second baptism is not necessary."[18] I insisted that God's Word once spoken can never be rescinded.

---

13 LW 40:229.

14 LW 40:234.

15 LW 40:241–42.

16 LW 40:239.

17 LW 40:240.

18 LW 40:246.

Consider my final word to the two pastors: "If the first, or child, baptism were not right, it would follow that for more than a thousand years there was no baptism or any Christendom, which is impossible. . . . For over a thousand years there were hardly any other than child baptisms."[19]

I was not a revolutionary who promoted or enjoyed change for the sake of change. My principle, as valid in your day as in mine, I put in these words, "For if we are going to change or do away with customs that are traditional, it is necessary to prove convincingly that these are contrary to the Word of God."[20]

With those words I return to my rest.

---

19 LW 40:256–57.

20 LW 40:241.

Letter 98

As early as 1525, letters were flying around Germany in an attempt to arrange a personal meeting between me and Ulrich Zwingli from Zurich. The purpose was to resolve our different understandings of the Lord's Supper. I had no interest in such a meeting. We had both presented our different understandings, very clearly, in what we had written. I was certain that nothing positive would be accomplished by a personal meeting. I had affirmed that the body and blood of Jesus Christ is bodily, as well as spiritually, present in the sacrament; Zwingli called the Holy Meal a symbol. There is no room for compromise between reality and a symbol.

One who spends his life researching these issues has said, "In 1527 [Landgrave] Philip of Hesse, in the interest of his political plan [to form a political federation of reform-minded territories], proposed a colloquy with Zwingli to Luther."[1]

When I discovered that a political motivation drove the movement, I became more firm in my opposition.

The Second Diet of Speyer convened in 1529 with a stronger desire (than at the First Diet of Speyer in 1526) to stop the reform movement. Philip of Hesse led a group of reform-minded nobles in offering a formal protest. That was the origin of the word *protestant* that is so frequently used in your day by people who have no idea about the nature of the protest.

The same researcher, noted above, said, "The landgrave believed that the time was now ripe for making a broader political alliance with the Swiss."[2]

I wrote to my sovereign, Duke John, in May 1529 and cautioned against the landgrave's intent. I said, "Through our prayers Christ our Lord will grant that . . . Your Electoral Grace may nevertheless not let yourself get involved in this and caught up in it."[3]

---

1 LW 38:6.

2 LW 38:7.

3 LW 49:225.

Landgrave Philip was more persuasive with the elector than I. When my sovereign approved of the alliance, I felt obligated to write positively to the landgrave and reluctantly accept the invitation to meet with Zwingli in Marburg.

I, Melanchthon, and a few others arrived in Marburg the end of September. Zwingli, Oecolampadius, and a small contingent arrived to represent the Swiss. A third party arrived from Strassburg. They were led by Martin Bucer, who thought he could provide a middle way. He could not see that a middle way was impossible; he and his group were with the Swiss party whether or not they chose to be.

On 1 October, informal private meetings were scheduled between Zwingli and Melanchthon and between Oecolampadius and me. They were productive, to a point.

Two very long days began at 6:00 a.m. on Saturday, 2 October, and concluded the evening of the following day. No notes were allowed to be taken by the participants or the several dozen who were permitted to be present as observers. However, after the conclusion of the colloquy, about a half dozen reports were written from memory by some attendees.

Most agreed that the discussions were civil and without acrimony. All sides agreed with fourteen important points of Christian teaching, but on the fifteenth we could not agree.

We made our public confession in what has been called the Marburg Articles.[4]

Even in article 15, in which we shared our understanding of the Lord's Supper, we agreed on five of six points. On one point we could not agree: Does the whole person of Jesus Christ come to us in the sacrament, or is it only a spiritual Jesus that we receive?

I credit Zwingli with this: he did move from saying that the sacrament is only a memorial to confessing that Jesus is really present in the bread and wine, if only a spiritual presence.

On 4 October, informal discussion continued. A respected student of the Reformation has said, "The common confession had failed. But then the Swiss proposed that despite the disagreement intercommunion be practiced, and to this 'Luther momentarily agreed.' This we know on the testimony of Bucer, 'until Melanchthon interposed out of regard

4 LW 38:85–89.

for Ferdinand and the emperor.'" He then added, "This statement is extremely significant. It means that Luther did not play the role of utter implacability commonly ascribed to him, and was disposed to join the Swiss until Melanchthon made him aware that to coalesce with the left would estrange the right."[5]

I may have said what Bucer recounted, but I am not certain. It doesn't sound like something that I would have said, and I cannot imagine changing my mind on matters of Christian confession or practice simply to please a politician, even the emperor.

Was anything accomplished by our meeting in Marburg? It may be easier for me to say it now than at the time: Yes, a great deal was accomplished. I have already noted the fourteen articles of agreement, and Zwingli's move from understanding the sacrament as merely symbolic to a confession that Jesus Christ is really present in the sacrament, although, regrettably, only spiritually.

In addition, one of your historians has said, "The colloquy had succeeded, however, in eliminating much of the former personal enmity and discord exiting between the opposing parties and made further cooperation much more likely."[6] I am delighted to see moves toward cooperation and understanding in your day.

Another historian said, "The Marburg Articles have thus become a masterpiece among the confessions of Lutheran origin."[7] That may be true, but I seriously doubt that many pay much attention to them. I expect that if you asked most pastors who bear my name to identify the Marburg Articles they would be stumped. I further expect that not one "Lutheran" (I thoroughly dislike such reference to my name) layperson in a thousand has even heard about them. Such is life in the Christian community.

---

5 Bainton, 320.

6 Schwiebert, 714.

7 Bornkamm, 650.

Letter 99

I had known for a long time that educational materials were needed for Christians, both adults and children. There were catechisms before my time, but almost exclusively for adults, and they were mostly instructions on what was required of Christians.

To explain how I became acutely aware of the immediate need, I must tell you something about church visitations that began in 1528.

The reform movement created problems even with churches that had accepted the Reformation heritage. Remember, there were no evangelically trained clergy; all were converts from the Roman Church. It would take many years to provide evangelical pastors for all the congregations.

Our sovereign, Duke John the Constant (Frederick the Wise had died 5 May 1525), sent teams to visit all the congregations in his territory. Each team consisted of a theological professor from the University of Wittenberg, a representative of the Saxon court, and a prominent parish pastor. The teams were to report on the competence of the pastor, both in terms of understanding the faith and his lifestyle. In order to provide guidance for the visitors, Melanchthon wrote *Instructions for the Visitors of Parish Pastors in Electoral Saxony*.[1] Someone noted that I wrote a preface for the instructions.

The results of the visitations were tragic. One who has studied the reports has said, "The first task of the visitors was to determine the worthiness of each individual [pastor] and to remove the incompetent."[2] He added, "In many regions the clergy had opportunely left the Roman Church and called themselves Lutherans, but when questioned as to their beliefs, they were colossally ignorant concerning Luther's writings. Many could not repeat the Ten Commandments, or the Lord's Prayer and knew little or nothing of the Bible."[3] The lifestyle of many clergy was as bad as their educational and spiritual incompetence. Again, the same historian wrote, "In one region in the lands of the former Duke George [Albertine Saxony], Menius reported the conditions so dreadful that out

---

1 LW 40:263–320.

2 Schwiebert, 617.

3 Schwiebert, 618.

of 200 clergymen all but ten lived in open fornication. It was not unusual to find pastors in gambling places and beer chambers, and distinguishable from the laity only by the title of clergyman."[4] On the first visit, the teams had to be very lenient or there would have been no pastors remaining. They were provided time for change and were eventually provided with my catechisms for elementary Christian teaching.

I need not tell you more to demonstrate how critical the need was for Christian teaching material.

In 1529, I wrote two catechisms: one for adults, including clergy, and the other for the youth. I never distinguished between the two, but some have called the one for adults the Large Catechism and the other one for youth the Small Catechism.

I was not original in my writing. The Ten Commandments, the Creed, and the Lord's Prayer had been at the heart of Christian nurture from the first century. Of course, the Creed had not been formulated at that early date, but the content of the Creed was certainly confessed in the first century. To those three essentials: the Ten Commandments, what God requires of each son and daughter of Adam; the Creed, what God has done for humanity because each has failed in fulfilling God's requirement; and the Lord's Prayer, the privilege given to people to address God as Father, I added the two sacraments: Baptism and the Lord's Supper.

To each commandment, each part of the Creed, and each section of the Lord's Prayer, in the Small Catechism, I provided simple explanations and meanings. For the two sacraments, I asked and answered four questions that are pertinent to each sacrament. In the Large Catechism, I did almost the same, but the answers were much more extensive.

Many have noted that in my comments on the meaning of the Creed, I placed great emphasis on God's action of making people righteous by faith alone, and also how personal I made it for each individual who reads my comments. I did the latter by using the first person singular pronoun. If you have studied my catechism, you will recall that I wrote the explanation of the First Article of the Creed with these words: "I believe that God has made *me* and all creatures. . . . All this He does out of fatherly, divine goodness and mercy, without any merit or worthiness in *me*."

The Second Article explains redemption: Jesus Christ "has redeemed *me*, a lost and condemned person, purchased and won *me*."

---

4 Schwiebert, 619.

The Third Article confesses: "I believe that *I* cannot by *my* own reason or strength believe in Jesus Christ. . . . But the Holy Spirit has called *me* by the Gospel."

I'm glad that many have recognized the personal nature of faith. It is not stale doctrines to be affirmed or a moral life to be lived, but a living relationship with your Creator, your Savior, and the blessed Spirit that God has given to every believer.

My heart beats with joy knowing that the catechism has been taught to youth for five hundred years. I regret that in your day it is no longer taught in most homes. In the Small Catechism, I said repeatedly, "As the head of the family should teach it in a simple way to his household."

Next to the Bible, the catechism was my lifeline to God. I repeated the catechism every day. I regarded the elements so highly that another of your historians has noted, "Luther said that he would be glad to have all his works perish except the reply to Erasmus [*The Bondage of the Will*] and the catechism."[5] He noted correctly.

Read the Bible daily, but memorize the catechism; it is short and simple. Carry it with you in your mind and recite it to yourself repeatedly. The entirety of the Christian faith is contained in that little booklet.

---

5 Bainton, 337.

LETTER 100

Every politician from emperor and pope to bishops and city officials stood in constant fear of the Muslim Turks as they moved westward toward the Holy Roman Empire. By the summer of 1529, the army of Islam, under the leadership of Suleiman, stood at the gates of Vienna, already within the eastern boundary of the empire.

A massive collective sigh of relief covered Western Europe when word was received that in October the defenders of Vienna had prevailed; the Turks had retreated, and the empire was spared.

The emperor, now freed from the threat of Islam, could focus on the reunification of the empire. In January 1530, he called for a diet to meet at Augsburg on 8 April. Explicit instructions accompanied the summons. One from your day noted that the summons "called upon the princes and cities to give an account of their faith."[1] Note very clearly that it was the princes and cities that were to give an account, not theologians. The heat was on the politicians. Another student of your day quoted the emperor's words, "That the holy empire of the German nation might once again be brought to unity."[2] The same student noted that the summons implied neutrality on the part of the emperor. He wrote, "The use of force was to be avoided, however. Together with the imperial estates, pope and emperor were to do 'what was right and honorable'; to that end, 'everyone's opinion and viewpoint' were to be 'heard and weighed carefully.'"[3]

What a ruse! Everyone knew that it was my teachings that were under examination, or more acutely, under condemnation. Neutrality of pope and emperor? What a joke. In January 1521, the pope had excommunicated me as a heretic; in May of the same year, the emperor had declared me an outlaw. Now they were going to allow "everyone's opinion and viewpoint to be heard and weighed carefully"? Not a chance.

The princes and political representatives of the cities were in no position to formulate theological statements. They had their own simple faith; that's all that God requires. But popes and politicians require more.

---

1 Grane, 15.

2 Mauer, 10.

3 Mauer, 16.

The elements of faith must be presented polished, clean, and clear, without contradiction or ambiguity.

Duke John did not receive the summons to the diet until 11 March, less than a month prior to the date of the diet's convening.

"In the spring of 1530," says one of your researchers, "the elector gathered the leading Lutheran theologians together to prepare a defense brief which could be presented to the diet."[4]

No time could be lost in preparing that defense.

When the elector left Saxony for Augsburg, he took with him several theological advisers: Melanchthon, Spengler, Justus Jonas, Johann Agricola, me, and one other from outside Wittenberg. I could not accompany the contingent beyond Coburg, the most southerly city in Saxony. Remember, I was still considered an outlaw and could be captured if outside my sovereign's territory. From Coburg, I could send messages to Augsburg and receive reports on the proceeding.

We arrived at Coburg on 15 April, and all but I continued to Augsburg on about 22 April.

The formulation of the Augsburg Confession included words from previous statements of faith, as well as a variety of contemporary voices. But for all practical purposes, Melanchthon was the author.

The elector sent Melanchthon's draft of the confession to me and requested my opinion. He also asked me to make any changes that I thought useful.

One of your historians copied what I said when I returned the draft to Elector Duke John. "[It] pleases me very much; I know nothing to improve or change in it, nor would this be appropriate, since I cannot step so softly and quietly [as Melanchthon]."[5] I am quite aware that I was always blunt and outspoken; Melanchthon was much gentler in his use of language. I always admired that trait in Philip, although at times I was frustrated by it.

On 25 June, the evangelical princes and other dignitaries who had signed the confession—not one theologian's name was included—presented the confession to the emperor.

4 Grane, 15.

5 Mauer, 12.

There were two parts to the confession. The first twenty-one articles affirmed the Christian faith as it had been believed, taught, and confessed from apostolic times. By those articles our leaders demonstrated that they and we affirmed the historic catholic faith. In articles twenty-two through twenty-eight, seven contemporary abusive practices of the Roman Church that needed correction were presented.

Finally on 3 August, the Roman Catholics presented their *Confutation*. Another of your students wrote, "The emperor thereupon declared the *Augsburg Confession* refuted and threatened as 'overseer and protector of the church' to proceed against the disobedient."[6] So much for "everyone's opinion and viewpoint were to be heard and weighed carefully."

It is of little note that while at the Coburg castle, I had time to write. My thoughts and prayers were constantly with my friends in Augsburg. In that lonely castle, I wrote *Exhortation to All Clergy Assembled at Augsburg*.[7] I would not have mentioned that writing if there had not been two comments made about it. One who read it said, "This treatise might be considered Luther's own Augsburg Confession."[8]

On 7 June, the first five hundred copies of the *Exhortation* were available for sale in Augsburg. They sold out almost immediately. Your reviewer wrote, "[The Roman Catholic] Cardinal Campeggio was impressed and commanded a secretary in his service to turn the *Exhortation* into Latin. The man whom he commissioned to make the translation wrote to a friend on 21 June, 'It is a summary of all Lutheranism. If you wish to see the whole of Luther, you ought to buy it.'"[9] I had not known about Cardinal Campeggio's impression until someone who lives where I live told me about it.

If you call yourself a "Lutheran," you should at least be familiar with the Augsburg Confession.

---

6 LW 34:6.

7 LW 34:3–61.

8 LW 34:7.

9 LW 34:8.

Letter 101

I spent endless hours translating the Bible for my dear German people. Sometimes I struggled for several days to find just the right German word or phrase to translate only a few lines.

When you do something to help others, you can be sure that someone will criticize your efforts, and the more people you help, the louder the criticism.

I had completed translating the New Testament in September 1522, while at the Wartburg; in 1530, I was still working on the Old Testament.

I had heard complaints from some papists that in translating I had added a word that was not in Paul's original writing. I had added "alone" to the words of Paul when I translated Romans 3:28. That verse reads, "We hold that a man is justified without works of the law, by faith alone."

From the Coburg castle, I sent a reply to an unidentified friend. (I had friends in Roman Catholic territories whose identities I thought should be kept confidential.) I wrote *On Translating: An Open Letter*[1] that explained a little about the task of translating.

Today I am going to limit my comments and let the words I wrote in 1530 speak directly to you. I have nothing more to say today about translating than I did then.

First, I stated the issue. "You tell me . . . that the papists are making a tremendous fuss, because the word *sola* (alone) is not in Paul's text, and this addition of mine to the words of God is not to be tolerated."[2]

My first response was an emotional disdain for the critics who knew nothing about translating and cared nothing about the German people getting a Bible they could understand. My comment was "And please give these asses no other and no further answer to their useless braying about the word *sola* than simply this, 'Luther will have it so, and says that he is a doctor above all the doctors of the whole papacy.'"[3]

---

1 LW 35:175–202.

2 LW 35:182.

3 LW 35:187.

I am quite aware that sounds arrogant and is really no answer at all, but I would say it again to those know-nothings.

I did give a more responsible answer when I showed how important, and really how necessary "alone" is, to complete Paul's meaning in Romans 3:28, mentioned above. I wrote,

> Here, in Romans 3 [:28], I knew very well that the word *solum* is not in the Greek or Latin text; the papists did not have to teach me that. It is a fact that these four letters *s o l a* are not there. And these blockheads stare at them like cows at a new gate. At the same time they do not see that it conveys the sense of the text; it belongs there if the translation is to be clear and vigorous. I wanted to speak German, not Latin or Greek, since it was German I had undertaken to speak in the translation.[4]

I then gave a few illustrations how Germans use the word *allein* (alone) to emphasize a point.

The German people were my audience. Therefore I continued, "We do not have to inquire of the literal Latin, how we are to speak German, as these asses do. Rather we must inquire about this of the mother in the home, the children on the street, the common man in the marketplace. We must be guided by their language, the way they speak, and do our translating accordingly."[5]

As I drew close to the end I spoke a bit about the difficulty of translating. "I have learned by experience," I said, "what an art and what a task translating is. Therefore I will tolerate no papal ass or mule to be my judge or critic, for they have never tried it. . . . If it is to be criticized, I shall do it myself."[6]

The hours that I spent, and the intellectual struggles that I endured, in translating the Bible were all done for my Lord, *SOLA* (alone). I wrote,

> This I can testify with a good conscience—I gave it my utmost in care and effort, and I never had any ulterior motives. I have neither taken nor sought a single penny for it, nor made one by it. Neither have I sought my own honor by it; God, my Lord, knows this. Rather I have done it as a

---

4 LW 35:188–89.

5 LW 35:189.

6 LW 35:193.

> service to the dear Christians and to the honor of One who sitteth above, who blesses me so much every hour of my life that if I had translated a thousand times as much or as diligently, I should not for a single hour have deserved to live or to have a sound eye. All that I am and have is of his grace and mercy, indeed, of his precious blood and bitter sweat. Therefore, God willing, all of it shall also serve to his honor, joyfully and sincerely. Scribblers and papal assess may blaspheme me, but real Christians—and Christ, their Lord—bless me![7]

As for you, thank God that you have His Holy Word in your own language; thank God for those who have spent years and a great deal of money to learn the ancient languages in order to translate that life-giving Word so that you can understand it. Above all, read the divine Word. It does you no good sitting on a shelf or covered with dust on a table.

Read it! For your own blessed sake, read it!

---

7 LW 35:193.

Letter 102

This will be not much more than a short note. Two items I wish to address in this letter, one of which I did not write, and the other should be of great value to you. When I share the two with you, I will explain why I am including them.

The first, *Sayings in Which Luther Found Comfort*,[1] I did not write. Four years after my death, my physician, Mathaeus Ratzeberger, visited the Coburg castle, says one of you scholars. "He made a point of inspecting the room Luther had used as a study and meticulously noted down the verses which Luther had written on the wall."[2] I include this comment because I want you to know how important the Word of God was to me; I wanted to be surrounded by it at all times. Others had collected short sayings from my time in Coburg that are included in the above-mentioned *Sayings*.

It would be of no value to you if I were to recite the Bible verses or other short sayings that I wrote on the wall or other places. The words that were spiritual nourishment for me might not be for you. Better than writing Bible verses on the wall—I have heard that such practice is an absolute taboo in your day—memorize the parts of God's Word that speak particularly to your need. You thereby carry the Word of God with you wherever you go. Imitate the writer of Psalm 119 [:11]: "I have stored up Your word in my heart, that I might not sin against You."

The second item for you today is of as much value to you as it was for me. It was a very short writing, only four pages: *That a Christian Should Bear His Cross with Patience*.[3] Suffering is intrinsic to Christian living. In my short comments, I said that we have a need to suffer, thereby entering into the suffering of Christ. Jesus said that it would be so. Endure it with patience. Second, suffering does not come from your heavenly Father, but from His enemy, and yours, the devil. That diabolical one does all that he can to disrupt, discourage, and destroy believers. Therefore I said, "Indeed, a Christian can no more do without the cross than without

---

1 LW 43:167–77.

2 LW 43:169.

3 LW 43:179–86.

food or drink."[4] Finally, I said, "The touch of Christ sanctifies all the sufferings and sorrows of those who believe in him."[5]

The first that I shared with you is useful to you. It should remind you of the high priority that every believer must put on the Word of God. Bear it with you at all times. Nevertheless, because it reflects my own experience, it is not critically important for you. The second is crucial for your life with God. If you are not personally suffering, tens of thousands of your brothers and sisters are. It is for you to participate in that suffering by sharing your wealth for their relief. Recall the words of St. Paul sent to the church in Galatia, "Bear one another's burdens, and so fulfill the law of Christ" (Galatians 6:2).

---

4 LW 43:184.

5 LW 43:184.

Letter 103

The emperor did not move against us immediately on 3 August 1530, when he accepted the Roman Catholic *Confutation* as a clear refutation of our Augsburg Confession. He continued to put pressure on the evangelical princes and nobles to abandon the reform movement and submit to his imperial edict. Your historian has noted one of these examples. He wrote,

> The Emperor employed every strategy to win over the evangelical princes and induce them to forsake the *Augsburg Confession*. He brought particular pressure on the Elector of Saxony, threatening to withhold his investiture, whereupon Elector John informed his Imperial Majesty that, though it was his lawful right, he would forego that right rather than deny his God.[1]

When strong-arm tactics did not accomplish his purpose, the emperor established a commission with equal representation from both sides in the hope of accomplishing a reconciliation. Nothing was accomplished. We said that everything was open to compromise except the Word of God. On that we could not and would not change our position.

On 22 September, the emperor declared a "recess" and gave our party until 15 April 1531, "for the benefit and prosperity of the Holy Roman Empire, for the restoration of peace and unity, and for the purpose of manifesting His Majesty's leniency and special grace"[2] to return to the Roman Church ". . . until a general council shall be convened."[3]

Our party was not paralyzed by the Roman *Confutation*. Melanchthon began immediately, and worked feverishly, to write an Apology (defense) of our *Confession*. He completed it on the day the "recess" began and was prepared to present it to the emperor, but as your historian has noted, "Upon the whispered advice of Ferdinand [Charles's brother and archduke of Austria] he [the emperor] refused to accept it."[4]

---

1 Schwiebert, 732.

2 Schwiebert, 734.

3 Schwiebert, 734.

4 Schwiebert, 734.

I was not lounging in Coburg. In early October, I began to write a *Commentary on the Alleged Imperial Edict*[5] and *Dr. Martin Luther's Warning to His Dear German People*.[6] In the *Commentary*, I simply asserted again the elements of the Christian faith that are at stake. I have previously shared those elements with you; I need not repeat them here. I concluded that *Commentary* by saying that I had never wanted the position that had been thrust upon me.

> However, I, Dr. Martinus, have been called to this work and was compelled to become a doctor, without any initiative of my own, but out of pure obedience. Then I had to accept the office of doctor and swear a vow to my most beloved Holy Scriptures that I would preach and teach them faithfully and purely. . . . And this which has been begun during my lifetime will be completed after my death.[7]

The *Warning* was of a different nature. We could not abide the conditions placed upon us by the imperial "recess" of 22 September. We had to prepare for what might happen after 15 April 1531.

I could see the storm clouds gathering. Armed force would most probably be used against us. I did not fear for my own life; I had been prepared to die for over a decade. But what about my dear German people? How should I advise them? I had always preached and taught against rebellion and insurrection. Could I maintain that position if the Gospel would be suppressed by God's own civil authority? Early in my *Warning*, I wrote,

> It is not fitting for me, a preacher, vested with the spiritual office, to wage war or to counsel war or incite it, but rather to dissuade from war and to direct to peace, as I have done until now with all diligence. . . . If war should come now, I will surely hold my pen in check and keep silent and not intervene as I did in the last uprising [the Peasants Revolt].[8]

I gave three reasons why the German people should not support the emperor's efforts to suppress the Gospel; on the contrary, they should actively resist. "The first reason . . . is . . . you vowed in baptism to

---

5 LW 34:63–104.

6 LW 47:3–55.

7 LW 34:103–4.

8 LW 47:18.

preserve the gospel of Christ."[9] "The second reason is . . . by such fighting you are taking upon yourself a part of the guilt before God of all the abominations which have been committed and will yet be committed by the whole papacy."[10] "The third reason . . . you would also lend a hand in overthrowing and exterminating all the good which the dear gospel has again restored and established."[11]

Should they resist with arms? I could not bring myself to say that they should, but I did say, "Furthermore, if war breaks out—which God forbid—I will not reprove those who defend themselves against the murderous and bloodthirsty papists, nor let anyone else rebuke them as being seditious, but I will accept their action and let it pass as self-defense."[12]

While Melanchthon and I were writing in support of the Gospel, the princes and nobles were preparing for any conflict that might arise after 15 April. Led by Elector John of Saxony and Philip, landgrave of Hesse, in February 1531 a league was formed in Smalcald. One of your students noted that the Smalcaldic League "grew to embrace electoral Brandenburg and Saxony, Prussia, Hesse, Mansfeld, Brunswick, Anhalt, and other territories containing twenty imperial cities."[13]

I fully expected war, but God granted us a reprieve through the Turks. They again became a threat on the Eastern front of the Holy Roman Empire. To coalesce all forces in the empire, the emperor was forced to relent against the evangelical nobles. In July 1532, the emperor declared a truce between the two religious parties—"The Peace of Nürnberg." That era of toleration lasted a full decade. It provided the evangelical movement time to expand and strengthen.

Actual war, called the Smalcaldic War, did not begin until 1546, only a few months after my death. God spared me from witnessing the tragedy. The war lasted until 1555, one side gaining an advantage, then the other. Finally the war was ended on 25 September with the *Peace of Augsburg*. An agreement included a Latin phrase that has become well known, *cuius regio, eius religio* (whose the realm, his the religion). In simple terms, it meant that if the ruler was Lutheran, his territory

---

9 LW 47:35.

10 LW 47:36.

11 LW 47:52.

12 LW 47:19.

13 Ozment, 256.

would remain Lutheran; where the ruler was Roman Catholic, his territory would be exclusively Roman Catholic.

The evangelical reform had taken root and was reluctantly accepted, within limits.

I have watched the terrible acrimony between the Roman Church and the Evangelicals over the past five hundred years. (By Evangelicals, I do not mean anything other than the Lutheran and Reformed parties.) I have also noted a renewed attempt at understanding each other during the past sixty years. I give thanks to God for Pope John XXIII, whom God used to open the door to more open dialogue between the two parties. I pray that God will heal the Body of Christ, which was fractured because of the tragic necessity of the Reformation as one of your scholars has called it.

Letter 104

My barber, Peter Beskendorf, asked for a simple way to pray. I suppose that I could have given him a short answer—pray the catechism—but instead I wrote a whole book, *A Simple Way to Pray*,[1] and dedicated the book "to a good friend . . . for Peter the master barber."[2]

I recognize that personal prayer, distinct from corporate prayer within a community of believers, is so intensely personal that no one can tell another how to prayer. My first words to Peter: "I will tell you as best I can what I do personally when I pray."[3]

I begin the day with prayer, and conclude the day in the same way. Make prayer your first item of business every day. To postpone prayer is to neglect prayer.

The way I told Peter how I prayed may also be helpful to you. I take the Small Catechism and use the Ten Commandments, the Lord's Prayer, and the Creed as the basis for my prayer. My words cannot be your words, nor Peter's, but I begin by taking each part of the Lord's Prayer, mediating on it, and extending each section as my needs, as well as the needs of my associates, my community, and the world, require. Each day those needs change.

"Our Father": Stop to consider, and give thanks, for the unparalleled privilege of calling your Creator Father.

"Hallowed (holy) be Your name": This is the only section of the Lord's Prayer in which you ask for nothing; these are exclusively words of worship. Take time to simply adore your heavenly Father for all the good He has done for you.

That's enough to get you started. As you make requests through the rest of the Lord's Prayer, remember that you never demand anything from your Father; you are totally dependent on Him. Sinful child that you are, you deserve nothing. However, never forget that you are a child of God; God has called you to live under Him and has asked you to make requests from Him.

---

1 LW 43:187–211.

2 LW 43:190.

3 LW 43:193.

What I do with the Lord's Prayer, I do also with the Ten Commandments. Focus on each of the ten, and, as you do, an honest reflection will certainly lead you to pray, "Forgive me, heavenly Father, for I have sinned; forgive me for Jesus' sake." Then trust that your sins have been forgiven, and live as a grateful child.

The Creed is a great way to bring your prayer to a close. Affirm your faith in God, your Father, as your Creator; remember that you owe your life to Him. Affirm your faith in Jesus Christ, your Savior. Remember that you haven't a ghost of a chance to share eternity with your heavenly Father, and all the saints, apart from Jesus Christ. Affirm your faith in God's Holy Spirit, who lives in you and every believer.

I also used words from the Bible that came to mind as I was praying. Of course, if you don't read the Bible and immerse yourself in God's Word, none will come to you while you pray. You can also use hymns of the church that express your inner desires, either of worship or request.

When you pray, don't be locked into a certain form that becomes mere repetition; let the Spirit of God guide your prayer. One of your reviews of *A Simple Way to Pray* said, "Of course, the reader is not supposed to repeat Luther's meditative prayers word for word, and if the Holy Spirit should kindle the heart, all method and scheme should be abandoned to listen to the 'sermon of the Spirit.'"[4]

I told Peter, "A good prayer should not be lengthy or drawn out, but frequent and ardent."[5] Therefore, perhaps you need not pray the entire catechism every day, but take one part today, another part tomorrow.

Well, that's how I pray. If that is helpful to you, I would be pleased. But remember that how you pray and when you pray is not nearly as important as that you pray and that you pray "in Jesus' name." Your access to God, your heavenly Father, is only through His only-begotten Son, Jesus.

---

4 LW 43:191.

5 LW 43:209.

Letter 105

In June 1536, Pope Paul III called for a general council of the church. It was to meet in Mantua, Italy, in May 1537. One of your historians knew the mind of the pope. He wrote, "Paul III also realized that the Lutheran movement could be arrested only by some much-needed reforms in the Roman Church."[1] Regrettably, the pope thought that nothing more than a moral reform was needed; I knew differently. Morals do not threaten the Gospel; false and faithless theology do.

When a representative of the Roman pontiff invited me to attend, I agreed to be present. I agreed for two reasons, one personal and the other political. For almost two decades, I had called for a general council of the church to resolve my dispute with Rome, although in my debate with Eck in Leipzig, I said that I did not have much confidence in councils. Nevertheless, at that early age, I was still naive and optimistic. I believed that if the bishops of the church could hear the blessed, liberating Gospel they would all join the reform movement. By 1536, I was more certain that nothing good would come from a council. However, having asked for one, I felt compelled to attend. The political reason related to the Peace of Nürnberg. That "recess" granted by the emperor for political reasons could be lifted anytime. I sensed that the council might authorize military action against us.

In preparation for the council, Elector John Frederick (Elector Frederick the Wise had died in 1525 and Elector John the Constant in 1532) asked me, in August, to prepare a personal statement of faith. I had written enough, and Melanchthon's Augsburg Confession and subsequent Apology were available and adequate. But, as one researcher has noted, "In the light of Luther's ill health and because of the council, the elector wanted a final and definitive theological statement from Luther."[2]

I complied with the request because of my respect for the elector. One historian said, "On the one hand, he had never been quite satisfied with the Augsburg Confession or the Apology, as he felt Melanchthon

1 Schwiebert, 740.

2 Brecht 3:178.

had tried to minimize the differences between the Roman and the Protestant teachings."[3]

But he spoke too strongly. If I had been dissatisfied with Melanchthon in 1530, I would have said so. Melanchthon and I spoke with one voice, but in a different pitch. My pitch was higher and sharper. I know that my pitch irritated Melanchthon a bit, as his softer tone gave me some stress. I'll say more about Melanchthon's irritation later.

Members of the Smalcaldic League met in February to formulate a position relative to the anticipated council. They would agree to participate in a council providing that four conditions were met: (1) the council was free of papal control, (2) all the estates were represented on equal terms, (3) the Bible was made the sole basis of judgment, and (4) the council met on German soil.

It was to the representatives of that league meeting in Smalcalden that I presented my confession of faith. Consequently, my confession has been known as the Smalcald Articles. That confession could be used by the league at the impending council. I know now, but did not know then, that the council did not open until 1546, in Trent, a few months after my death. Trent was located in the German lands.

The articles were definitely mine, but in December the elector had asked several of the local theologians to assist me with the preparation. The assistance proved providential. One of your historians noted, "On 18 and 19 December, however, he [Luther] suffered one or more heart attacks (*angina pectoris*), and had to dictate the remaining articles and thus keep them brief."[4] The pain (*angina*) subsided, and by the end of January, I felt well enough to travel to Smalcalden. With Melanchthon and Bugenhagen, I arrived on 7 February. About forty other theologians had already arrived.

The worst was yet to come. On the day after our arrival, I passed a kidney stone. That was only the beginning. Again, your researcher noted, "On 19 February Luther was unable to urinate, and this persisted for eight days."[5] Need I tell you about the pain of eight days? The physicians could do nothing. The same researcher wrote, "They also tried, from the

---

3 Schwiebert, 740.

4 Brecht 3:181.

5 Brecht 3:185.

Dreckapotheke (excrement pharmacy), remedies made from garlic and raw manure."[6]

I was certain that death was imminent. I was not only ready—I wanted to die. The pain was excruciating. My companions thought the same as I, but I wanted to die in Saxon lands.

On 27 February, I was loaded onto a wagon to be transported to my beloved home territory. That trip over a bumpy road may have saved my life. "During the night," says the same source, "the urinary blockage finally ended."[7] Further, he said, "On the evening of that day [1 March] he passed six stones, one of them as large as a bean."[8] When I finally arrived at my home in Wittenberg, in mid-March, I was still passing stones. My kidneys must have been a gravel pit.

Back in Smalcalden the league was still considering my articles. Almost all of the theologians present signed the articles as truly representing their faith, although my closest colleague added a caveat, "However, concerning the pope I maintain that if he would allow the gospel, we, too, may (for the sake of peace and general unity among those Christians who are now under him and might be in the future) grant to him his superiority over the bishops which he has 'by human right.'"[9]

The league might have acted differently if I had been present. But I believe that they were influenced by Melanchthon's softer tone. The league decided not to accept my articles, but to use the Augsburg Confession at the council, if necessary.

Nevertheless, more than twenty years after my death, the Smalcald Articles were accepted as one of the basic Lutheran confessions of faith to be included in the Book of Concord.

Some may not be able to identify the Book of Concord; I was not aware of it as it was published some thirty-four years after my death. It is a collection of eight (or ten) written statements of faith that most Lutherans around the world accept as a faithful witness to the historic Christian faith. Included are the three ecumenical creeds (Apostles', Nicene, and Athanasian), the Augsburg Confession, Apology of the Augsburg Confession, the Smalcald Articles, Treatise on the Power and

---

6 Brecht 3:185.

7 Brecht 3:187.

8 Brecht 3:188.

9 *The Book of Concord*, 326.

Primacy of the Pope, the Small Catechism, the Large Catechism, and the Formula of Concord.

One who wrote an introduction to the Book of Concord said, "These three [the electors of Saxony, Brandenburg, and the Palatinate], joined by eighty other princely and municipal governments, led 8,188 theologians into subscription of the Formula of Concord by 1580, and the Formula and other confessions were published as the Book of Concord on 25 June, the fiftieth anniversary of the presentation of the Augsburg Confession."[10]

10 *The Book of Concord*, 2.

Letter 106

In 1537, I was sick and tired. In my last letter, I told you how sick I was—at death's door. I was also tired. Tired of writing hundreds of treatises, sermons, and articles, and thousands of pages, in long hand, with no machines to write as you have; tired of countless hours of struggle with the devil and my own sinful nature, all to profess and defend the gracious Gospel of my Lord Jesus Christ against thick-skulled theologians and would-be theologians.

I longed to get back to the basics and write for my dear German people. I wanted nothing more to do with academic controversies. The basics of the faith are no better defined than in the ancient creeds of the Church. Therefore I wrote *The Three Symbols or Creeds of the Christian Faith.*[1] You are familiar with the Apostles' Creed, which I called "the finest of all,"[2] and the Athanasian Creed. Some may not be familiar with *Te deum laudamus* (you God we praise), a song of praise to God from the fourth century. At the conclusion, almost as an afterthought, I did include the Nicene Creed but made no comment about it.

My comments in the treatise centered almost exclusively on Jesus. The whole Christian faith stands or falls on the person and activity of Jesus. I said, "I have perceived and noted in all histories of all of Christendom that all those who have correctly had and kept the chief article of Jesus Christ have remained safe and secure in the right Christian faith."[3] Shortly thereafter, I wrote, "On the other hand, I have also noticed that all error, heresy, idolatry, offense, misuse, and evil in the church originally came from despising or losing sight of this article of faith in Jesus Christ."[4]

The devil attacks the heart of the faith by denying that Jesus is truly God or that He is truly human or that His death had no saving effect. I said, "Thus the devil has work to do and attacks Christ in three lines of battle. One will not let him [Jesus] be God, another will not let him be man, and the third will not let him do what he has done."[5]

Believers through the centuries have resisted the devil's lies and have confessed that Jesus is entirely true God and truly human, and that His

1 LW 34:197–229.

2 LW 34:201.

3 LW 34:207.

4 LW 34:207.

5 LW 34:210.

death has a salvific effect. To have Jesus is to have everything. I wrote, "For whoever stands correctly and firmly in the belief that Jesus Christ is true God and man, that he died and has risen again for us, such a person has all other articles added to him and they firmly stand by him."[6]

I could accept a little heresy in the church as long as the basic articles of the faith are maintained. I confirmed that by writing, "Therefore whoever desires to see the Christian Church existing in quiet peace, entirely without crosses, without heresy, and without factions, will never see it thus, or else he must view the false church of the devil as the real church."[7]

Reason scoffs at the God-man, Jesus, and ridicules His sacrificial death and resurrection. When I wrote about reason and faith, I mentioned the Jews, but what I said is just as valid for fellow travelers in the church in your day and mine. I said, "For they consider us to be vain, silly ducks and geese who are unable to sense or notice what foolishness it is to believe that God is man and that there are three distinct Persons in the one Godhead. No (praise God), we sense it indeed that such a doctrine neither will nor can appeal to reason."[8] I followed by saying, "It is not even comprehensible to the angels, who nevertheless constantly behold it joyously."[9] But I may have challenged reason best near the close of the treatise when I wrote, "The Scriptures are God's testimony of himself, while reason can know nothing at all about the divine substance. Shall then reason try to judge concerning that of which it knows nothing? That is really what might be called a blind man's attempt to judge colors!"[10]

The creeds of the Church and the *Te deum laudamus* mean nothing to unbelievers whose lives are oriented exclusively to this world. We who are believers join all humanity in using our reason and five senses for life here and now, in this world. But God has promised a new and better life beyond our earthly journey. We participate in that New World already, through faith. Because there is a distinction between believers and unbelievers, I wrote, "For whoever has no hope of a future life needs Christ just as little as the cows and other beasts in paradise did."[11]

For you, my dear fellow believers, keep the faith; for all others, good luck.

---

6 LW 34:207.
7 LW 34:215.
8 LW 34:216.
9 LW 34:218.
10 LW 34:227.
11 LW 34:211.

Letter 107

Can anyone complete a career, or even navigate through the years of life, without deep regret for words spoken or actions taken? Think about your own life. Are there secret, or not so secret, events from long ago, now forgiven by the grace of God, that still return to bring you grief? You are not alone.

I would prefer not to mention two items that I regret, but the issues are public knowledge. I know that I have been forgiven, but regrets remain. Remember, God can forgive only real sinners, never only theoretical sinners.

I will share one item with you in this letter and the second in a subsequent letter.

The first issue relates to Landgrave Philip of Hesse who had joined the evangelical reform movement. As a young man, he was wed to Christina, daughter of Duke George of Albertine Saxony, for political purposes. Political marriages were commonplace in my day and have been arranged even as late as your own day. Philip had no desire for the marriage and no affection for the girl. Consequently, it was not a happy marriage, although they had seven children. In his mid-thirties, Philip's affection was drawn to a young lady, Margaret von der Saale, nearly twenty years younger than he. The landgrave had engaged in an adulterous affair with his newly beloved. Much later, I discovered that he had also engaged in several other promiscuous relationships. Those actions so bothered Philip that he would not receive Holy Communion. Philip asked for my counsel. I could not counsel divorce because Jesus allowed divorce only on the grounds of adultery, not the adultery of the offending party. I counseled him to marry the young lady but to keep the marriage a secret. I knew very well that I was counseling bigamy; the penalty for bigamy in the empire was death. My excuse, really it was simple rationalization, was that God had allowed bigamous relationships among the patriarchs of the Old Testament. King David also had several wives. I should have known better. Rationalization is self-justification, and I had discovered the Gospel of justification through faith in Jesus' death for sinners. I had discovered that Gospel nearly twenty years earlier. My first sin was to counsel bigamy and to keep it a secret; my second sin was to justify my actions. I think that my second sin was worse than my first.

Keep the marriage a secret? I should have known that to be impossible. The new bride's mother spread the word. I then told Philip to lie about the marriage. I was now guilty of another sin, another failure. To justify that action, one of your historians wrote, "Then Luther counseled a lie on the ground that his advice had been given as in the confessional, and to guard the secrets of the confessional a lie is justified."[1]

I need not tell you how seriously my actions hurt the evangelical reform movement, but your same historian did. He said, "The whole episode had disastrous political consequences for the Protestant movement because Philip, in order to secure pardon from the emperor, had to dissociate himself from a military alliance with the Protestants."[2] I think that was not the worst consequence. The papists made a great issue of the morals of the so-called reformer. God preserved the movement in spite of me.

After five hundred years, I have no intention of continuing in self-justification. I was a sinner and knew it even then. I join myself to the words of the apostle Paul in Romans 7: "Wretched man that I am! Who will deliver me from this body of death? Thanks be to God through Jesus Christ our Lord!"

Again, your same historian noted my last word on bigamy. He wrote, "Luther's final comment was that if anyone thereafter should practice bigamy, let the Devil give him a bath in the abyss of hell."[3] My advice to myself was too late.

Remember to be faithful to Jesus Christ, not to Martinus.

---

1 Bainton, 374.

2 Bainton, 375.

3 Bainton, 374.

Letter 108

My counsel to Philip of Hesse [see Letter 107] carried the "mark of the beast" in my day and had disastrous consequences for the reform movement; in your day, the issue is passed over as a bit of stupid advice. The second great regret of my life has been identified as my attitude toward the Jews. In my day, that attitude was considered temperate; in your day, I have been vilified and excoriated for some of the things that I said about the Jews.

I have learned a good deal since my flesh was placed in the ground in 1546, and I deeply regret some of the things I said. But please do not judge me on the values and prejudices of your day.

I have no interest in justifying anything that I said; I have a Savior who has done that for me. But I do want to clarify a few things.

Those who have studied my life and work recognize that my comments about the Jews were always motivated by a religious concern; they were never a racial or ethnic issue. One said, "His position was entirely religious and in no respect racial."[1] Nevertheless, he also said, "One could wish that Luther had died before ever this tract was written."[2] The tract to which he referred was, I think, my lengthy treatise *On the Jews and Their Lies*.[3] I'll say more about that treatise later.

Those who castigate me in your day for my comments about the Jews do not consider all my writings but limit themselves to some terrible things that I said late in life.

In 1523, I wrote *That Jesus Christ Was Born a Jew*.[4] A reviewer noted correctly that rumors about my teaching were poisoning the atmosphere. "It was charged among other things," he said, "that Luther taught that Jesus was conceived of the seed of Joseph."[5] I had to respond to those vicious lies. The first part of the treatise proved from the Old Testament Scriptures that Jesus was born of a virgin. I taught the faith of the

---

1 Bainton, 379.

2 Bainton, 379.

3 LW 47:121–306.

4 LW 45:195–229.

5 LW 45:197.

church that continued from the first century. Toward the latter part of the treatise, I said, "While we are on the subject, however, we wish not only to answer the futile liars who publicly malign me in these matters but we would also like to do a service to the Jews on the chance that we might bring some of them back to their own true faith, the one which their fathers held."[6]

Whether Jews or Turks or Anabaptists or Papists, my only aim was to bring all back to my Lord Jesus Christ, whose Gospel had set me free.

My concluding words in the treatise included the following: "Again, when we forbid them to labor and do business and have any human fellowship with us, thereby forcing them into usury, how is that supposed to do them any good? If we really want to help them, we must be guided in our dealings with them not by papal law but by the law of Christian love."[7]

Those words were countercultural. Very few in my day had anything good to say about any Jew.

Perhaps it would have been best if I had stopped with that treatise, but I did not. Many things change over the course of nineteen years. In 1542, I wrote *On the Jews and Their Lies*.

I had hoped and prayed that the Jews would accept my Lord, but that happened so rarely as to be inconsequential.

One from your day who digs through ancient writings discovered that in 1539 I had read a book written by Anthony Margaritha, a converted Jew. The lengthy title of the book is *The Whole Jewish Faith, Together with a Thorough and Truthful Account of All the Regulations, Ceremonies, and Prayers Both for Family and Public Worship, as Observed by the Jews throughout the Year, with Excellent and Well-Founded Arguments against Their Faith*.[8] The researcher then noted, "Out of which in part he [Luther] drew his critical arguments against the Jews."[9]

Indeed, that book was part of the impetus for the treatise, along with the failure of the Jews to convert and a vile, bitter spirit that engaged me in my old age.

On the Jews and Their Lies includes three sections. The same researcher said, "The first part dealt with the advantage of which the Jews

6 LW 45:213.

7 LW 45:229.

8 Brecht 3:339.

9 Brecht 3:339.

boasted."[10] The second part, he said, was the main portion, "which dealt with the promised Messiah."[11] "The concluding third part, sadly, has achieved infamy in connection with modern anti-Semitism."[12]

In the third part of the treatise, I made some recommendations that I thought right and appropriate at the time. I now hesitate to share them with you because of my shame, but Christian honesty impels me to bare my soul to you. There were seven recommendations:

> First, to set fire to their synagogues or schools and to bury and cover with dirt whatever will not burn . . .
>
> Second, I advise that their houses also be razed and destroyed . . .
>
> Third, I advise that all their prayer books and Talmudic writings . . . be taken from them . . .
>
> Fourth, I advise that their rabbis be forbidden to teach henceforth on pain of loss of life and limb . . .
>
> Fifth, I advise that safe-conduct on the highways be abolished completely for the Jews . . .
>
> Sixth, I advise that usury be prohibited to them, and that all cash and treasure of silver and gold be taken from them and put aside for safekeeping . . .
>
> Seventh, I recommend putting a flail, an ax, a hoe, a spade, a distaff, or a spindle into the hands of young, strong Jews and Jewesses and letting them earn their bread in the sweat of their brow, as was imposed on the children of Adam (Gen. 3 [:19]).[13]

My greatest regret is that almost four hundred years after I wrote those words, they were used by a leader in Germany to promote a culture of hatred toward the Jews that resulted in millions of Jews being slaughtered for no other reason than their ethnic identity.

Regret changes nothing. I pray, dear fellow believers, be careful what you say. Words once spoken can never be retrieved. Many of my words, I have been told, have been a blessing to millions. But a few short sentences, taken out of their religious context and inserted into

---

10 Brecht 3:341ff.

11 Brecht 3:342.

12 Brecht 3:343.

13 LW 47:268–72.

a cultural cauldron of hate to promote an evil social experiment, meant death to millions.

I cannot say whether I grieve now in my new abode, but I can ask those who carry my name to grieve for me.

Letter 109

I have not yet introduced you to Johann Agricola, one of my best friends, perhaps second only to Melanchthon. John was nine years younger than I and came from the town of my birth; therefore I sometimes called him Master Eisleben.

Agricola had a religious experience similar to mine. One of your historians wrote, "The concept of judgment, and the strict demands of late medieval piety appear to have oppressed him."[1] That was precisely my experience before I discover the life-liberating Gospel. Agricola came to the University of Wittenberg in 1516, and the same historian said, "Luther became his mentor (*Seelsorger*), and Luther's theology was liberating for him."[2] Yes, we became very close friends. I appreciated his liberated spirit and keen mind.

Some people can be so overwhelmed by the Gospel because of its sheer liberating power that they become transfixed on the Gospel and no longer recognize the need for God's Law. Agricola was one of them.

That issue with Agricola appeared for the first time in 1527. Elector John Frederick directed a visitation of all churches in his territory, with instructions for evangelical preaching and practice. Melanchthon drew up the *Articles of Visitation*. In those articles, he instructed that God's Law be preached along with the Gospel.

Lest there be any doubt or confusion about what constitutes Law as distinct from the Gospel, I will make the distinction clear. God's Law demands what God requires of us. When I wrote *The Freedom of a Christian* in 1520, I said, "The commandments [law] show us what we ought to do but do not give us the power to do it."[3] The Gospel tells us what God has done for us because we do not do what is required. The Law is a demand; the Gospel is a promise, a gracious gift.

One who has read Melanchthon's *Articles* wrote, "Many now talk only about the forgiveness of sins and say little or nothing about repentance."[4] He continued, "But true repentance and contrition for sin—which are to

1 Brecht 3:156.

2 Brecht 3:156.

3 LW 31:348.

4 LW 47:101.

be instilled by the rigorous preaching of the law—are the necessary preconditions for genuine faith."[5]

Agricola objected to the preaching of the Law. He believed that the love of God, reflected in the Gospel, is all that is necessary to lead one to repentance. I agreed with Melanchthon. My friendship with Agricola was strained, but not broken.

Agricola was absent from Wittenberg for several years, teaching in Eisleben, but he returned in 1536 with the hope of receiving a professorship at the university. I did use him in 1537 to do some lecturing and preaching for me while I was away. His preaching and teaching showed that he was up to his old tricks of minimizing God's Law. For the next three years, our friendship was further strained. Several times he returned and confessed that he believed as I, but it was only verbal.

The contention between Agricola and me has become known as the Antinomian Controversy (*anti* means against, or apart from, and *nomos* means law). In 1539, I wrote a short treatise *Against the Antinomians*.[6] Even at that late date, I affirmed my friendship with Agricola. I wrote, "But since it is generally known that he was one of my best and closest friends, I shall leave this to someone else, so that no one will suspect that I am not in earnest about it."[7]

I know my need of God's Law; it shows me my sin and drives me back to Jesus Christ daily for forgiveness. In the treatises, I wrote, "I myself, as old and as learned as I am, recite the commandments daily word for word like a child."[8]

Agricola thought that I had changed my tune because I had preached the Gospel with such force and fervor against the papist in the late teens and early 1520s. He was right that I had powerfully preached the Gospel. I wrote, "To be sure, I did teach, and still teach, that sinners shall be stirred to repentance through the preaching or the contemplation of the passion of Christ, so that they might see the enormity of God's wrath over sin, and learn that there is no other remedy for this than the death of God's Son."[9]

---

5 LW 47:101.

6 LW 47:99–119.

7 LW 47:109.

8 LW 47:109.

9 LW 47:110.

But preaching must not be stale, dead doctrine; the preacher must know to whom he is preaching. The devil is a master trickster. I identified that trait by writing, "But the devil devotes himself to making men secure, teaching them to heed neither law nor sin, so that if sometime they are suddenly overtaken by death or by a bad conscience, they have grown so accustomed to nothing but sweet security that they sink helplessly into hell."[10]

Indeed, there are hearers who are overwhelmed, even near despair because of their sin. To such I wrote that the dear Jesus can never be portrayed sweetly enough. They need much more of this, as I discovered in many of them, to say nothing of myself. But other hearers are too secure and comfortable; they need to hear the condemning word of God's Law. I have heard a saying from the previous century that quite well defines my attitude toward preaching the Law and the Gospel. The task of a preacher, it is said, is "to comfort the afflicted (that's the work of the Gospel), and to afflict the comfortable (that's the work of God's Law)."

Eventually the conflict between Agricola and me became political. In late 1539 and early 1540, Agricola brought charges against me with the university; my pastor, Johann Bugenhagen; the Mansfeld clergy; and the congregation in Eisleben. Finally, in March 1540, he brought a complaint against me to the elector.

Later, proceedings were begun against Agricola. Before the proceedings were completed, Agricola left Wittenberg and took a preaching position in the court of Elector Joachim II in Berlin.

Both Joachim II and Agricola wanted the conflicted situation healed. Your historian noted, "On 1 October Melanchthon was able to transmit Luther's conditions for peace to Joachim II: Agricola would have to withdraw his complaint against Luther, acknowledge in writing his error to the Eisleben congregation, and retract his criticism of *Against the Antinomians*."[11] He continued by saying that Agricola immediately accepted the conditions.

I was still not convinced that Agricola had changed his tune. I had received reports from Berlin about his teaching, that he was still minimizing God's Law. When he returned to Wittenberg and wanted to visit me, I refused to see him; only his wife, Elsa, was allowed entry.

---

10 LW 47:111.

11 Brecht 3:169.

I have no doubt that Agricola was saved by faith in Jesus Christ, just as I was, but his theology was flawed. It has had the potential to lead many into a false security without a recognition of sin and the need for repentance.

Letter 110

When I was very ill in 1537 [see Letter 105] and away from my home in Wittenberg, I decided to write something to take the place of a properly executed legal will. A historian from your day said, "Luther wrote a brief statement referred to by some authorities as his 'first will.'" He then said, "But in reality this was more of a confession of faith and farewell message than anything like [a] last will and testament."[1] That may be. I never had anything more precious to leave to my beloved Katie and my children than my faith in the glorious Gospel of Jesus Christ that had set me free a couple of decades earlier. What little material possessions I could leave to my family would be gone in a few years, but faith lasts eternally. If only faith could be transferred so easily as in a will.

Melanchthon made a will in 1539 and suggested that I should do the same. Someone noted my response, "I have no intention in making a will. My books which are extant I leave to my children. May they understand that they are not smarter than their forbears. I appoint you, Katie, as universal heiress. You bore the children and gave them your breast. You will not manage their affairs to their disadvantage."[2]

The Saxon laws of my day allowed a widow to inherit no more than her dowry and personal belongings. That would leave Katie destitute; I could not endure that thought. Consequently, in 1542, I decided to prepare something more formal to protect my dear wife.

I cared little for legal formulations so I took it upon myself to write what I thought to be best for her and our children. That which I wrote has been discovered and published as simply *Luther's Will*.[3] I'll share with you only the opening statement of what I wrote.

> I, Martin Luther, doctor, etc., acknowledge with this my own handwriting that I have given to my beloved and faithful housewife Katherine as an endowment (or whatever one can call it) for her lifetime, which she will be at liberty to manage according to her pleasure and to her best interest,

---

1 LW 34:292.

2 LW 34:291–92.

3 LW 34:295–97.

and give it to her by the authority of this document on this very present day.[4]

I added a few specifics, and said that the mother would be the best guardian for the children. After asking that all accept this handwritten will to be authoritative, the will was witnessed by Philip Melanchthon, Kaspar Cruciger, and Johann Bugenhagen Pomeranus.

A reviewer wrote, "Luther's trust, however, was vindicated, and on April 11, 1546, shortly after his death, Elector John Frederick confirmed the will with the statement that 'although the registered document was deficient in refinement and formalities which the law requires,' he would graciously confirm it and would not fail to validate it."[5]

In early 1545, I discovered that a dirty lie about my death was being circulated; it had originated among the papists in Italy. Ghoulish comments were made about my grave and the foul smell of hell that was present there. I had the tract printed with the title *An Italian Lie Concerning Dr. Martin Luther's Death.*[6] I added a single, short paragraph to the tract. I said, "And I, Dr. Martin Luther, acknowledge and witness with this writing that on March 21 I received this passionate fabrication of my death and have read it almost gladly and happily, with the exception of the blasphemy attributing these lies to the exalted Divine Majesty."[7]

Less than a year later, I died; greed killed me. Not my own greed. I had many sins, but greed was not one of them. It was greed between brothers, the counts of Mansfeld. It all had to do with mining rights and the profits that could be made from those rights. I was asked to come and help negotiate a resolution to the conflict. I had no training in law and no interest in business. Late fall in 1545 was cold, and I was old, only a month before my sixty-second birthday. Reluctantly, I agreed to go to Eisleben, the town of my birth, to be nothing more than a fatherly presence among the quarrelers. Your historian noted correctly, "Luther did not act as an arbitrator, but he wanted to assist the counts in reaching an agreement through his sermons, admonitions, and suggestions."[8] Some success was achieved. There was an agreement to seek a settlement, but not all parties were present; a postponement was necessary. I could not

4 LW 34:295.

5 LW 34:292.

6 LW 34:361–66.

7 LW 34:366.

8 Brecht 3:370.

wait for all to be present; I had to return to Wittenberg because Melanchthon was ill.

In the depth of a cold winter, in late January, I again reluctantly traveled the eighty miles to Eisleben to assist with the negotiations. I left Wittenberg with my two sons Martin and Paul on 23 January and arrived in Eisleben the evening of 28 January. I was tired, really worn out.

One of your researchers wrote, "The following three weeks proved very trying. The tangled affairs of the princes and incessant wrangling of their lawyers taxed Luther's patience exceedingly."[9]

I rejoiced on 17 February when an amicable solution was reached between the brothers. My final battle had been fought and brought to a peaceful conclusion.

I must have had a premonition of my end, because someone recalled that a day earlier I had said, "If I go back home to Wittenberg, I'll lie down in a coffin and give the maggots a fat doctor to eat."[10]

After dinner on 17 February, I had severe chest pains. About nine o'clock, I went to sleep and slept for about an hour. I got up and went to another room; there I slept again until about two o'clock in the morning, when I had another severe attack of chest pain. I returned to sleep until a third, and even more severe, pain awakened me. Those close to me knew that my earthly life was swiftly ebbing to a close. My dear friend and colleague at the University of Wittenberg, Justus Jonas, spoke loudly and clearly and asked me, "Reverend Father, are you willing to die in the name of the Christ and the doctrine which you have preached?"[11] My last words in this world were a resounding "Yes!"

So I died only to gain life that for the past five hundred years has been more marvelous, more wonderful, more restful, and more peaceful than words can convey.

I long to meet you, my friends from the New World. Until then, keep the faith.

---

9 Schwiebert, 749.

10 Brecht 3:372.

11 Schwiebert, 750.

Resources

Bainton, Roland. *Here I Stand: A Life of Martin Luther*. Nashville and New York: Abingdon-Cokesbury Press, 1950.

The Book of Concord: Confessions of the Evangelical Lutheran Church. Editors: Robert Kolb and Timothy J. Wengert. Minneapolis: Fortress Press, 2000.

Bornkamm, Heinrich. *Luther in Mid-Career 1521–1530*. Philadelphia: Fortress Press, 1983.

Brecht, Martin. *Martin Luther*. Vol. 1, *His Road to Reformation of the Church, 1483–1521*. Trans. James L. Schaaf. Philadelphia: Fortress Press, 1985.

———. *Martin Luther*. Vol. 3, *The Preservation of the Church, 1532–1546*. Trans. James L. Schaaf. Philadelphia: Fortress Press, Minneapolis, 1993.

Decrees of the Ecumenical Councils. Editor: Norman P. Tanner, S.J. 2 vols. London: Sheed and Ward, and Washington DC: Georgetown University Press, 1990.

Grane, Leif. *The Augsburg Confession: A Commentary*. Minneapolis: Augsburg Publishing House, 1987.

Grimm, Harold J. *The Reformation Era, 1500–1650*. New York: The Macmillan Company, 1954.

Gritsch, Eric W. *Martin—God's Court Jester: Luther in Retrospect*. Philadelphia: Fortress Press, 1983.

Hillerbrand, Hans J. *Christendom Divided: The Protestant Reformation* (Theological Resources). New York: Corpus; Philadelphia: Westminster; London: Hutchinson, 1971.

Kittelson, James. *Luther the Reformer: The Story of the Man and His Career*. Minneapolis: Augsburg Publishing House, 1986.

Loewenich, Walther von. *Martin Luther: The Man and His Work*. Minneapolis: Augsburg Publishing House, 1986.

Luther, Martin. *Luther's Works: American Edition*. General editors: Jaroslav Pelikan, Helmut T. Lehmann, and Christopher Boyd Brown. 82 vols. St. Louis: Concordia Publishing House, and Philadelphia: Muhlenburg Press/Fortress Press, 1955–. [Cited as LW.]

Luther, Martin. *The Works of Martin Luther*. Holman Edition. 6 vols. Philadelphia: A. J. Holman Company and Castle Press/Muhlenburg Press, 1915–32. [Cited as PE, the Philadelphia Edition.]

Markwald, Rudolph K., and Marilyn Morris. *Katharina von Bora: A Reformation Life*. St. Louis: Concordia Publishing House, 2002.

Mauer, Wilhelm. *Historical Commentary on the Augsburg Confession*. Philadelphia: Fortress Press, 1986.

Olivier, Daniel. *The Trial of Luther*. St. Louis: Concordia Publishing House, 1971.

Ozment, Steven. *The Age of Reform, 1250–1550: An Intellectual and Religious History of Late Medieval and Reformation Europe*. New Haven and London: Yale University Press, 1980.

Schillebeeckx, Edward, O. P. *Christ, the Sacrament of the Encounter with God*. New York: Sheed and Ward, 1960.

Schwiebert, E. G. *Luther and His Times: The Reformation from a New Perspective*. St. Louis: Concordia Publishing House, 1950.

Smith, Preserved. *Luther's Correspondence and Other Contemporary Letters*. 2 vols. Philadelphia: The Lutheran Publication Society, 1913–18.